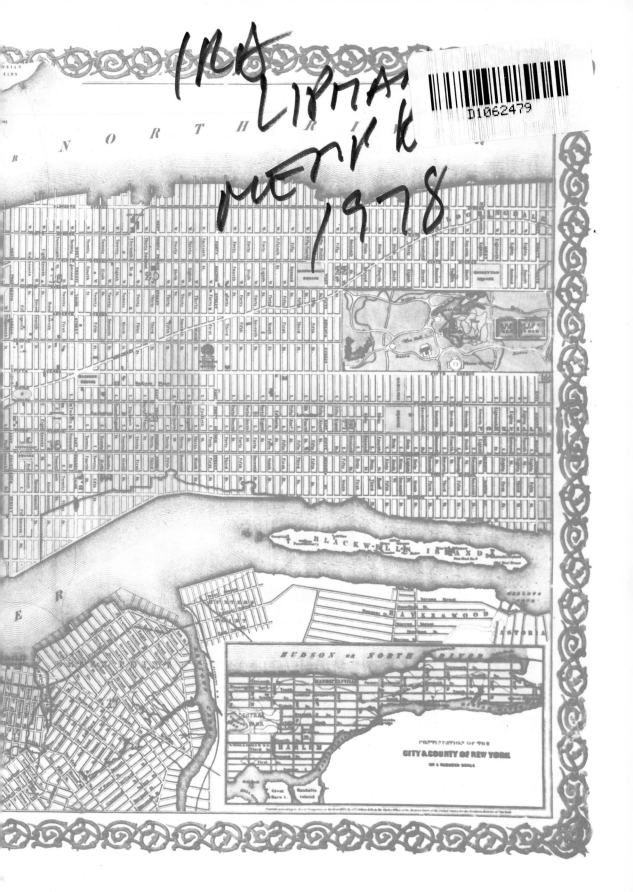

Manhattan Moves Uptown

Books by Charles Lockwood

Bricks & Brownstone

Manhattan Moves Uptown: An Illustrated History

Manhattan Moves Uptown

An Illustrated History

Charles Lockwood

Houghton Mifflin Company / Boston / 1976

Book design by Edith Allard

Library of Congress Cataloging in Publication Data

Lockwood, Charles.
    Manhattan moves uptown.

    Includes index.
    1. Manhattan (Borough)   2. New York (City) — History.
3. Architecture — New York (City) — History.   4. Real
property — Valuation — New York (City)   I. Title.
F128.3.L8   974.7'1   76-22487
ISBN 0-395-24674-1

Printed in the United States of America
M 10 9 8 7 6 5 4 3 2 1

for Robert Sincerbeaux

Acknowledgments

After my history of the New York row house, *Bricks &
Brownstone,* was published in November 1972, I received a
grant from the Eva Gebhard-Gourgaud Foundation to do
further work on New York's architecture and growth. Because
I was already familiar with books and articles in this field, I
decided that nineteenth-century New York newspapers were
the best source of new information in this area.

Because of the generosity of the Eva Gebhard-Gourgaud
Foundation, I was able to devote a year and a half to research
for this book and to induce a friend, Alexander Cassie, to leave
Boston and help me in this work. Together we searched
through every issue of the New York *Daily Tribune* and *Herald*
published from the late 1830s to the 1870s. We read scattered
dates of the *Evening Post, Mirror,* and *Times* to find additional
information about stories uncovered in our research in the
Daily Tribune and *Herald.* I could not have asked for a better
research assistant than Alex Cassie. His sharp mind and good
humor made our newspaper research pleasant and productive
work.

All the research for this book was done in the library of the
New-York Historical Society. James J. Heslin, the director,
and James Gregory, the librarian, encouraged my work on this
book and made several suggestions that became a part of the
research and the text. I owe a great deal to the library staff: Sue

Adele Gillies, Roger N. Mohovich, John A. Lovari, Howard J. Schaetzle, Philip Klingle, Thomas J. Dunnings, Jr., and Reynold J. Yuska. Roger N. Mohovich, the newspaper librarian, was particularly helpful, carrying out volume after unwieldy volume of bound newspapers from the stacks, and bringing to my attention books and periodicals that I did not already know about.

Although I relied on newspapers for the bulk of my research, I did look through such magazines as *Frank Leslie's Illustrated Newspaper* and *Godey's Lady's Book,* which are listed fully in the Bibliography. George Templeton Strong's *Diary* was another valuable source of information, as was Philip Hone's *Diary,* which I read in the complete unpublished manuscript at the New-York Historical Society. I must acknowledge my debt to I. N. Phelps Stokes' *Iconography of Manhattan Island,* which is indispensable to anyone studying the history of New York.

When it was time to select illustrations for this book, Charlotte La Rue at the Museum of the City of New York and Wendy Shadwell and Jan B. Hudgens at the New-York Historical Society assisted my search for suitable photographs. Curtis Roseman shot most of the engravings used in this book from old magazines and books.

I must thank Grant Ujifusa, the book's editor, for seeing it from manuscript to published work and for suggesting, in the first place, the growth of New York as a book subject best suited to my interests and research material. Kent Barwick, Charles Gillispie, and Nathaniel Thayer gave me moral support and suggestions for this project from the beginning. Marshall Davidson told me about some nineteenth-century engravings, which were included in this book just before it went to the publisher. To Frances Apt, many, many thanks for painstakingly editing the manuscript line by line and also to Candy Allgaier for her help with proofreading.

My friend Patrick Daniels remained stalwart during my writing of the book in 1975. The problem of telling the story of Manhattan's growth in just over one-hundred-thousand words was the first instance where his advice helped me to reach a decision about the manuscript. He criticized portions of the book as they were completed, and gave me some of the ideas for its conclusion.

My greatest thanks go to Robert Sincerbeaux. His interest and support of my work since 1970 have enabled me to write this and other books, and it is fitting that I dedicate *Manhattan Moves Uptown* to him.

Illustrations

City Hall — *page* 2
Courtesy of The New-York Historical Society, New York City

View of lower Manhattan, ca. 1842–1845 — 4
Courtesy of The New-York Historical Society, New York City

St. John's Chapel and St. John's Park, ca. 1840 — 8
Museum of the City of New York

Dutch house — 10

Wall Street: view west from Broad Street, ca. 1820 — 12
Courtesy of The New-York Historical Society, New York City

Collapse of a warehouse, 1832 — 16
Museum of the City of New York

Pearl Street: typical countinghouse of 1840s — 17
Courtesy of The New-York Historical Society, New York City

Walton House, ca. 1830 — 19
Museum of the City of New York

Shipyard on the East River — 21
Courtesy of The New-York Historical Society, New York City

South Street — 22
Courtesy of The New-York Historical Society, New York City

Wall Street, winter of 1833–1834 — 26
Courtesy of The New-York Historical Society, New York City

The Battery and view of New York Bay, 1830 — 32
Courtesy of The New-York Historical Society, New York City

Bowling Green, 1826 — 35
Courtesy of The New-York Historical Society, New York City

Broadway: view from foot of City Hall Park, 1819 — 37
Museum of the City of New York

Collect Pond, 1798   39
Museum of the City of New York

Lispenard Meadows, 1785   40
Courtesy of The New-York Historical Society, New York City

Warren and Greenwich streets, 1809   41
Museum of the City of New York

Philip Hone   44
Museum of the City of New York

Broadway from Park Place to Barclay Street,
with Philip Hone's residence, 1831   46
Museum of the City of New York

Bond Street   51

Bleecker Street   53
Courtesy of The New-York Historical Society, New York City

"Colonnade Row," Lafayette Place   55
Courtesy of The New-York Historical Society, New York City

Lafayette Place, 1866   56
Courtesy of The New-York Historical Society, New York City

"The Row," Washington Square North   63
Courtesy of The New-York Historical Society, New York City

West Eleventh Street, 1825, showing open fields   65
Museum of the City of New York

69 Downing Street: a little Federal house   67
Courtesy of The New-York Historical Society, New York City

Map of Greenwich Village, 1822   69
Courtesy of The New-York Historical Society, New York City

Sixth Avenue near Eighth Street, 1862   70
Courtesy of The New-York Historical Society, New York City

Delmonico's restaurant, 25 Broadway   83

Trinity Church   84
Museum of the City of New York

Interior of A. T. Stewart's store   86–87

A. T. Stewart's store, Broadway and Chambers Street   88
Museum of the City of New York

John Cox Stevens' residence   92
Museum of the City of New York

Rebuilding of Liberty Street, 1854   97

Park Place, ca. 1855   99

Worth Street: typical warehouses of the 1850s and
1860s   101
Courtesy of The New-York Historical Society, New York City

Five Points, ca. 1870   109
Museum of the City of New York

A rear building on Roosevelt Street   112
Museum of the City of New York

Tenement district, ca. 1860   114

Slum dwellers, ca. 1860   115

Garbage on East Fifth Street   115
Museum of the City of New York

Broadway: view north from Spring Street, 1867   124
Museum of the City of New York

A New York belle   128
Museum of the City of New York

A Broadway stage   130
Courtesy of The New-York Historical Society, New York City

Broadway traffic, 1854   132

Lord & Taylor, Broadway and Grand Street, 1860   134
Museum of the City of New York

Tiffany & Co., 550 Broadway, 1855   137
Courtesy of The New-York Historical Society, New York City

Ball, Black & Co., 247 Broadway: interior
of the jewelry store, 1850   139
Courtesy of The New-York Historical Society, New York City

Taylor's restaurant, 365 Broadway   140
Courtesy of The New-York Historical Society, New York City

"Hooking a Victim"   145
Museum of the City of New York

St. Nicholas Hotel: façade   153
Courtesy of The New-York Historical Society, New York City

St. Nicholas Hotel: dining room   155
Courtesy of The New-York Historical Society, New York City

Broadway (Spring to Prince streets), ca. 1855   160–161
Courtesy of The New-York Historical Society, New York City

A Bird's-Eye View of New York, 1849   166
Courtesy of The New-York Historical Society, New York City

Union Square, ca. 1855   169
Courtesy of The New-York Historical Society, New York City

Brevoort residence, Fifth Avenue and Eighth Street   174
Museum of the City of New York

Grinnell mansion   176
Courtesy of The New-York Historical Society, New York City

Fifth Avenue: view north from Twenty-eighth Street,
ca. 1865   179
Courtesy of The New-York Historical Society, New York City

Gramercy Park   180
Courtesy of The New-York Historical Society, New York City

Croton Reservoir   185

High Bridge   187

A plumber's advertisement, 1848   188

A bathroom, ca. 1860   190

Trade card for a furnace manufacturer 194
Courtesy of The New-York Historical Society, New York City
Johnson's Gas Fittings advertisement, 1848 198
General Theological Seminary, Ninth Avenue
and Twentieth Street 204
Sixth Avenue and Twentieth Street: Gothic row
houses, 1854 205
Breakfast room in Fifth Avenue mansion, ca. 1860 206
Residence of Madame Restell, 657 Fifth Avenue 209
Museum of the City of New York
Union Club, Fifth Avenue and Twenty-first Street 213
Courtesy of The New-York Historical Society, New York City
After-church promenade on Fifth Avenue, ca. 1875 218
Brick Presbyterian Church, Fifth Avenue
and Thirty-seventh Street 224
Museum of the City of New York
Waddell villa, Fifth Avenue and Thirty-seventh Street 226
Museum of the City of New York
The Samuel P. "Sarsaparilla" Townsend residence,
Fifth Avenue and Thirty-fourth Street, 1860 228
Museum of the City of New York
Park Avenue: view north from Thirty-fifth Street 230
Property map: Park Avenue 230
Courtesy of The New-York Historical Society, New York City
"The Bottom Out" 235
Courtesy of The New-York Historical Society, New York City
"Dutch Hill" shantytown, Forty-second street,
near the East River, ca. 1860 237
Museum of the City of New York
Cattle drive: a cartoon 239
Fifth Avenue and Twenty-first Street, 1865 241
Courtesy of The New-York Historical Society, New York City
A mansion next to a shack: cartoon, ca. 1868 243
A crowded "street railroad," 1867 245
View of the East River shoreline from the foot
of Fifty-third Street, ca. 1860 247
Museum of the City of New York
Stryker's Cottages, West Fifty-second Street 249
Courtesy of The New-York Historical Society, New York City
322–350 West Forty-sixth Street, a row of brownstones 251
Museum of the City of New York
A parlor filled with typically elaborate furniture, 1854 255
Fifth Avenue: view north from Forty-second Street,
ca. 1882 258
Courtesy of The New-York Historical Society, New York City

Madison Avenue: view north from Fifty-fifth Street,
ca. 1870   260
Museum of the City of New York

Western Union Building   264
Courtesy of the New-York Historical Society, New York City

Nassau Street: view north from Wall Street   266
Museum of the City of New York

Wall Street, 1864   267
Museum of the City of New York

Wall Street: view west from William Street, ca. 1872   268
Courtesy of The New-York Historical Society, New York City

Trinity Building   271
Courtesy of The New-York Historical Society, New York City

Broadway Bridge, 1864   275
Courtesy of The New-York Historical Society, New York City

Clustered skyscrapers, 1881   277

"King's Dream" skyscrapers, 1908   278
Courtesy of The New-York Historical Society, New York City

The Blizzard of 1888   281
Museum of the City of New York

Trial trip of the elevated railroad, 1867   283
Museum of the City of New York

The el: view south on Columbus Avenue, 1879   285
Museum of the City of New York

Bleecker Street, a slum   291
Courtesy of The New-York Historical Society, New York City

Eighteenth Street apartments   295
Museum of the City of New York

The "Ladies' Mile," Broadway, 1875   297

Bums at a fountain in Madison Square, 1877   298

Thirty-fourth Street and Fifth Avenue   300
Museum of the City of New York

Fifth Avenue and Fifty-first Street   303
Courtesy of The New-York Historical Society, New York City

Old frame house, 3 East Eighty-third Street   306
Museum of the City of New York

Marsh drugstore, One hundred twenty-fifth Street,
1865   307
Museum of the City of New York

Park Avenue vicinity, south from Ninety-third Street   308
Courtesy of The New-York Historical Society, New York City

Houses in open fields, West One hundred thirty-third
Street   309
Courtesy of The New-York Historical Society, New York City

Fifth Avenue: view north from Sixty-fifth Street   311
Museum of the City of New York

Bloomingdale Road, 1862 312
Museum of the City of New York

Charles Ward Apthorpe mansion, 1892 314
Museum of the City of New York

Central Park West, ca. 1873: open fields 316
Courtesy of The New-York Historical Society, New York City

Shanty on Riverside Drive 318
Courtesy of The New-York Historical Society, New York City

King Garbage: cartoon, 1891 321

Pennsylvania Station 325
Museum of the City of New York

Endpapers: Cotton's map of New York and the Adjacent
Cities, New York, J. H. Cotton, 1862
Courtesy of The New-York Historical Society, New York City

Introduction

Americans once idolized New York as the nation's richest, most powerful, most exciting city. It also had a greater population than any of our cities, as proved by the 1820 census, which counted 123,706 people living in Manhattan.

At first, New Yorkers were surprised by their city's surging growth. They remembered how demoralized and badly damaged the city was after the seven-year occupation by the British Army during the Revolutionary War. Nearly half New York's buildings were destroyed or in disrepair, its trade was in ruins, and half of its residents had been scattered into the countryside or to other towns. But New York quickly recovered, and by 1820 the memory of those times only heightened New Yorkers' swelling pride in their city and their expectations for its future.

Yet the growth that took place in the early nineteenth century seemed small when compared with that of later years. By 1860 Manhattan's population was 813,660, over six times as large as it was in 1820. And fifteen years later it had crossed the one million mark; with the consolidation of the five boroughs into one city, the population of Greater New York was over 3.4 million. Because of this burgeoning population, Manhattan experienced a feverish building boom, which slowed, but never completely stopped, for occasional depressions and wars. A solid line of row houses and paved streets marched northward up Manhattan, obliterating the farms, the outcroppings of rock, and the hills and streams of its vanishing rural past. At the same time, one-time family residences in built-up areas several miles downtown from the city's northern edge were altered or demolished for the ever-expanding demands of trade. Entire districts that had once been solidly residential were given over to count-inghouses and warehouses, shops, hotels, even bars and brothels.

At the end of the Revolution, New York was clustered around Wall Street and did not extend more than ten blocks northward up Manhattan Island from the Battery. By 1820, thirty years later, the city had grown another ten or fifteen blocks to the north, near the vicinity of the present-day City Hall. But by around 1850 New York's outermost edge had pushed nearly two miles farther; it reached Fourteenth Street.

That was just the beginning of the city's wondrous growth. In 1864 more than half of Manhattan's population lived north of Fourteenth Street. By then, adventuresome builders were already erecting rows of houses in the streets of today's Upper East Side and in the village, at the inter-section of One hundred twenty-fifth Street and Third Avenue, known as Harlem. By the 1890s the city had en-gulfed all but the northernmost reaches of Manhattan, and those built-up areas several miles downtown that were not yet taken over by trade were becoming more densely popu-lated as tenements and apartment buildings replaced single-family row houses.

Manhattan Moves Uptown will describe this march of growth up Manhattan Island from the end of the Revolu-tionary War in 1783 to the years at the beginning of the twentieth century. It will show how growth overtook most areas of Manhattan and what these areas were like through-out the nineteenth century: the streets around the Battery and Bowling Green, which were once New York's most de-sirable residential neighborhood; Wall Street; ill-fated St. John's Park, a private park that occupied the spot where motorists now enter the Holland Tunnel; the Five Points, which simultaneously became the city's first slum district and the most popular tourist attraction; Greenwich Village; Lafayette Place, with its famed white marble Colonnade Row; Tompkins Square, which seemed for a time to have a splendid future; the Lower East Side; Union Square; Fifth Avenue, which surprised most New Yorkers by emerging as the city's most fashionable address in the 1840s and 1850s; Chelsea; Gramercy Park; Murray Hill; today's midtown district, between Forty-second and Fifty-ninth streets, whose streets were once solidly lined with brownstones; the Upper East Side, which everyone expected to become a working-class and middle-class area, except for a row of mansions along the stretch of Fifth Avenue opposite Central Park; and the Upper West Side, which New Yorkers at the turn of the century expected would become the most fashionable neighborhood of them all.

Manhattan Moves Uptown will reveal almost-forgotten aspects of various neighborhoods' pasts: Wall Street's years as a residential street; the ponds and marshes, just north of City Hall, that had to be drained and filled before the city could push any farther northward; the time when Greenwich Village actually was a village, dotted with country estates, some distance from town; SoHo's service as the city's busiest red-light district; the shortage throughout the city of decent reasonably priced housing for the middle class 120 years ago; and the shantytowns, garbage dumps, and slaughterhouses which once dominated what is now midtown Manhattan.

But a history of Manhattan's growth must include more than the story of the spread of the city up Manhattan Island and the histories of the various areas that were developed along the way. As the nation's largest and most cosmopolitan city, New York introduced building types that later became incorporated into cities across the country. *Manhattan Moves Uptown* describes in some detail the nation's first department store, A. T. Stewart & Co.; the first enormous luxury hotel, typified by the St. Nicholas; and the first men's club to have its own clubhouse and self-perpetuating membership, the Union Club. But New York also led the nation in erecting buildings that capitalized on human misery; this book describes the appearance of tenement houses in New York and the growth of the first sprawling slum, as well as the early efforts to combat these housing evils with "model tenements."

Rapid growth and extravagant building are not enough to make a modern city or one that is pleasant to live in. Despite the handsome appearance of its leading streets and its ever-rising wealth, the New York of 1840 was little more than a vastly overgrown medieval village. Although the city's population reached 312,710 in 1840, its citizens still lived much as they had a hundred years earlier. Indoor plumbing was still virtually unknown in the finest houses. Sewers were almost nonexistent, and garbage collection infrequent and irregular, so New Yorkers often threw their household waste, including the contents of chamber pots, into the middle of the unpaved streets. The pigs that roamed the city were the object of considerable ridicule, particularly from European tourists, but at least they ate some of the garbage, which otherwise would have lain rotting in the street. Not surprisingly, cholera and yellow fever epidemics regularly swept the city, killing hundreds of its residents and sending many others into the countryside for the duration of the contagion.

But ten years later everyday life had become far easier for most New Yorkers, and their city had taken the first steps to becoming a well-functioning modern metropolis. New York had an ample supply of pure water from the Croton Reservoir, indoor plumbing and central heating in most houses, and gas lights for homes and street lamps. In the following decades New Yorkers rid Manhattan of the slaughterhouses and stockyards that fouled not only the outskirts of the city but many built-up neighborhoods, started to pave the streets and keep them free of garbage, introduced telephones and electric lights, and built the elevated railroad so that people could get around the city without using trolleys and omnibuses on the crowded streets.

For all its wealth, large population, and grandeur at the beginning of the twentieth century, New York still lacked one thing that is the mark of a great city: the affection of its citizens. They were proud of New York, but few of them felt the love that residents of Paris or San Francisco expressed for their city.

New York showed the effects of not being loved. Even at

the turn of the century, its streets were still too dirty, its slums too appalling and widespread, and the amenities that make for a pleasant life too scarce for a city of its wealth, talent, and pride. Perhaps this absence of affection was the price New York paid for its remarkable growth.

Or maybe New Yorkers were too busy making money, often in real estate, to attend to the things that make living in any one place enjoyable and satisfying. The decision, in the 1850s, to set aside Central Park, and Samuel Ruggles' laying out Gramercy Park when he developed his family's former farm, are wise, generous acts, all too rare in the history of New York. *Manhattan Moves Uptown* tells how real estate speculators exploited New York, as early as the 1830s and 1840s, in the construction of tenements and rear buildings in poor areas, for example, or in the destruction of the Park Place district for block after block of dry goods warehouses.

These matters make the lesson of history particularly important to New Yorkers of today, beyond satisfying our curiosity about our city's or our neighborhood's past. New York has always been plagued by problems — an inadequate water supply 150 years ago or the financial crises of the present day — but New York has great resiliency as a city and thousands of gifted, hard-working people willing to help their city, if only given the chance. This was true when the city overcame crises 100 or 150 years ago; it must be so now if New York is to continue to thrive.

Manhattan Moves Uptown

1

When City Hall was completed in 1811 at
Broadway and Chambers Street, New Yorkers found their
sentiments expressed in *Blunt's Stranger's Guide*: the building
was "the handsomest structure in the United States; perhaps, of its size, in the world." Its light French Renaissance
detail was a novelty to New Yorkers, who were accustomed
to the Georgian architectural tradition, and the white marble
walls facing south, east, and west were a startling sight in a
city built of red brick and wood. No one complained that the
city fathers had saved some money by facing the north wall
in common brownstone. The building stood at the outskirts
of the city, and the north side, everyone figured, "would be
out of sight to all the world" for years to come.

The city fathers were very wrong. Less than ten years later
the 1820 census named New York the most populous city in
the nation, and small town modesty vanished forever. Now
New Yorkers boasted about their city and predicted a splendid future. "It almost amounts to a certainty," declared
James Hardie in his 1827 *Description of New York*, "that
unless we shall be afflicted with war, pestilence, famine,
earthquake, or some other dreadful visitation of Divine Providence, we shall, at the close of the present century, not only
equal but far surpass either of the great cities of London or
Paris in population, trade, commerce, navigation, arts, science."

In 1823 John Pintard, a merchant and civic enthusiast,
brashly predicted that the city's population — 123,706 by the

1820 census — would reach 260,000 by 1840, 520,000 by 1860, and 800,000 by 1875. Such growth appeared impossible to New Yorkers who remembered the badly damaged, demoralized city of 12,000 that the British Army, after a seven-year occupation, left at the end of the Revolutionary War. But Pintard warned the skeptics that his prediction was "no fond, delusive anticipation," and he was right. His figures, in fact, erred on the low side. New York's population actually reached 312,710 in 1840, 813,660 in 1860, and crossed the one million mark by 1875, an eightfold increase in fifty years.

This fast-rising population led to a building boom and the rapid growth of the city northward up Manhattan Island. By 1820 the city had already engulfed City Hall, whose plain brownstone north wall was now a daily sight to the thou-

City Hall

sands of New Yorkers coming to work down Broadway from their homes uptown. The northward rush of the city up Manhattan Island thrilled them; they believed that their city would be impressive and lovely as well as simply populous. "What enormous and magnificent edifices will . . . be erected!" boasted one newspaper in 1836. "What charming private residences! What majestic city halls, courts, colleges, libraries, academies . . . What fine rows of buildings! What streets and squares! What parks, theaters, opera houses, arcades, and promenades! . . . Will not this become one of the most wealthy, populous, and splendid cities of the globe?"

In the early nineteenth century the 200-foot spire of Trinity Church was the favorite spot for New Yorkers and visitors wishing to admire the sweep of the city. Trinity, located at Broadway and Wall Street, was not the brownstone church now at that location but its predecessor, a modest "plain Gothick" structure built in 1788–1790. Nor was its spire the tallest in the city. The tower of St. Paul's Chapel, a few blocks north, at Broadway and Fulton Street, and the one on St. John's Chapel on Varick Street at the outskirts of the city, were each nearly a hundred feet higher. But Trinity's location was one of the best known and busiest in the city, surrounded by the finest residences, hotels, shops, and business buildings.

The site, furthermore, was one of the best loved in the New York of the 1820s. The parish of Trinity Church first conducted services there in a small wooden building in 1697. That building was long gone, as was the lovely stone church completed in 1737 and burned in 1776 during the British occupation. The churchyard, however, had remained intact all these years, and in 1827 the New York *Mirror* called it "one of the most ancient in this city, having been the resting place of successive generations for upwards of 130 years."

Trinity Church's tower was not officially open to the public, but the sexton or a vestryman was usually willing to show visitors the way to the spire for a modest gratuity. A winding stairway, with benches along the way for the weary, led to the top. There, more stairs and several ladders led people to a small room at the top of the tower with windows on four sides.

3

The view more than justified the trouble of the long climb. There lay New York, a "mammoth beehive" of right-angled brick walls and pitched slate roofs, stretching out in all directions, 200 feet below. The noise of the city was just a busy hum at this height, but the people in the spire could see the brightly colored omnibuses making their way up and down Broadway, tiny pedestrians hurrying along the sidewalks, and horses pulling heavily loaded wagons through the unpaved streets. Visitors and even New Yorkers were surprised at the size and vitality of the city. "I was not prepared to find such a large and populous city on a coast where two hundred years ago there was only an insignificant village," declared Baron Axel Leonhard Klinckowstrom, a Swedish naval officer and writer, in 1818.

To the south one could see several blocks of rooftops and chimneys, ending abruptly at the trees of the Battery. These blocks were largely residential, the mansions of the rich and the boardinghouses of the poor intermixed on the narrow, irregular streets, which had been "made as the wants of the inhabitants required, or the owners of large tracts of land laid them out, selling their lots fronting on the new streets,"

View of lower Manhattan, ca. 1842–1845

wrote the *Herald* years later. Broadway, which started at the Battery, was eighty feet wide, lined with poplars, and, viewed from the church tower, it "cut through the inhabitations of men . . . like a deep channel" on its northward route.

The Battery was an oasis of grass and quiet in the already bustling New York. Philip Hone, a businessman who became Mayor of New York in 1825, wrote "A more delightful scene can nowhere be found." And even the acerbic and critical Mrs. Frances Trollope admitted that "no city could boast . . . a public promenade . . . more beautiful." Here New Yorkers passed afternoons and evenings, strolling along curving, tree-shaded paths and enjoying the sea breezes and the sight of New York Bay. The Bay's waters "must be the most beautiful in the world," thought the English actress Fanny Kemble, who also delighted in the sight of hundreds of sailing ships "glancing like graceful seabirds, through their native element."

To the east of Trinity Church, the city sloped gently down toward the East River. The streets east of Broadway had been largely residential at the end of the Revolution; in the 1820s, however, the countinghouses and warehouses, which served the rising demands of shipping and trade, were displacing the last residences. One hundred years earlier, Pearl Street had run along the shore of the East River, but landfill operations had extended Manhattan into the river, first as far as Water Street, then Front Street, and finally South Street. So many ships from the transatlantic trade docked along the East River that by the 1820s the east shore of Manhattan was "a forest of masts." Beyond that lay the unspoiled farmland of Brooklyn, the rolling hills, open meadows, and stands of trees so different from the closely built rooftops of the city below the church tower.

To the west of Trinity Church were several blocks of pleasant residences, which ended at the Hudson River, sometimes called the North River. The farms and forests of New Jersey extended beyond the opposite shore. Shipping had also taken over the Manhattan shoreline here, although there were fewer sailing vessels than along the East River. Domestic shipping had settled along the Hudson, and its skiffs and flatboats, though not as glamorous as the transatlantic vessels, carried on a thriving trade with the South and now trafficked with upstate New York and the Midwest by the Erie Canal, which opened in 1826.

But it was the view to the north that excited the greatest wonder of visitors to Trinity Church's tower. By the 1820s, New York had already begun its fabled march uptown, slowing only for war or depression, obliterating the hills, farms, and streams that once dotted Manhattan. Carpenters and masons were erecting thousands of modest but handsome red brick row houses every year, but the city's population was growing so fast that houses were in short supply and families often moved into half-finished buildings. Other New Yorkers were even less fortunate in their search for a place to live and, when their leases expired, moved into the jail, on Chatham Street, until they found other homes.

By the same decade, the city was solidly built as far as Canal Street, and scattered development had pushed so far north that, in 1825, the *Commercial Advertiser* declared: "Greenwich is now no longer a country village. Such has been the growth of our city that the building of one block more will completely connect the two places; and in three years' time, at the rate buildings have been erected the last season, Greenwich will be known only as a part of the city, and the suburbs will be beyond it."

The panorama from Trinity Church thrilled New Yorkers because they were proud of the city's growth and new buildings. A fine mansion or an extravagant shop, in their eyes, was more than a sign of the owner's private wealth; it was a reflection of the public's well-being and New York's rising greatness. Standing in the tower, they proudly pointed out the greenery of St. John's Park, a mile to the north. Its successful development in the 1820s proved that New York had the daring and vision, as well as the people and wealth, to become a great city.

Back in 1803 Trinity Church had tried to introduce the delights of the residential squares of London's West End to a piece of land it owned along the Hudson River beyond the city. It laid out St. John's Park, which was bounded by Varick, Beach, Hudson, and Laight streets, and then offered the lots around its perimeter for ninety-nine-year leases, subject to restrictions that would permit only first-class row houses to be constructed. The church even built St. John's Chapel on Varick Street, facing the square. The site, however, was too far beyond the city at that time, and rich New Yorkers, who were expected to move in, were put off by the leasehold nature of the lots and St. John's Park's frankly British inspiration. The development of the park did not get underway, and the lovely chapel stood virtually alone among cow pastures and marshland, for twenty years.

In the mid-1820s New Yorkers transformed Trinity's failed urban vision into "the most desirable residence" and "the fairest interior portion of this city." The church decided to sell rather than lease its property in the area, and in 1827 it deeded the square itself to the owners of the sixty-four surrounding lots. Within a year these landholders had fenced in the square for the princely sum of $25,000, thereby reserving the park for their sole enjoyment. Catalpas and cottonwoods, horse chestnut and silver birch trees were planted throughout, and gravel paths wound among them and the ornamental shrubs and flower beds.

Encouraged by successes like the development of St. John's Park, New Yorkers were bold enough to question who is so blind as not to see that New York would always be the great city of the western world. But the sight from the tower of Trinity Church in the 1820s and 1830s was deceptive. "New York viewed from a distance," declared one English visitor in 1824, "has the air of a metropolis . . . A walk through it, however, dissipates much of the idea of grandeur excited by the distant view."

New York had much to do before it truly became one of the leading cities of the world. Despite its soaring population and geographical expansion, the city had changed little, during the past hundred years, in such basic services as water supply, sanitation, fire fighting, and public health. The streets were "the dirtiest in the Union," the *Evening Post* admitted in 1821, and were littered with ashes, bits of food, even dead animals. City garbage collection and street cleaning were sporadic at best. "Multitudes of rats infested almost every building," according to Englishman James Boardman, and scavenging pigs were "quite at home" in the streets

everywhere in the city. Slaughterhouses, distilleries, glue works, and stables were a nuisance in all but the finest neighborhoods. Sewers were unknown, and raw sewage was often thrown into the streets along with household garbage.

Because of these nearly medieval conditions, yellow fever and cholera epidemics regularly ravaged the city. New Yorkers usually fled the infected neighborhood at the first sign of disease, and the city spread quicklime and coal dust in the streets and kept fires burning night and day in hopes of cleansing the air of contagion. The bonfires, however, were nearly as great a threat to the city as the epidemics they were intended to combat. Fires were one of the sights of New York, according to most European visitors; the city was so densely built and the water supply so limited that the volunteer fire companies were fortunate if they lost just one building and kept the fire from spreading to its neighbors.

St. John's Chapel and St. John's Park, ca. 1840

Still, New Yorkers displayed a passionate pride in their city that amused visitors, particularly those from Great Britain, who had a more objective view of its strengths and weaknesses. Alexander Mackay, a British journalist, recalled that "Americans are justly very proud" of New York and "its residents passionately attached to it." One winter day, after landing in New York, Mackay shared a sleigh going to the Astor House with "a young New Yorker, who had been in Europe for more than a year . . . 'There goes the old city!' said he in his enthusiasm, as we entered Broadway. 'I could almost jump out and hug a lamp-post.' "

Anyone who was away from New York for more than a year or two was amazed, on his return, by the changes in the city. "The time that you have been abroad has made great changes, in everything that meets the eye," wrote James Fenimore Cooper to his friend W. B. Schubrick in 1833. "To us they have been gradual and almost unperceived, but will strike you with great force; even in your own New York, you will scarcely recognize some of the places with which you were most familiar."

The growth and change delighted most people. "New York never saw such days as the present since it was a city," boasted the *Evening Post* in 1825. "The streets are so ob-

Dutch house

structed by the great number of buildings going up and pulling down, that they have become almost impassable, and a
scene of bustle, noise, and confusion prevails that no pen can
describe, nor any but an eye witness imagine." New Yorkers
were gratified by the demolition of old buildings that reminded them of their city's less prosperous, less powerful
past. By 1824 Cooper thought that fewer than 500 buildings
dating before 1783 survived in New York, and according to
one British visitor, the few Dutch dwellings that "still continue to disgrace the city" were disappearing rapidly.

But ruthless change, exciting as it was, exacted a toll from the people living in its midst. The New York of 1833 reminded Fanny Kemble of a country fair, it was "an irregular collection of temporary buildings, erected for some casual purpose . . . not meant to endure for any length of time." It offered little solace and stability for those living, working, and raising families there. "A man born forty years ago finds nothing, absolutely nothing of the New York he knew," observed *Harper's Monthly* in 1856. "If he chance to stumble upon a few old houses not yet leveled, he is fortunate. But the landmarks, the objects which marked the city to him, as a city, are gone." The rush of change was affecting the appearance of the city and the quality of life. New Yorkers were always proud of their city, but few of them loved it. "Why should it be loved as a city?" asked *Harper's Monthly*. "It is never the same city for a dozen years altogether."

2

Few places in New York were changing as rapidly in the 1820s and 1830s as the streets around Trinity Church. On the stretch of Broadway near the church, the one-time homes of some of the city's richest families were being demolished or altered to make stylish boardinghouses, hotels, fine shops. "The spirit of pulling down and building up is abroad," observed Philip Hone after a walk in the area in 1839. "Brickbats, rafters, and slates are showering down in every direction. There is no safety on the sidewalks, and the head must be saved at the expense of dirtying the boots."

Around the corner from Broadway, this "spirit" was obliterating the last vestiges of Wall Street's splendid residential past. After the Revolution, Wall Street had been the home of such prominent families as the Dennings, Jaunceys, Ludlows, Pintards, and Verplancks as well as political figures like Samuel Otis, Secretary of State; John Lawrence, the first Congressman from New York City and later a United States Senator; General John Lamb, Collector of the Port; Richard Varick, the Mayor; and Alexander Hamilton, Secretary of the Treasury.

Their homes, whether mansions or three- and four-story row houses, were built "in the English style," differing "little from those of London," in the opinion of a British visitor. The pleasingly proportioned red brick façades were almost spare of ornament, except for the delicately leaded sidelights and fanlight window beside and above the front door. The windows had the small panes of glass traditionally

Wall Street: view west from Broad Street, ca. 1820

associated with the period hung six over six, and shutters painted dark green or black. The roofs were pitched, with dormer windows lighting the attic.

Wall Street was the first fashionable downtown street to fall to trade. For one thing, it had never been entirely residential. At various times in the eighteenth century the City Hall, temporary United States Capitol, and Merchants Exchange were on Wall Street, but these public buildings did not annoy the street's residents nearly as much as the intrusion of commerce around 1820. Pearl Street, which intersected Wall Street three blocks east of Broadway, and the nearby East River waterfront were so crowded and so prosperous that trade spilled into nearby Wall Street, even if it meant the tradesmen's violating one of the city's finest streets and paying enormous prices for property there. Trade did not advance into any other costly residential streets at this time; they were in the still unspoiled area around the Battery or west of Broadway.

Merchants needed more and more countinghouse and warehouse space every year because New York had become "the great commercial emporium of North America" after the War of 1812. The city was the leading port of entry for Europe's exports to America, and in the 1820s New York paid more duties on these goods than rivals Boston, Philadelphia, Baltimore, Norfolk, and Savannah combined. Likewise, in some years more packet ships sailed to Europe from New York than from all other American cities put together. On January 1, 1824, the *Evening Post* counted 324 vessels in New York harbor, a staggering figure for the time though it would be nothing to boast of a few years later.

The opening of the Erie Canal the following year offered an easy water link between New York and the Great Lakes. Before, it took $120 and three weeks to ship a ton of wheat, worth $40, from Buffalo to New York along narrow, rutted dirt roads. Once the canal opened, shipping costs dropped to $6 a ton and shipping time to eight days. New York became the outlet for the Midwest's crops and, in later years, its manufactured goods, whether they were destined for domestic sale or export to Europe. The Erie Canal route worked both ways, and foodstuffs, dry goods, and merchandise, made in America or imported, passed through New York on its way to the Midwest. One success in trade led to another, and soon the South's planters no longer sent their cotton directly to mills in New England or Great Britain but to New York wholesalers, who took their commission and then shipped it on to the mills. No wonder New Yorkers in the late 1820s saw "no limits" to the city's "lucrative extensions of trade and commerce."

Pearl Street, the focal point of New York's trade in the 1820s and 1830s, began at the Battery and ran northward, roughly parallel to the East River three blocks inland. Indeed, it had been the "principal merchants' mart of the city" since the seventeenth century, when each Dutch mercantile family lived above its countinghouse or in another house nearby. The East River shoreline had always been better for sailing ships than that of the Hudson. Because of the prevailing winds, ships could get underway quickly in the East River, whereas along the Hudson tugs frequently had to pull them into the Bay. The Hudson also froze occasionally in winter, but the East River remained clear of ice because of tidal action and the salt from New York Bay.

Pearl Street's residential character began to disappear after the Revolutionary War. Even though some of the city's grandest houses still stood on or near the winding thoroughfare, the Dutch families were leaving their traditional quarter for Wall Street, the Battery, and lower Broadway, which had emerged as fashionable addresses soon after the British seized New Amsterdam in 1664. Rich English families felt uncomfortable with the Dutch, and therefore established desirable locations other than Pearl Street for their homes. In the late eighteenth and early nineteenth centuries, the streets along the East River lost population as trade demanded more space.

By the 1820s the narrow streets along the East River were the most exciting in the city, crowded with workmen, carriages, countinghouse clerks, and wagons carrying merchandise from one firm to another. Imported goods were unloaded at the docks, moved to the auction house or import-export firm's warehouse by wagon, then to the wholesale warehouse by wagon, and, after their sale, back to the waterfront for shipment to the new owner. The wholesale warehouses were often so busy or filled with goods that boxes and bales of merchandise sat in the streets for hours before being taken inside or loaded on wagons.

The sidewalks were no less an obstacle course than the streets. Open cellar doors "yawn to receive the unwary" and broken paving stones "threaten to trip him up . . . break his legs, or inflict some grievous injury," wrote Alexander Mackay when he visited New York in the 1840s. Merchandise was stacked up on the sidewalks, too, so "you have no alternative but to jump over boxes, or squeeze yourself as best you can, between bales of merchandise." Pedestrians were usually too busy to look up, which was just as well because "heavy and bulky masses are dangling . . . from many lofty cranes . . . in a way which makes you feel nervous for your head," wrote Mackay. Then, too, all the building and demolition meant "lofty piles of building material towering, tottering, and leaning over the heads of passersby."

The countinghouses looked like dwelling houses of the period, which is not at all surprising since many of them were former residences with another floor and an extension at the back added for more space. Even those built as countinghouses were twenty or thirty feet wide, rose three or four

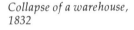

Collapse of a warehouse, 1832

16

stories, and had simply ornamented red brick fronts and pitched roofs. The first floor was the merchant's counting-house or office. Copyists and clerks sat on high stools and wrote the firm's letters and orders by hand, often writing the same item several times, because carbon paper had not yet been invented. The office staff also included several boys who ran errands and delivered letters; they were paid several dollars a week for six ten-hour days. The back room on this floor was the merchant's office, and the two or three floors above the first were warehouse space.

The Pearl Street wholesalers had not established branch offices in other cities, and traveling salesmen were virtually unknown in the 1820s and 1830s. So twice a year, in the spring and fall, storekeepers swarmed to New York from across the nation, from "almost every place that is a place," to buy their merchandise for the coming six months. Visiting wholesaler after wholesaler, the country buyers tried to find the best deal, but the wily Pearl Street merchants were several steps ahead of them. "Selling goods is an art, but accosting men is a science," observed the *Daily Tribune*, "and nobody understands it better than the New York merchant."

The wholesalers did everything they could to gain the confidence of the country buyer. "One they grasp cordially by the hand, ask affectionately after his wife and the bairns he left behind him, offer him a cigar warranted genuine, shake out for him the morning paper, and make him feel more at home than he *were* at home," reported the *Home Journal*. "Another they regard with a cool polite expression of inquiry. They ready beg pardon; they don't quite recollect him; countenance familiar, and all that, and all the while they know him better than they do their own grandfathers." Were the Pearl Street wholesalers that forgetful? No. "The first comer is a good customer; he pays cash; he *always* pays. The other is a little, just a *very* little doubtful, and the secret of thaw and frost is out in a twinkling."

To encourage trade, the city occasionally tried to relieve the impassable streets along the East River. In 1825 the Common Council ordered Pearl Street widened and straightened at Coenties Slip. That move meant the destruction of the old *stadt huys*, the old Dutch city hall. But New Yorkers did not mourn the "ancient Knickerbocker edifice which has for nearly a century and a half obtruded itself far too much into the street," commented the *Commercial Advertiser*.

Several mansions from Pearl Street's eighteenth-century residential heyday were still standing in the 1820s. One survivor was the William Walton house, 326 Pearl Street, at Franklin Square. Walton, a leading merchant and shipowner, built the house in 1752 when that stretch of Pearl Street was open land sloping down to the grassy banks of the East River. By building in the then-unsettled location,

Walton House, ca. 1830

Walton enjoyed some countrified delights that would have been out of the question in the more crowded streets to the south. His grounds, bounded by present-day Pearl Street, Cherry Street, Peck Slip, and the East River, were enclosed with a picket fence and boasted flowers, vegetable gardens, grape arbors, and shrubs. Gravel paths led down to a summerhouse and boathouse along the river. The entire property had cost £2200.

The house was three stories tall, had a high roof pierced by dormer windows, and was built of yellow-hued "Holland brick" with brownstone trim. The front door was framed by a portico with richly carved columns and the Walton family coat of arms. The interior represented "the then most elegant style known." The hallways were paneled in ornately carved English oak. The drawing rooms, paneled in black walnut, had marble fireplaces with lovely tiles, and crystal chandeliers hung from the lofty paneled ceilings. A ballroom took up one corner of the second floor. This mansion and its parties were so splendid for the time that when American representatives to the British Parliament in the 1770s pled poverty as an objection to additional taxes, more than one Member of Parliament recalled the extravagant entertainments royal officials had enjoyed at the Walton mansion.

After Walton's death, in 1768, his descendants occupied the mansion until a grandnephew, James DeLancey, died there in 1834. By then, the mansion, the *Times* recalled in the 1870s, was "so much surrounded by business establishments that it is unattractive . . . as a residence" to the heirs. Not wanting to demolish the mansion so that more warehouses could be built, the family chose the other, less painful alternative: the building became a boardinghouse for sailors and immigrants. After a few years of this abuse, however, the Walton mansion had become a dilapidated mockery of its former glory, almost forgotten in the commotion of the surrounding commerce.

All the activity on Pearl Street was "only a drop in the bucket compared to that on the wharves and slips, the warehouses, docks, shipyards, and auction stores, on South, Front, and Water Streets," according to Anne Royalle, an Englishwoman, in 1826. Twenty years later Alexander

Mackay agreed that "one needs to come down to the river quays to see the greatness of New York." Sailing ships jammed the East River shoreline, their slender bowsprits and elegantly carved figureheads looming over South Street and nearly touching the other side of the street. Hundreds of American flags and standards of merchant houses floated from the masts in the breeze, adding a spirit of pageantry to the scene. Few New Yorkers failed to recognize the red, white, and blue swallowtail of Grinnell, Minturn & Company; the yellow, red, and yellow horizontal bars with the letter *L* in the center for A. A. Low; or the thirteen blue and white squares of N. L. & G. Griswold. The Griswolds prospered so mightily that many New Yorkers said dryly that the

Shipyard on the East River

"N. L. & G. G." stamped on boxes of their merchandise had to mean "No Loss and Great Gain."

In good years, ships were loaded and unloaded in fair weather from early morning until late at night. Hydraulic or steam-powered cranes were unknown in the 1820s, so horses hauled the boxes and bales from the ships' holds by pulley. Stevedores then loaded the merchandise on small hand trucks or horse-drawn wagons to go to the import-export firm's warehouse on South Street or one of the sidestreets off the waterfront.

The wealth accruing from the waterfront led the city's merchants to brag, in 1823: "The City of New York — The emporium of America; commerce her glory, rivalship hopeless." These merchants also knew that there was a "jealous opposition" among Boston and Philadelphia businessmen to New York's rise in trade. They, too, started packet lines to link their cities with European ports and readied turnpikes, canals, and railroads for tapping the riches of the interior. New York's rise must have been especially galling to Philadelphia. Besides being the nation's capital from 1790 to 1800, Philadelphia had been America's most populous city in the eighteenth and nineteenth centuries. It lost this distinction to New York in the 1820 census, and in 1824 the British consul reported that its trade, once the greatest in the nation, was "on the decline in all its branches." Philadelphia, for one thing, lacked New York's natural geographical advantages. Its distance from the Atlantic Ocean, 130 miles, added days to a ship's journey from Europe, and the Delaware River sometimes froze over for two or three months at a time. Its decline also reflected a loss of spirit. "Commercial men here seem to have lost all their accustomed enterprise," reported the consul.

Boston was a more serious trade rival of New York. Although Boston could not, like New York, draw upon a thriving interior, its harbor was magnificent and, in the days of sailing ships, several days closer to Europe than New York. Its merchants were spirited men, ready with ideas and hard work. Boston was the first East Coast city to complete its rail lines to the West in the 1830s and, for a time during the next decade, had the best communications with Europe, because

South Street

23

the crack Cunard Line ships docked there. New England was the center of the nation's emerging textile industry, and Boston became the leading wholesale market for domestic cloth.

Because of Boston, merchants in New York did not believe that their city's supremacy was inevitable or necessarily permanent. No sooner had New York achieved commercial leadership in the 1820s than its merchants worried about losing it to another city. "The tide of prosperity threatens to be checked by the superior enterprise of other cities on the seaboard," warned the *Merchants' Magazine*. "Without great outlays of capital and enterprise, beyond what has already been made, New York must soon lose her proud pre-eminence among the cities of the Union."

One problem that New York merchants did not face was a "decayed spirit of enterprise." The busy, hard-driving spirit of the waterfront spread far beyond the East River and influenced the tempo of life for all New Yorkers. Indeed, New York had the "air of a town sacrificed to trade," according to an English visitor. After visiting America in 1832, Charles Latrobe described Philadelphia as the "most symmetrical" city in the nation, Baltimore as the "most picturesque," Washington as the "most bewildering," and New York the "most bustling." No one disputed the words of the Swedish visitor Gustav Unonius that on Broadway the pedestrian had "need of a pair of eyes in the back of the neck and of an eye at each ear, in order to escape being run over or trampled down [by the] surging throng." The city's growth reflected, in a way, this bustling spirit. Its obsession with trade influenced the mood of its people as well as the tempo of their lives. Because of the continual communication with Europe, New Yorkers were among the first in the nation to get new ideas and inventions, few of which were not tested and talked about. And New York was one of the most cosmopolitan cities in America. "With perhaps the exception of New Orleans," wrote James Fenimore Cooper in 1828, it was "the only city in the Union that has not the air of a provincial town." All the "customs, nations, society, and manners" of Europe were present, "all tempered without being destroyed, by the institutions and opinions of the country."

Yet trade, for all its influence on New York's wealth and spirit, had not, by the 1830s, rooted out vestiges of the residential past of the streets along the East River. Frame and brick houses, some dating back to the days before the Revolution, still survived in the alleys that crisscrossed the area or stood on a busy street, dwarfed by stone-front warehouses next door. Very few of the houses remained one-family residences. Because of the proximity of business, they were ideally suited to boardinghouse keepers, who paid more rent than families intending to occupy the premises alone or with one or two boarders. The prediction that a street would soon be filled with boardinghouses usually was a self-fulfilling prophecy. Rents rose in the expectation of the event, driving families to cheaper areas and leaving the homes to boardinghouse keepers.

The conversion of dwellings to countinghouses, or their outright destruction to make way for new buildings, did not keep pace with the increasing demands of trade in the Pearl Street area. So merchants and real estate speculators looked beyond the traditional boundaries of commerce. "It is no longer possible for the mercantile community to be pent up within a few blocks," wrote the *Commercial Advertiser* in 1836. "We are glad to see a disposition to enlarge the circle of business." Thus was Wall Street engulfed by the expansion of business from Pearl Street.

Several banks had moved to Wall Street by 1810, but rather than erect new buildings they took over the lower floors of one-time residences for their offices, and rented out the upper floors as offices or fashionable boardinghouses. Lawyers, insurance companies, and stockbrokers next came to Wall Street to be close to the banks. Wall Street's destiny as financial center of the nation was so clear by 1822 that the United States Government bought the Verplanck mansion, on Wall Street at the head of Broad Street, and erected the Customs House, modeled on a Greek temple; it later became the Sub-Treasury building and still stands there. By 1825 the *National Advocate* declared that the "Ludlows, Verplancks, and Jaunceys are all bought out there . . . Almost every house is a bank or insurance company, and the cellars filled with brokers instead of potatoes, cabbages, and old wine."

Some residents of Wall Street resisted the tide of commerce. Daniel McCormick, an elderly merchant, had lived at 57 Wall Street since the 1780s. He was "generous in his style of living, simple in his manners, and courteous in his intercourse with society," wrote his friend Philip Hone, and the front stoop of his home had been "a sort of lounge . . . for important men" of his day. By the mid-1820s, McCormick was in his eighties and refused to leave his beloved home despite high offers for the property. "He adhered pertinaciously to his old domicile and would not suffer the least alteration in its arrangements . . . resisting the encroachment of banks and insurance offices," wrote Hone. McCormick died in 1834 at the age of ninety-one, and his heirs sold the old house for $60,000 several months later.

Just a year later, on December 16, 1835, a fire left so much of lower Manhattan in ruins that New Yorkers wondered if

Wall Street, winter of 1833–1834

their city's prosperity had been dashed. The blaze started at the Comstock & Adams' dry goods warehouse at Pearl and Hanover streets. The streets here were so narrow and crooked and the buildings so tall and closely packed, according to Hone, that the flames jumped "like flashes of lightning . . . in every direction." The firemen were "almost incapable of performing their usual services," because the night was so cold that the water froze in the hydrants, leaving just an icy trickle. The firemen, furthermore, were exhausted from fighting a blaze the night before, and their numbers were reduced by the recent cholera epidemic.

Soon the fire was "unmanageable," recalled Hone, and "the crowd, including the firemen, appeared to look on with the apathy of despair." About the only thing a merchant could do, if his warehouse was in the path of the flames, was move his goods to a nearby location. But the flames spread so fast and so far that "little or nothing was saved" this way. Believing Wall Street safe from the fire, some merchants had moved their merchandise to the new Merchants Exchange, but that too fell to the fire. The next morning only its columned façade along Wall Street was standing, and the remains of the "noble building," wrote Hone, "resemble the ruins of an ancient temple rather than the new and beautiful resort of the merchants."

That was just the beginning of the destruction. The fire had destroyed nearly 700 buildings on seventeen blocks along the East River. At least a thousand mercantile houses had lost their buildings and, most likely, all their merchandise. About four thousand clerks were out of work, at least temporarily, along with thousands of cartmen and porters. The losses in buildings and merchandise totaled $20 million, much of it lost when the city's insurance companies went bankrupt.

The fire, however, did not ruin New York. In a curious way, it was a nineteenth-century version of urban renewal. Trade no longer had to remove residences one by one from the area along the East River. In one night the flames had completely cleared the area, so merchants could build warehouses as densely set and as up-to-date as they wished. Within a month after the fire, lots in the "burnt district," wrote Hone, were bringing "enormous prices, greater than they would have brought before the fire, when covered with valuable buildings." On the first anniversary of the fire, Hone noted that "the whole is rebuilt with more splendor than before . . . to the honor of the merchants and as an evidence of the prosperity of the city."

The start of construction of a new Merchants Exchange on Wall Street in 1836 speeded the street's transition from residence to business. The $750,000 paid for the site, bounded by Wall, William, Exchange, and Hanover streets, and the "certainty of the accomplishment of this magnificent project" once construction began, sent land values along Wall Street soaring to heights unimaginable ten years earlier. The banks and insurance companies demolished the former residences they had occupied for as long as twenty years, and erected three- and four-story Greek Revival stone-front buildings. Considering the demand for offices on Wall Street, the old houses were economically impractical; they wasted space on broad halls, front yards, high ceilings, and back gardens. Graciousness had no part in commerce. Besides, the red brick houses with their fanlight doorways and dormer windows now seemed clumsy and old-fashioned to a city charmed by Greek Revival architecture and the unparalleled wealth of the era.

New Yorkers now saw startling signs of Wall Street's transformation other than the demolition of the residences for bank buildings. Women and children were a rare sight there. Well-dressed gentlemen, talking earnestly with each other or striding purposefully to their offices, filled the sidewalks throughout the day. The number of people in the neighborhood, working inside or walking along the street, had jumped sharply since the early nineteenth century, and, consequently, so did traffic, noise, and garbage in the street. The new buildings blocked the sun, which had once streamed over the pitched rooftops and through the gardens into the street.

One landmark of the past, Trinity Church, had reassuringly survived all the changes in the neighborhood. But in 1839 it, too, was demolished. The vestry planned to repair the fifty-year-old building and remodel the interior in a grander, more modern style, "leaving the venerable exterior and noble-looking spire in their original integrity." Once work began, the building was found to be in far worse condition than anyone had expected. Rather than spend great sums to renovate a building that was small and old-fashioned, the vestry decided to build a new church that would be more fitting for the fashionable congregation and would enhance an increasingly impressive-looking city.

Although Philip Hone was excited by the plans for the brownstone Gothic Revival church that now occupies that site, the sight of "the dark mass of ruins" of the old church filled him with "melancholy reflections." Like many New Yorkers, he felt a close tie to the city and its buildings. The loss of Trinity led him, now that he was nearing sixty, to ask if "I not also see in this dilapidation a type of my own decay and speedily approaching removal?"

But the loss of the church also excited Hone. "Think of the changes which have occurred there during the time the venerable spire which is now removed has thrown its shadow over the place 'where merchants most do congregate,' " he wrote. The destruction of Trinity Church in 1839 marked the end of Wall Street's residential past and symbolized the street's emergence as the financial capital of the nation; in the words of the *Herald*, "a street of palaces . . . great, gaudy, splendid, Corinthian, scheming, magnificent, and full of all kinds of roguery."

As trade displaced the residences along
Wall Street and the blocks leading down to the East River in
the 1820s and 1830s, the streets around the Battery or running west of Broadway down to the Hudson River remained
quiet, tree-shaded, almost solidly residential. The loss of
Wall Street to trade strengthened the remaining residential
neighborhoods in lower Manhattan, which now attracted
families who had fled the commercial advance east of Broadway but did not wish to move to the newly developing areas
a mile or two to the north. Some of these families built new
homes downtown, asserting a street's continuing desirability and often replacing a ramshackle shop or a dwelling remaining from the area's less elegant past of fifty or a hundred
years earlier.

In the growth of New York, church congregations have
been both astute judges of real estate trends and slaves to its
shifting fashions. In the 1830s the downtown churches expected that much of lower Manhattan would be residential
for years in the future. When the First Presbyterian Church,
at 5 Wall Street just off Broadway, burned in 1834, the tower
fell into the nave and only the thick stone walls were standing the next morning. The church had been the oldest in the
city, built in 1719, enlarged in 1748, and partly rebuilt in
1810. Philip Hone, who attended nearby Trinity Church,
thought that the "site is so valuable and new buildings have
encroached upon it in such a manner that it is presumed the
ground will now be sold, and the Congregation erect a new

The Battery and view of
New York Bay, 1830

church in some other situation." Hone, who avidly watched real estate developments thought that residences would virtually disappear from lower Manhattan in ten years. The members of the congregation, most of whom lived within walking distance of Broadway and Wall Street, thought otherwise, and decided to build another church on that site the following year.

The most handsome location for a residence downtown was the neighborhood around the Battery. "What a beautiful spot it is!" wrote Hone after an early evening walk there with his wife in the spring of 1835. "The grounds are in fine order. The whole bay, with the opposite shores of New Jersey, Staten Island and Long Island, vessels of every description, from the noble, well-appointed Liverpool packet to the little market craft and steamer, arriving from every point, give life and animation to a prospect unexcelled by any city view in the world." The houses on State Street and Battery Place, facing the Battery and just around the corner on Broadway, were some of the grandest and most sought-after in New York. An 1827 real estate advertisement for a "substantial house" on lower Broadway declared that " 'tis seldom a house is offered for sale in so central and desirable a situation."

The Battery had been a fortified place, as its name indicates, since the Dutch settled New Amsterdam. As early as 1697 Benjamin Bullivant, a Boston physician, praised the Battery as "a most lovely prospect." In 1785 a letter in the *Packet* suggested that the Battery be landscaped so that New Yorkers could have a quiet spot for walking and viewing the harbor, and a few years later the city planted trees and flowers, built a walk at the water's edge, and added winding gravel paths through the lawns. Rich New Yorkers now began to build their houses around the Battery to take advantage of the view, the sea breezes, and the isolation from city noise.

Just around the corner from the Battery was the grassy oval of Bowling Green and the beginning of Broadway. Bowling Green had been a cattle market in the days of the Dutch and, under British rule, a parade ground for troops in the fort at the nearby Battery. In 1733 the Common Council leased the land for eleven years to John Chambers, Peter Bayard, and Peter Jay at the annual rent of one peppercorn "to make a Bowling Green thereof with walks therein, for the beauty and ornament of the said street as well as for the recreation and delight of the inhabitants of this city." Bowling Green became a favorite promenade, and in 1742 the Common Council renewed the lease for another eleven years. The rent, however, had gone up; it was now twenty shillings a year.

In 1756 Archibald Kennedy, the colony's Receiver-General and later Earl of Cassilis, purchased the land known as 1 Broadway from Abraham De Peyster for £600. Soon after, he tore down several small houses on the site and purchased the property to the rear so that his land could stretch to the Hudson River. There, sometime before 1760, he built one of the finest mansions in the city. Bowling Green, opposite his home, was anything but quiet for the next few years. In 1765 a mob protesting the Stamp Act burned the British Governor in effigy at Bowling Green, along with his coach, which they had stolen from his stables. On July 9, 1776, another mob of patriots gathered there and pulled down the equestrian statue of King George III in the middle of the oval. Three days later the British fleet briefly shelled New York, hitting several houses near the Kennedy mansion and filling the neighborhood with smoke and the smell of powder. The six people killed in this attack were hastily buried that night in a mass grave in Bowling Green. After the British Army landed in New York on September 15, 1776, Sir William Howe and other British officers made the Kennedy mansion their headquarters, as George Washington had done during the early days of the war. Sir Guy Carleton, the last British Governor of New York, also used it as his residence. At the end of the Revolution, the Kennedy mansion was a girl's boarding school and then a fashionable boardinghouse. Archibald Kennedy returned to his ill-fated home in 1798, but in 1810, after his death, his heirs sold the mansion to Nathaniel Prime, partner in the Wall Street bankinghouse Prime, Ward, & King, whose family lived there for several decades.

Philip Hone envied the families living so close to the Battery, with its fine view and breezes, but his own home, 235 Broadway, opposite City Hall Park, had an equally pres-

Bowling Green, 1826

tigious address. Hone was one of the great self-made men of his era. The son of a carpenter, he was born in 1780 in a frame house at Dutch and John streets. In 1797, at the age of seventeen, he joined his elder brother, John, in his fledgling auction house. From the beginning the firm, which sold anything from woolens to works of art to wines and spirits, was "the first in business, uniformly prosperous and in the enjoyment of unbounded credit," recalled Hone. In 1815 the profits were $159,007, of which he received seven-twentieths, or $55,652. Other merchants respected Hone not only for his business acumen but also for his unbending honesty, open and frank manner, and pleasing sociability.

Despite this enviable life, Hone regretted that he had sacrificed education and experience to begin work at seventeen, and in 1821 he retired from the auction house with a handsome fortune. Now he sought out the great men, places, and events of his time. Neither his respectable but ordinary-looking home nor its location at 44 Cortlandt Street, a block and a half from the Hudson River, suited these goals. So, soon after his retirement, Hone purchased his handsome Broadway mansion for $25,000, and in 1825 served as Mayor of New York.

Broadway was the most desirable address in the city from its beginning among the secluded mansions of Bowling Green to the area around Canal Street, where the red brick row houses, slate sidewalks, and poplars gave way to decaying farmhouses and neglected fields. A Broadway address meant that a family was probably one of the richest in the city. In 1828 well over a hundred of the city's 500 richest men lived on Broadway, over three times more than on the nearest rival, Greenwich Street.

Since the 1780s, visitors to New York, like the Duke de La Rochefoucauld-Liancourt, had written that "there is not in any city in the world a finer street than Broadway." It was not just the "extremely handsome" houses that won his praise; Broadway was also the most well-known street in New York, the distillation of the city and its variety at its best. Goodrich's *Picture of New York* called Broadway the "handsomest street and greatest thoroughfare" in the city, and the *Mirror* wrote, "Broadway opens a grand thoroughfare through the city." The city's most fashionable shops now occupied the first floors of quondam dwellings near Wall Street. From 11:00 A.M. to 3:00 P.M. this stretch of Broadway was the favorite strolling place of the "fashionable, the gay, the idle," according to Anne Royalle in 1826. Baron Klinckowstrom added that "you then have a chance to see serious Quaker and Methodist costumes and grotesque Dutch dress, which contrast sharply with the modern costumes."

Broadway was more than the preferred residential and shopping street of New York society. Because of its eighty-foot width and route up the central spine of Manhattan, it became a favored road for pedestrians and carriages going north and south. Early in the morning, clerks, shopkeepers, and laborers filled its sidewalks on their way to work on Wall Street or along the East River. Thousands of men walked uptown at the end of the workday, but hours later Broadway was still filled with people on their way to the boarding-houses, hotels, restaurants, and theaters that were also dis-

Broadway: view from foot of City Hall Park, 1819

placing the homes on Broadway around Wall Street. The *Mirror* wrote, "We doubt if there is another street in the world which presents such a confused assemblage of high, low, broad, narrow, white, gray, red, brown, yellow, simple, and florid."

Broadway had always been one of the city's leading streets. Its route followed one of the Indian trails that once crisscrossed Manhattan. It appeared on maps of New Amsterdam as early as 1639, and the Dutch settlers called it *heere Straet* or *heere Wegh*, the highway. Around 1668 the name was Anglicized to Broadway. A few fine houses already had been built along lower Broadway, and in 1707 the Common Council ordered the street paved from Bowling Green to Wall Street with "pebble stones," which were somewhat smaller than cobblestones. The "regulated" or open and graded portion of Broadway did not stretch past Wall Street in 1700; the city didn't go any farther north at that time. Beyond that, Broadway was, at best, a rutted country road that ended at the fifty-foot hill near present-day Duane Street. In 1712 the Common Council ordered the street opened from Etienne De Lancey's house at 115 Broadway, near Trinity Church, and a well at the present corner of Ann Street. New York grew far enough northward in the following twenty years that Broadway was regulated in 1723 a few blocks farther north to the area of City Hall Park.

At the close of the Revolutionary War, the northern boundary of Broadway was the hill at Duane Street, then called Barley Street. In 1795 an advertisement in the *Argus* for a "new two-story house, brick front" on Broadway near Chambers Street suggested that "it will suit a genteel private family who would wish to reside in the country." The unsettled area just north of today's City Hall was best known for Collect Pond, now the site of Foley Square. The spring-fed pond was sixty feet deep in spots and was often used for skating in winter and boating in summer. In 1796 John Fitch, an inventor, tried out his eighteen-foot-long screw propeller–driven steamboat before a crowd of curious New Yorkers. Collect Pond drained westward into the Hudson River, and much of the land between Broadway and the river was wet marshland known as the Lispenard Meadows.

Although New York had not yet grown past Fulton Street, the city began to extend Broadway northward into the country in expectation of future growth. Around 1800 it leveled the hill at Duane Street and regulated Broadway several blocks farther north to Canal Street. In 1805 Broadway was extended to Prince Street, in 1806 to Great Jones Street, and in 1807 to Astor Place, where it ended at a farmer's picket fence.

In 1806 one New Yorker offered a Lutheran church in financial difficulty the gift of four acres of land at Broadway and Canal Street. The church, though hard-pressed, turned down the marshy land because it was not worth the expense of fencing. The church made a mistake. Collect Pond blocked city growth along the eastern side of Manhattan, and workmen were already filling it in. In 1809 the city had laid out

Collect Pond, 1798

Canal Street, with a sewer underneath to drain the spring, which had fed the pond, into the Hudson River. All traces of Collect Pond were gone in 1811, and real estate speculators were planning to build in the old Lispenard Meadows, no longer marshland.

Because Broadway formed a central axis, growth swept along it ahead of the northward move of the built-up city. In the early nineteenth century, New Yorkers were not at all surprised to see fine red brick row houses at the outskirts of Broadway with nothing but fields and rural shacks beyond. The sidestreets running into Broadway were already laid out but would not be built up until the city's growth caught up to the area several years later. New Yorkers were so captivated by Broadway's reputation as a residence that they paid high prices for these houses at the edge of the city. In 1807 one builder quickly sold a row of houses on Broadway between Worth and Leonard streets, despite their proximity to Collect Pond and the Lispenard Meadows. And a few years after that, a row of costly residences replaced several frame cottages on the east side of Broadway between Franklin and White streets, two blocks to the north.

Lispenard Meadows, 1785

LITH. BY G. HAYWARD 120 WATER St. N.Y.   FOR O. T. VALENTINE'S MANUAL 1858

LISPENARD'S MEADOWS
taken from the site of the present St. Nicholas Hotel Broadway

Living at the edge of the city presented problems not found in the areas already settled. The prominent New Yorkers who moved to the houses on Broadway between Worth and Leonard streets in 1807 endured the stench and disorder that accompanied the filling of Collect Pond. Years later John Randall recalled that the dirt and garbage thrown into the pond, "being of greater specific gravity than the debris, or mud at the bottom of 'the Pond,' caused it to rise and mix with the rubbish and stand out; forming a very offensive and irregular mound of several acres; which appeared to me, as seen from Broadway, between which and it there were no buildings, to be from twelve to fifteen feet in height above the level of the tide, and of the water remaining in the Pond."

By buying his home at 235 Broadway, Philip Hone avoided all the indignities that accompanied living at the edge of the city. His house faced City Hall Park; in the rear, the side-streets running slightly downhill from Broadway to the Hudson River contained some of the most desirable residences in the city. But the area around Park Place had not always been so fashionable. In 1809 the Baroness Hyde de Neuville, banished with her husband from France by Napoleon, painted a watercolor showing Warren and Greenwich streets in the

Warren and Greenwich streets, 1809

snow. The scene is charming — frame Federal houses, children sledding down the street, people on the sidewalks bundled up against the cold, and horse-drawn sleighs in the street. The neighborhood is distinctly middle-class. Houses such as these had disappeared in the 1820s and 1830s as well-to-do families rebuilt Barclay Street, Park Place, Murray Street, Warren Street, and Chambers Street with what the newspapers called "elegant three-story private dwellings." The newspapers described the remaining frame houses, by then a bit run-down and old-fashioned, as "the most miserable tenements in the city."

The upgrading of the Park Place area was an unusual phenomenon in nineteenth-century New York. Most respectable neighborhoods at this time eventually decayed into slums or gave way to trade. The Park Place area, however, had several advantages over most other neighborhoods. Several blocks downtown, the streets west of Broadway around the Battery and Trinity Church had always been fashionable. The streets west of Broadway were wider and laid out in a more regular pattern than those east of Broadway, and in warm weather they enjoyed cool breezes off the Bay and the Hudson River. In nineteenth-century New York, one type of land use, whether for trade or by a social class in search of homes, did not usually leapfrog from one location to another but generally moved into an adjacent spot from an area already dominated by that use. So it was by a logical sequence of events that Park Place and its neighboring streets took on the social characteristics of the streets west of Broadway just a few blocks downtown. The Park Place district was also fortunate in having Columbia College as a neighbor; it occupied a two-block-square campus, bounded by Barclay Street, Church Street, Murray Street, and College Place (now called West Broadway). Park Place stopped at the Church Street boundary of the campus and resumed its course a block to the west at College Place under its original name, Robinson Street.

An advertisement for a "valuable leasehold property" at the northwest corner of College Place and Robinson Street, which appeared in the *Commercial Advertiser*, gives an idea of the size and splendor of the houses being built in the area in the 1830s.

House 25 feet by 60 deep — Lot 25 feet by 130 feet. The house is three stories with attic, high basement and counter cellar seven feet in the clear and perfectly dry, paved, etc.

The house has been well finished, with marble mantels throughout and mahogany doors. It is roomy, with numerous closets and pantries, and in this respect is very convenient...

From the Southern exposure of the house, it is cool and pleasant in summer and warm in winter. The view in front, particularly from second and upper stories, over College Green, up Park Place and across the [City Hall] Park, is exceedingly beautiful, particularly in summer . . . A large portion of the purchase money can remain on bond and mortgage.

For further particulars, inquire on the premises.

This property, grand as it sounds, was nothing extraordinary for the Park Place area. Few New Yorkers boasted a home or lifestyle as grand as the bachelor merchant William Douglass, who lived at 28 Park Place, at the corner of Church Street, overlooking Columbia College. In 1840 Douglass began to hold *déjeuners à la fourchette* on Thursday afternoons between one o'clock and four. Hone and his daughters, Margaret and Mary, joined the "throng of beauty and fashion" at the second such entertainment, and afterward he pronounced the party "something of a novelty in this country [but] the last imitation of European refinement." In fact, "this series of breakfasts . . . can hardly be called *imitation*, for in taste, elegance, and good management it goes beyond most things of the kind in Europe." At two o'clock the guests ate a breakfast of meat pies, ice cream and pastries, coffee and hot chocolate, French wines and cooling lemonade. The first two floors of the house were open to the guests, who particularly admired the conservatory and singing canaries, bullfinches, and mockingbirds. A band at the top of the main stairs played all afternoon, and once the meal was over "the young folk" danced waltzes and cotillions "until the reluctant hour of departure."

Hone was one man in the area who lived as well as William Douglass. Seven years after moving into 235 Broadway in 1828, Hone began a diary, which he kept with dogged regularity until his death two million words later in 1851.

Philip Hone

Whether Hone hoped that his diary would preserve his memory after his death is uncertain, but it is clear that he relished recalling his friendships and good times with men like John Jacob Astor, James Fenimore Cooper, Washington Irving, Daniel Webster, and Henry Clay. He also enjoyed the comfort and tranquillity of his home and liked nothing better than spending an afternoon in his library, reading one of his many books or writing in his diary. But in the 1830s life on Broadway became less pleasant for the Hones. Every year brought more pedestrians and vehicles, and the shops and hotels, which were once located around Trinity Church, had crept northward and engulfed the blocks around Hone's residence.

The Fourth of July was always a trial for residents of this

stretch of Broadway. Thousands of New Yorkers gathered in City Hall Park to set off fireworks, drink beer and hard liquor sold in booths, and wander around the adjoining streets shouting and singing patriotic songs late into the night. The American Hotel, next door to the Hones', at the corner of Park Place, was another occasional nuisance. In May 1834, for instance, the Young Whigs held a dinner at the hotel for Davy Crockett, described by Hone as "the Tennessee member of Congress so celebrated for eccentricity and strong natural talents." During the dinner, "there was speaking, singing, toasting, and shouting until a late hour; very much to the annoyance of my household, for we are so near that the noise of the carouse disturbed such of us as wished to sleep." A group from the dinner came next door to invite Hone to join them, but "I was not at home and I presume it was lucky for me."

The influx of shops and hotels and the noise of traffic did not upset him that much. It was to be expected if one lived in so prominent a spot. If Hone had wanted seclusion as well as a fashionable address, he could have bought a similar home for $25,000 around the Battery or on St. John's Park. But he did not want to live with the demolition and construction that accompanied Broadway's transformation from homes to shops and hotels. In 1834 John Jacob Astor began to build the fabled Astor House on the blockfront of Broadway just south of Hone's residence. The hotel, Hone realized, was "probably intended as a monument to its wealthy proprietor." Astor, then seventy-three, lived on the projected site and wanted to build his hotel at almost any cost. He was able to purchase the rest of the block, except for John G. Costar's home, 227 Broadway. The elderly Costar refused Astor's offer of $30,000, the market value of the house. Astor raised his offer to $40,000, but Costar again turned him down. He had lived there for years and didn't need the money. Finally, Astor revealed his plan to Costar.

According to an account written by James McCabe years later:

"I want to build a hotel," said [Astor]. "I have got all the other lots. Now name your own price."

Mr. Costar replied that he would sell for $60,000 if his wife would consent, and that Mr. Astor could see her the next morning. Mr. Astor was punctual to the appointment, and his offer was accepted by the good lady, who said to him, condescendingly, "I don't want to sell the house, but we are such old friends that I am willing for your sake."

Astor used to remark with great glee that anyone could afford to exhibit such condescension after receiving double the value of a piece of property.

Hone praised the planned hotel as "a great public advantage" and "an ornament to the city." But its construction made him and his neighbors miserable. During the demolition of the houses on the site, "the dust from the immense mass of rubbish has been almost intolerable . . . " Then, with the start of construction, Hone faced more dust, piles of building materials blocking the sidewalks and even spilling into Broadway, noisy traffic jams in the street because of these blockages, and crowds of rowdy workmen in the area. Hone and his family started to look for a new home that year and left 235 Broadway before the Astor House opened for guests.

Broadway from Park Place to Barclay Street, with Philip Hone's residence, 1831

Hone regretted giving up his home of sixteen years. "I shall leave this delightful house with feelings of deep regret. The splendid rooms, the fine situation, my snug library, well arranged books, handsome pictures, what will become of them?" But he left his home for the same reason as his neighbor, Costar. Hone sold his house to Elijah Boardman, owner of the American Hotel next door, for $60,000. Boardman converted the lower floors into shops and joined the upper floors to the hotel. "I have turned myself out of doors," wrote Hone, "but $60,000 is a great deal of money."

4

Once Philip Hone decided that he and his
family should leave their home on Broadway facing City Hall
Park, he began to look uptown for another house or a well-
situated lot on which to build one to his specifications. One
day, after a meeting of the board of directors of the Bank for
Savings, Hone and fellow board member, Abraham Swan,
walked uptown to look at property on Second Avenue, St.
Mark's Place, Tompkins Square, and Lafayette Place. Just a
few years earlier this land had been "orchards, cornfields, or
morasses a pretty smart distance from town . . . a journey to
which was formerly an affair of some moment, and required
preparation beforehand," recalled Hone. Now this area was
"the most fashionable quarter of New York," attracting men,
like Swan and himself, who were selling their homes downtown to shopkeepers and hotel owners. "Almost everybody
downtown is in the same predicament. We are tempted with
prices so exorbitantly high that none can resist, and the old
downtown burgomasters, who have fixed to one spot all
their lives, will be seen during the next Summer in flocks,
marching reluctantly north."

Two weeks after this walk uptown Hone purchased a lot at
the southeast corner of Broadway and Great Jones Street.
Although the neighborhood was only partly built up and lay
at the outskirts of the city, *New York As It Is* had already
declared that "some of the rows of houses in Lafayette Place,
Bond Street, Bleecker Street, &c., may vie, for beauty and
taste, with European palaces." Hone was so delighted with

his new neighborhood that he rented 716 Broadway, opposite Washington Place, for $1600 a year while waiting for his new home to be finished. His temporary residence was "a fine house, delightfully situated," he wrote. "The distance to walk downtown is not by any means so fatiguing as I apprehended, and if I prefer riding, I can always get an omnibus in a minute or two by going out of the door and holding up my finger." The Tompkins Market, a few blocks away on Third Avenue, had over a hundred meat and vegetable stalls, and the "grocery stores abound in this region equally as good as any downtown."

Perhaps the best-known street in this neighborhood was Bond Street, which ran for just one thousand-foot-long block between Broadway and the Bowery. Jonas Minturn built the first house on Bond Street, Number 22, in 1820. Its white marble front was one of the first for a house in New York. Other affluent families and builders followed Minturn to outlying Bond Street, and by the late 1820s fine row houses occupied nearly twenty of the street's sixty lots. Real estate advertisements in New York newspapers described the grandeur of these houses and a rich family's lifestyle. An advertisement in the *Evening Post* in 1826 read:

To Let in Bond Street — the two elegant three-story marble houses on the north side of Bond Street, being the second and third from Broadway, with large brick stables in the rear on Great Jones Street. The lots are twenty-six feet wide and 200 deep. The houses are finished throughout in the best manner, having marble mantels and grates in nine rooms, stoves in the halls, vaults front and rear — in the yards are wells of excellent water, large brick cisterns, and a variety of fruit trees, vines, &c. The house can be seen and terms known by applying at the first house in Bond Street, or to the subscribers, 63 Pine Street,

Lambert, Brothers, & Co.

By the time Philip Hone moved into his mansion in 1837, Bond Street was almost completely lined with three- and four-story row houses, some of them Federal, others Greek Revival. Property owners along Bond Street had planted two trees in front of every lot in the 1820s and soon the foliage was so dense that in summer only the stoops and front doors of each house could be easily seen from the street.

In the 1830s and 1840s Bond Street was the residence of
some of New York's best-known citizens, including Dr. Gardiner Spring, beloved pastor of Brick Presbyterian Church
for sixty-three years; Albert Gallatin, Secretary of the Treasury for twelve years under Presidents Jefferson and Madison; General Winfield Scott, hero of the Mexican War; Coventry Waddell, the lawyer who built the magnificent Gothic
Revival country house on Fifth Avenue between Thirty-seventh and Thirty-eighth streets in the 1840s; and Samuel B.
Ruggles, who laid out Union Square and Gramercy Park
when he developed his family's real estate holdings north of
Fourteenth Street at this time.

Bleecker Street, one block south of Bond Street, was just
as fashionable an address and the location of houses more
distinguished architecturally than was its perhaps better-
known neighbor. Fine row houses lined Bleecker Street from

51

its beginning, at the Bowery, to Sixth Avenue, nine blocks to the west. Beyond Sixth Avenue it turned northward and was lined with modest houses and shops as it ran through the West Village.

New Yorkers admired Bleecker Street's long sweep across town, one of the features of the uptown grid street plan. The width and rectangular layout of streets in the Bond Street district were a distinct improvement over the narrow, twisting streets south of Houston Street or in the West Village. "The streets in the lower and older portion of the city are very narrow and crooked, and what is more immediately inexcusable, are kept in very bad order," observed an English visitor. "The more modern streets are greatly superior in every respect; they are in general wide and straight, and the footwalks comparatively free from projections and encumberances."

The sweep of Bleecker Street was a suitable setting for the terraces or monumental blockfronts of houses that New Yorkers began to admire in the 1820s. The first such terrace built in New York was Le Roy Place on both sides of Bleecker Street, between Mercer and Greene streets. In 1827 Isaac G. Pearson, a builder, purchased the land for $400 to $600 a lot and renamed that one block of Bleecker Street in honor of Jacob Le Roy, one of the leading merchants in the trade with India and the East Indies. Over the next few years, Pearson built large, granite-faced, Federal houses, each of which cost between $11,000 and $12,000.

A print drawn by architect Alexander Jackson Davis shows one side of Le Roy Place a year or two after its completion. The row houses are identical, except for the two houses in the center; they are taller than the others and stand out a few feet from the blockfront. A continuous iron fence, railings at the second-floor windows, and a classical balustrade at the roofline reinforced the visual unity of the blockfront. The houses on the other side of the street, which were not drawn by Davis, formed a uniform, but nonetheless impressive, blockfront. To enhance the visual unity, Pearson set all the houses ten feet back from the front lot line, thereby leaving each house a small front yard and giving the street a greater width and dignity than was usually available on crosstown blocks.

The Le Roy Place terrace met New Yorkers' yearnings for architectural grandeur, which would reflect the wealth of their families and city. "A marked deviation from every rule of regularity is one of the most striking peculiarities in the streets of New York," declared Fay's *View in New-York*. "While some run in straight lines, others describe a circuitous course . . . The houses present numerous instances of the same inconsistency. A fine block may sometimes be observed wherein each house is of different height and composed of various materials." The houses of Le Roy Place, however, "have a uniform color, and present an imposing appearance, [and] afford a new evidence of the surprising improvements visible in the city." The acclaim that greeted Le Roy Place upon its completion and the easy sale of the houses at a profit encouraged other real estate developers to build impressive terraces, including several more on Bleecker Street.

The greatest terrace in New York, however, rose not on Bleecker Street but on Lafayette Place, several blocks away. La Grange Terrace, or the Colonnade Row, as it was more often called, was "universally allowed to be unequaled for grandeur and effect," according to the *Knickerbocker*. The houses, which sold for $25,000 to $30,000 at their completion in 1833, were "the most imposing and magnificent in the city." A two-story colonnade ran the full length of the row in front of the second- and third-story windows. A boldly rusticated basement and first floor provided a balance for the colonnade and the heavy cornice, which concealed the distinctly unclassical pitched roof. In the 1830s and 1840s Irving Van Wart, whose relative Washington Irving spent entire winters with him, lived at 33 Lafayette Place, in the Colonnade Row; Franklin H. Delano, grandfather of Franklin Delano Roosevelt, owned 39; and David Gardiner, whose daughter Julia married President John Tyler in 1844, lived at 43 Lafayette Place.

Even before the completion of the resplendent Colonnade Row, Lafayette Place was already a grand and lovely street. The spot had been well known for years before the opening of the street in 1826. Jacob Sperry, a Swiss physician who came to New York in 1748 at the age of twenty, purchased

Lafayette Place, 1866

what was then pasture land to grow flowers and hothouse plants. Sperry's gardens, a mile from the outskirts of town, became a pleasant destination for New Yorkers on their early evening and weekend walks and, according to the *Herald* years later, was "the great resort of belles and beaux for the purchase of their bouquets."

In 1804 Sperry sold his gardens to John Jacob Astor for $45,000. Astor, in turn, leased the property to a Frenchman named Delacroix, who turned the spot into a country pleasure grounds known as Vauxhall Gardens. Delacroix placed classical busts and statues along the winding gravel paths among Sperry's trees and flowers. Groups of people enjoyed juleps, wines, and ice creams in the summer pavilions and leafy alcoves he scattered throughout the gardens. The former greenhouse became a saloon for serious drinking. A band played almost continually in the center of the garden, and at night there were fireworks and theatrical entertainments. Vauxhall Gardens, recalled the *Herald,* had "no rival, no equal" as a "resort of the fashionable — the young and old."

When Delacroix's lease on the property expired in 1825, the streets just to the south, Bleecker, Bond, and Great Jones, were already becoming some of the most choice residential streets in the city. So Astor cut a broad street, several blocks long, through Vauxhall Gardens. This was Lafayette Place. Vauxhall Gardens was reduced to half its former size, beginning at the back of the lots of the houses along the east side of Lafayette Place and ending where it had before, at the Bowery. Astor sold the lots along both sides of Lafayette Place for many times more than the $45,000 he had paid for the entire property twenty-one years earlier.

The development of Lafayette Place shows what James McCabe called Astor's "regular system" of real estate speculation. Although Astor sometimes bought property in the built-up portion of the city if the price was right, he preferred to buy land far beyond its outskirts. The city was growing northward so fast that Astor's property was in the line of development years before anyone but he had dreamed possible. He then sold by the lot the property that he had bought by the acre ten or twenty years earlier.

In 1810 he sold a lot on Wall Street for $8000 in cash. Once the sale was made, the new owner asked Astor why he would sell for $8000 property that everyone said would be worth $12,000 in just a few years.

" 'That is true,' said Mr. Astor," according to McCabe's account, " 'but see what I intend doing with these $8000. I shall buy eighty lots above Canal Street, and by the time your one lot is worth $12,000, my eighty lots will be worth $80,000.' His expectations were realized," wrote McCabe.

Astor never lived on Lafayette Place. After demolishing his home of over thirty years at 223 Broadway to make room for the Astor House, he moved to 585 Broadway, near Prince Street, where he died in 1848. His son William B. Astor however, did live at 34 Lafayette Place, opposite the Colonnade Row, in a large but plain red brick mansion. Despite its outward simplicity, Philip Hone thought that the house was "magnificent . . . one of the finest in the city." Astor's family had a lovely garden in the rear and a private riding gallery.

The Bond Street area and Lafayette Place were just two of the uptown areas attracting rich New Yorkers from the increasingly commercial streets downtown. Philip Hone and his friend Abraham Swan, during their walk uptown, had looked around St. Mark's Place, Second Avenue, and Tompkins Square as well as Lafayette Place.

St. Mark's Place was the three blocks of Eighth Street between Third Avenue and Avenue A, which runs along the western edge of Tompkins Square, and was filled with fine row houses and mansions. But the block between Second and Third avenues was by far the most impressive. In 1831 Thomas E. Davis built two rows of identical, richly detailed red brick Federal row houses down both sides of the 800-foot-long block. The grandeur of these two rows was heightened by their standing virtually alone in the meadows and marshland of the Stuyvesant family's farm.

The farm's boundaries were present-day Third Street, Avenue C, Twenty-third Street, and the Bowery, once spelled *Bouwerie,* the Dutch word for "farm." The family had owned the land since the seventeenth century and the days of Peter Stuyvesant, the last Dutch Governor of New Amsterdam. As the city neared their property, the Stuyvesants were determined that the land be developed in a way that would be profitable for them and good for New York. As early as 1789, Petrus Stuyvesant, the great-grandson of the Dutch Governor, mapped out some of the land around his mansion, which stood at today's Second Avenue and Tenth Street, in a grid street plan running exactly north to south and east to west. Several of the houses built for this street plan still stand today: 21 Stuyvesant Street (1803–1804), the home of his daughter Elizabeth and her husband, Nicholas Fish, and 44 (circa 1795), home of Nicholas William Stuyvesant.

The city's 1807–1811 grid street plan, which guided the development of land north of Houston Street, varied considerably from the Stuyvesant family plan. The city's streets followed the axis of Manhattan rather than the east and west compass points. Other New Yorkers besides the Stuyvesants had laid out streets and built houses in the way of the city's street plan. As the city opened streets according to its plan, all the country lanes and streets at variance with its grid were closed, the houses demolished or moved, and the owners compensated for their losses in land or houses. The Stuyvesant family, however, was influential enough that the street where they had built their houses remained open "both for public convenience and for the accommodation of a large and respectable congregation attending St. Mark's Church as well as the owners and occupants of several large and commodious dwelling houses . . . all of which would be destroyed, or rendered of little value, if that street were closed," in the statement by the Common Council in 1830.

The city opened Third Avenue through the Stuyvesant holdings in 1812, Second Avenue in 1816, and Eighth, Ninth, Tenth, Eleventh, and Twelfth streets in 1826. Row houses and mansions, some costing as much as $30,000 or $40,000, began to rise on Second Avenue, and in the 1840s and 1850s it became one of the most desirable addresses in the city, under the guidance of the Stuyvesant family.

Another nearby spot that, surprisingly, attracted some prosperous families in the 1830s and 1840s was Tompkins Square, the ten-acre park bounded by Avenue A, Tenth Street, Avenue B, and Seventh Street. The city opened the park in 1834 and the next year built an ornamental cast-iron

59

fence around the periphery and planted shade trees on the grassy lawns. Two years later, Caroline Gilman, a Charleston author visiting New York, thought that Tompkins Square was "handsomely laid out and affords a fine view of the East River and opposite shore of Long Island." The park had become "a place of great resort during the warm season, especially on Sundays, and . . . a favorite parade ground for the military corps of the city."

All this open space in a city with almost no park land led New Yorkers to predict a brilliant future for the area around Tompkins Square. St. Mark's Place, which ended on the western side of the park, linked the neighborhood to fashionable Second Avenue and Lafayette Place. Throughout the 1830s and 1840s New Yorkers periodically heard of plans to build terraces of fine row houses around the park's edge. In 1839 "a well-known wealthy religious society" proposed that a church be built in the middle of each street facing Tompkins Square. The *Herald* thought that this idea would be "an ornament to the city" and even suggested that Trinity Church, then trying to decide what to do with its decaying old edifice, should erect a new church on Tompkins Square. All these proposals never got past the talking stage. Old shanties and stables marred the edges of Tompkins Square. When building operations got underway around the park in the mid-1840s, the new houses were decidedly not for the upper class which had, ten years earlier, been expected to live there.

Tompkins Square was too far east of the main course of expensive residences up Broadway to become a truly stylish neighborhood. Rich New Yorkers who wanted to live in houses facing a park instead chose Washington Square, three blocks west of Broadway. The Square had once been marshland, fed by the Minetta Brook, and after 1795 it was a potter's field and the site of the city gallows. In 1826 the city purchased some additional land here and turned the area into the Washington Parade-Ground and a public park. Two years later, Blunt's *Picture of New York* described Washington Square as "another great and most effective ornament to our city" and noted that "there have already been erected around it, many handsome private dwellings, and this vicinity has likewise become a most fashionable residence, although somewhat remote at present from the center of business."

Some of the first houses built on Washington Square indeed served as country homes for their owners. Number 20 Washington Square, the first house built on the north side of the Square, was the summer house of George P. Rogers, whose other home was 18 Broadway, opposite Bowling Green. The house was enlarged and altered in the 1880s and now accords visually with the row houses on either side. Rogers' home originally was a thirty-seven-foot-wide mansion, with the pitched roof and dormer windows typical of the Federal style, and stood alone on its own grounds with a carriageway on the west side leading to a stable in the rear.

Rogers' mansion soon lost its countrified setting. Builders were busy erecting row houses on the south side of Washington Square in the late 1820s, and in 1831 Sailors' Snug Harbor, the home for retired seamen, leased the north side of the Square between Fifth Avenue and University Place to James Boorman, John Johnston, and John Morrison. Under the terms of their lease, which ran for 100 years, the developers agreed to build "a good and substantial dwelling house, of the width of said lot, three or more stories high, in brick or stone, covered with slate or metal," set back twelve feet from the front lot line, and "to be finished in such style as may be approved of by" the lessor. The developer also had the right to build a stable at the rear of the lot as long as it did not become a "slaughterhouse, tallow chandelery, smith shop, forge, furnace or brass foundry, nail or other iron factory, or any manufactory . . . trade business which may be noxious or offensive to the neighbors."

Zoning regulations were then unknown in New York, and the restrictions in the Sailors' Snug Harbor leases for 1–13 Washington Square North were designed to protect the property owners from "nuisances," as they were called, which afflicted nearly all residential areas of the city. Sailors' Snug Harbor was looking after its own interests, too. In 1801 Captain Robert Richard Randall had bequeathed twenty-one acres of land north and east of what became Washington Square as the site for such a home for retired seamen. Randall's family, however, contested the will, and by the time the courts ruled in favor of Sailors' Snug Harbor the city had grown to the edge of its twenty-one-acre property. So the trustees voted to move the home to Staten Island and lease the valuable Manhattan property for income. Sailors' Snug Harbor had the good fortune to own land in the path of fashionable residential growth. The trustees added the restrictions against nuisances to the Washington Square deeds to help guarantee that the property would attract rich New Yorkers who would pay high ground rents for their lots.

The houses erected at 1–13 Washington Square North were among the first in New York to display the Greek Revival style, which was superseding the long-popular Federal style in the early 1830s. Their fronts were red brick, as with Federal houses, but the freestanding white marble porches supported by Doric columns had replaced the intricately leaded fanlight and sidelights as the front door's primary ornament. The stoop railings and front fences now displayed such Greek motifs as the anthemion, a stylized honeysuckle, and the fret, or Greek key. The houses along Washington Square North had a flat roofline, pierced by small windows to light the attic beneath the roof, which now sloped backward. The pitched roof and dormer windows, characteristic of Federal, were now considered "ugly projections . . . which in many streets disfigure almost every private building."

An 1833 real estate advertisement for the just-completed 2 Washington Square stated that this "elegant private residence . . . is believed inferior to no house in the United States, either in workmanship or convenience." But it was the monumental terrace formed by these houses that excited New Yorkers more than their individual splendor or Greek Revival style. The houses were known simply as "The Row" throughout the nineteenth century. The richly detailed front fence, extending several hundred feet, the evenly aligned front doorways and windows, and the even cornice line made for an impressive vista. The location — it faced Washington Square — and the twelve-foot-deep front yards, which were a part of the deed restrictions, gave the Row a grandeur and aloofness lacking in most row-house terraces built close to the sidewalk on the usual narrow crosstown street.

"The Row," Washington Square North

Occasionally residents of the Row were reminded of Washington Square's less-than-aristocratic past. In the late nineteenth century, E. N. Tailer, who had lived at 11 Washington Square North in the 1830s, wrote: "I remember when heavy guns were drawn over the Square, after it became a parade ground, that the weight broke through the ground into the trenches in which the dead were buried and crushed the tops of some of the coffins . . . At one time near Fourth and Thompson Streets, I saw a vault under the sidewalk opened and the body found there was still wrapped in the yellow sheet in which the yellow fever victims were buried." But living on Washington Square in the 1830s also had considerable advantages. Mrs. Emily Johnston de Forest recalled that "the houses in the 'Row' . . . all had beautiful gardens in the rear about ninety feet deep, surrounded by white, grape-covered trellises with rounded arches at intervals and lovely borders full of old-fashioned flowers." Beyond the back yards of Washington Square North were open fields and unpaved roads, where children played and families took their carriages for a ride in the country.

The streets west of Washington Square, however, were already filling up by the mid-1830s. After a visit to Sixth Avenue near Washington Square in 1835, a writer for the *Herald* "wondered that in so short a space of time so great a revolution could have taken place. Instead of the lanes and groves where we were wont to take a ramble, stand rows of splendid two, three, and four story buildings, embracing numerous stores, the appearance of which denotes the mind of enterprise." The red brick rows of buildings on Sixth Avenue ended at West Eleventh or West Twelfth Street, and at the corner of West Fourteenth Street stood the country house of a French-born gentleman. The *Herald* reported that "it reminded us of the Montgomery plantation on the banks of the Mississippi, deficient only in the scented rose, violet, and magnolia."

The growth of Greenwich Village, so goes the story, started with the yellow fever epidemic of 1822. "The malignant or yellow fever generally commences in the confined parts of the town, near the waterside, in the month of August or September," an English visitor wrote after the 1805 epidemic.

As soon as this dreadful scourge makes its appearance in New York, the inhabitants shut up their shops, and fly from their houses into the country. Those who cannot go far, on account of business, removed to Greenwich, a small village situated on the border of the Hudson River, about two or three miles from town. Here the merchants and others have their offices, and carry on their concerns with little danger from the fever, which does not seem contagious beyond a certain distance. The banks and other public offices also remove their business to this place; and markets are regularly established for the supply of the inhabitants.

As they had not done in earlier years, New Yorkers panicked in the 1822 epidemic. The yellow fever broke out in the stylish streets west of Broadway, just a few blocks north of the Battery, for the first time in anyone's memory. All earlier epidemics had first appeared in the crowded streets along

West Eleventh Street, 1825, showing open fields

the East River filled with warehouses, waterfront taverns, and the squalid homes of the poor. In the confusion, the city government declared everything below City Hall an "infected district" and removed those people from their homes who had not yet fled the city. Within a week, Greenwich Village was swarming with refugees. "Hundreds of wooden houses were reared up in a twinkling and even Sunday put no stop to the sound of the hammer or the saw," reported Peter Neilson, a Scotsman. New Yorkers talked of abandoning their city two miles downtown altogether and starting anew in Greenwich Village, but most people and businesses returned to their former locations with the first frost in October and the consequent disappearance of the yellow fever. Greenwich Village, however, was no longer the country. The wooden buildings, which had been hastily erected during the summer, now housed families who did not wish or could not afford to live farther downtown.

The epidemic of 1822 was not the only factor eroding Greenwich Village's country past. The city would have engulfed the area in the 1820s anyway; the epidemic only speeded up the process by several years. In the building boom following the War of 1812, builders began erecting modest red brick row houses in the streets leading to the Hudson River north of Canal Street. The following advertisement from the *Evening Post* describes one of these houses:

To Let, three elegant two-story brick houses, situated in Dominick Street, between Hudson and Varick Sts. The houses are finished in the most modern style, with vaults in front; the yards and walks are flagged with blue stone; the rooms are finished with marble chimney pieces, and grates for Lehigh coal, with folding doors, and Davy's patent locks. Also the brick front house and store 451 Greenwich, three doors from Canal Street. For further particulars, inquire of Azariah Ross, 36 Dominick Street, or A. Van Cleef, corner of Hudson and Dominick Streets.

Three blocks north of these newly finished houses stood Richmond Hill, which had once been a charming country house. "I remember it well," recalled one New Yorker in the 1830s, "a long, low venerable, irregular, white, cottage-like

69 Downing Street: a little Federal house

brick and wood building, pleasant notwithstanding, with a number of small, low rooms and a very spacious parlor, delightfully situated on a steep bank, some fifty feet above the shore, on which the waves of the Hudson and the sides of the bay dashed and sported. There was a fine orchard, too, and a garden on the north." At various times, Richmond Hill was the temporary headquarters of George Washington; the home of John Adams, the Vice President, when New York was the nation's capital from 1789 to 1790; and, after 1797, the home of Aaron Burr, whose parties were famed throughout the city.

Burr foresaw the eventual spread of the city into this vicinity as early as 1797. That year he mapped out present-day Vandam, Charlton, and King streets through the six-acre estate. Nothing came of these plans because the city was too far distant from the property, and Burr left the city that year in disgrace after his duel with Alexander Hamilton. In 1803 John Jacob Astor purchased the estate from Burr and over the next few years prepared the property for development. The estate's hill was cut down, and the house moved to the southeast corner of Charlton and Varick streets. In the early 1820s, Astor began to sell off building lots in the area, and row houses began to rise on the streets that followed Burr's twenty-year-old plan.

Like most other houses in the city, those in the Charlton Street area were erected on speculation by ordinary carpenters and masons or a professional builder with a crew of workmen, each man performing his own specialty, cellar digging, masonry, or carpentry. Few houses at this time were built for a particular family according to its specifications. Although professional builders accounted for many of the city's row houses, the buildings were still small and simple enough for a carpenter or mason to erect an occasional house or two on speculation. An Englishman who visited New York around 1820 described some aspects of row house construction at the time.

Building appears brisk in the city. It is generally performed by contract. A person intending to have a house erected contracts with a professed builder; the builder, with a bricklayer; and he, with all other necessary to the completion of the design. In some cases, a builder is a sort of head workman, for the purpose of overseeing the others; receiving for his agency seven-pence a day from the wages of each man; the men being employed and paid by him. There are occasional instances in which there is no contract, everything paid for according to measure and value.

The last sentence makes the distinction between "construction by contract," in which there was an incentive to finish the house as quickly as possible and start another one, and "day's work," in which workmen were paid by the day and were expected to do the highest quality work. The speculative builder, whether working for himself or a wealthy investor, usually worked by contract. Only a family commissioning a house for its own occupancy would pay for the "day's work" arrangement.

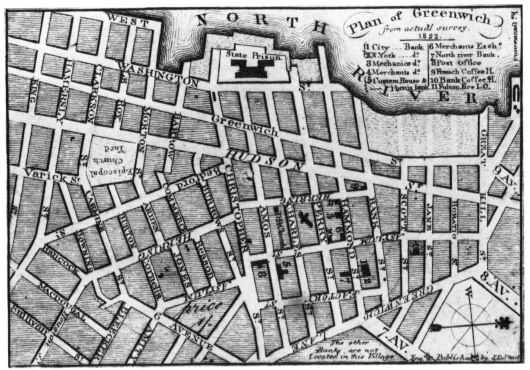

Map of Greenwich Village, 1822

The speculative builder usually began construction during the summer of one year and finished the house the following March or April so that it would be sold or rented before May 1, the traditional moving day in the early and mid-nineteenth century. Only unusually large and elaborately ornamented row houses or mansions took longer than one year to complete.

No sooner had row-house construction moved into the Charlton Street area than it swept into Greenwich Village, whose southern boundary had long been Houston Street. Speculative builders first worked on Sixth Avenue, Hudson Street, and Greenwich Street, which led to lower Manhattan and had been open for some time. Row houses, in general, appeared on the winding sidestreets only when the most eligible sites on the north-to-south routes were gone. An 1829 advertisement for a pair of houses on Hudson Street, near St. Luke's Chapel at Christopher Street, indicates the pleasant life of middle-class families at this time, as well as the charm of the surrounding neighborhood.

69

*Sixth Avenue near Eighth
Street, 1862*

Houses in Hudson Street . . . Nos. 359 and 353, near St. Luke's Church . . . having marble mantel pieces, and elegant brass grates to burn either Liverpool or anthracite coal . . . There are green Venetian shutters on all the windows in the houses, a vegetable vault near the kitchen, brick cisterns with pumps, and stone sinks in the yard, and woodhouses in the rear of the lots, having an entrance through an alley from Barrow Street, obviating the necessity of carrying fuel through the houses. The yards are partly paved, and have green plots in the center. There is a good well of water opposite, sufficiently soft for washing. The situation is delightful.

New Yorkers of the early and mid-nineteenth century liked Greenwich Village almost as much as have the city's residents in recent years. Greenwich Village, specifically the streets between Sixth Avenue and the Hudson River, was one of the few neighborhoods where middle-class families could live at a reasonable cost in their own homes on quiet, sunny, largely residential streets. James Fenimore Cooper, writing in his *Notions of the Americans,* described these row houses, which filled the western reaches of Greenwich Village:

There is a species of second-rate, genteel houses, that abound in New York, into which I have looked when passing with the utmost pleasure. They have, as usual, a story that is half sunk in the earth, receiving light from an area, and two floors above. The tenants of these buildings are chiefly merchants, or professional men, in moderate circumstances, who pay rents of from 300 to 500 dollars a year. You know that no American, who is at all comfortable in life, will share his dwelling with another. Each has his own roof, and his own little yard. These buildings are finished, and exceedingly well finished too, to the attics; containing, on the average, six rooms, besides offices, and servants' apartments. The furniture of these houses is often elegant, and always neat. Mahogany abounds here, and is commonly used for all the principal articles, and very frequently for doors, railings of stairs, &c. &c.

Middle-class New Yorkers, unfortunately, were never to live this pleasantly or cheaply for the rest of the nineteenth century.

5

As row houses spread uptown into Bond
Street and Washington Square in the 1830s, trade took over
more of the residential streets downtown. Even Bowling
Green and lower Broadway, whose row houses and mansions were so lovely and had once appeared so resistant to
change, slowly began to give way to trade. In 1837 the *Herald*
wrote that Bowling Green was "the only place in the lower
part of the city, whose rural, picturesque, and placid beauties still remain, in the midst of the mad mania of speculation
and improvement." Around Bowling Green, "the quiet air of
the old times still lingers — the trees — the shrubs — the
green grass — and the *tout ensemble* of nature, as yet redolent
of their ancient sweets, [while] every other part of Broadway,
up to its farthest extremity is filled with carts, carriages, omnibuses, dust, dirt, noise, and uproar."

The *Herald's* description doesn't tell everything that was
happening around Bowling Green. The mansions on both
sides of the oval fenced park, it is true, were still "quiet,
gentlemanly, elegant, and pleasing" in appearance, but they
had become stylish boardinghouses favored by bachelors,
widows, and visitors staying in New York for several weeks
or more. Although these boardinghouses did not harm the
genteel appearance of Bowling Green, they were business
properties, and when business dictated a more profitable use
for the property, the building would be altered or demolished for that purpose, even if the change might harm the
fashion of the neighborhood. By the mid-1830s real estate

speculators were already eyeing Bowling Green as a spot on which to build countinghouses and warehouses.

They did not worry about destroying the area's long-standing charm or paying enormous prices for the property. The city, like the nation, was enjoying unparalleled prosperity in the mid-1830s, and the rashest speculation in New York real estate often turned out to be the most profitable. "Our country is prospering beyond all precedent," Samuel F. B. Morse wrote James Fenimore Cooper, who was living in Paris, in 1833. "Everything is thriving, commerce, manufactories, agriculture . . . There is no country on Earth like our own. If we did but properly appreciate the blessings we enjoy, we should be the happiest."

Speculation in New York and Long Island real estate had become "one of the bubbles of the day," according to Hone. "Men in moderate circumstances have become immensely rich merely by the good fortune of owning farms of a few acres in this chosen land." He continued, somewhat enviously: "Abraham Schermerhorn has sold his farm of 170 acres at Gowanus, three miles from Brooklyn, at $600 per acre; four years ago, having got out of conceit of it as a residence, he offered it for sale at $20,000, and would have taken $18,000; to-day he pockets $102,000, and regrets that he sold it so cheap!"

The same speculative frenzy was sweeping Manhattan. The city had grown no more than three miles north of the Battery and its population was around a quarter of a million in the mid-1830s. Captain Frederick Marryat, the British novelist, who visited New York in 1837–1838, reported that "building lots were marked out for the other seven miles; and, by calculation, these lots, when built upon, would contain an additional population of one million and three-quarters. They were first purchased at from $100 to $150 each, but, as the epidemic raged, they rose to upwards of $2,000." Over in Brooklyn, which then had a population of thirty thousand, Marryat noted that "lots were marked out to the extent of fourteen miles, which would contain an extra population of 1,000,000, and these were eagerly speculated in."

Men who owned real estate did well in this period of ascending values. In 1836 Philip Hone was delighted to sell his home, for which he had paid $25,000 in 1821, for $60,000. But he complained about the inflation, which was raising his household costs as well as real estate prices. The year before he sold 235 Broadway, he wrote:

Living in New York is exorbitantly dear, and it falls pretty hard upon persons like me, who live upon their income, and harder still upon that large and respectable class consisting of the officers and clerks of public institutions, whose support is derived from fixed salaries. Marketing of all kinds, with the exception of apples and potatoes, is higher than I ever knew it . . . I paid to-day $30 a ton for hay, and not an old-fashioned ton of 2,240 pounds, but a new-fangled ton, invented to cheat the consumer, of 2,000 pounds. This is a cent and a half a pound, nearly three times the ordinary price. I paid also for my winter butter, 400 to 500 pounds, two shillings four pence per pound. In the long course of thirty-four years housekeeping, I never buttered my bread at so extravagant a rate.

Just a few months later, he complained: "The market was higher this morning than I have ever known it — beef twenty-five cents per pound, mutton and veal fifteen to eighteen cents, small turkeys $1.50."

Inflation did not affect his financial position though, because he was making much more money in real estate than he was losing in higher food prices or servants' wages. But late in 1836 real estate values in New York started dropping, while prices, in general, continued rising. "Real estate is a drug," wrote Hone. "There are no sales, there is no money to pay for it." By the beginning of the next year, real estate speculation had fallen sharply from the frantic levels of 1835 and 1836. Construction at the edge of the city and the rebuilding of the downtown area had almost come to a stop because of the difficulty in obtaining mortgages and selling properties. The "evil day has arrived which has been so truly predicted," declared Hone.

Far worse financial trouble was in the offing. Working-class New Yorkers had been badly hurt in 1835 and 1836 because their wages had not kept pace with inflation. Now, in 1837, their wages actually started to drop, and they began to protest their grievances in the streets. *Bread, Meat, Rent,*

Fuel! Their Prices Must Come Down. The Voice of the People Shall Be Heard, and Will Prevail! announced the handbill for a demonstration that took place in City Hall Park on February 13, 1837. *All Friends of Humanity, determined to resist Monopolists and Extortionists, are invited to attend.* This demonstration was peaceable enough, but shortly after its conclusion several hundred men and women set out for Eli Hart & Company's flour warehouse at 175 Washington Street. One of the speakers in City Hall Park had denounced Hart for hoarding hundreds of barrels of grain, waiting for even higher prices in the weeks to come. The mob overwhelmed the city police, broke into the warehouse, and emptied nearly 200 barrels of flour and 1000 bushels of wheat into the street. As the mob greedily scooped up the flour from the street, Mayor Cornelius Lawrence arrived on the scene and asked the mob to disperse. He "was assailed with a shower of barrel staves, stones, etc., and was compelled to retreat for his life," reported the *Evening Post.*

The riot at the Eli Hart & Company warehouse was just the beginning of the troubles about to beset New York's mercantile community. On March 17 Hone wrote, "The great crisis is near at hand, if it has not already arrived." The I. and L. Joseph bankinghouse on Wall Street had suspended payment. Its business, Hone wrote, had been "enormous," and he feared that many merchants, jobbers, and grocers would be dragged down with it to ruin. Just four days before, the Josephs' new building, nearly completed at Wall Street and Exchange Place, "came down with a crash like that of an earthquake." Its construction apparently had been as reckless as the operations of the firm.

In the subsequent days, the state of Wall Street affairs became worse. Hone wrote: "The accounts from England are very alarming; the panic prevails there as bad as here. Cotton has fallen. The loss on shipments will be very heavy, and American credits will be withdrawn. The paper of the southern and western merchants is coming back protested." With specie scarce, "money is exorbitantly dear. The bloodsuckers are beginning to be alarmed, and keep their unholy treasures locked up." By May 10 all the New York banks suspended specie payments. The next day the banks in Philadelphia, Baltimore, Albany, New Haven, and Hartford also suspended specie payments, and the banks in Boston, Mobile, New Orleans, Charleston, and Cincinnati followed suit within the week.

"The volcano has burst and overwhelmed New York," Hone lamented in his diary. "The glory of her merchants is departed." The Panic of 1837 had badly affected Hone's fortune. His son John had been one of the first merchants to fall at the onset of the Panic. Philip Hone not only lost the capital he had given his son to start his firm a year earlier, but was obligated to pay all the notes he had cosigned for him. As he struggled with his own and his son's distress, he complained, "I do not receive a dollar from any quarter where it is due me, and cannot raise anything upon my real estate which constitutes the bulk of my property."

Hone was far from alone in his financial embarrassment. All real estate in the city had declined in value with the start of the Panic, particularly unimproved lots at the outskirts of the city. Lots near Bloomingdale Village around West One-hundredth Street had cost $480 apiece in September 1836, but were selling for just $50 in April 1837. "The immense fortunes which we heard so much about in the days of speculation, have melted away like the snow before an April sun." Perhaps the most unsettling sights of the day for Hone were "the sales of rich furniture, the property of men who a year ago thought themselves rich and such expenditures justifiable, but are now bankrupt."

Five or six years passed before New York had completely recovered from the financial upsets of 1837, but signs of better times started to appear, in various ways, once the banks resumed specie payments on May 22, 1838. On that day, the *Evening Post* wrote hopefully, "We see commerce reviving — mechanics actively employed — buildings erecting — and in fact every avenue to prosperity filled with renewed enterprise." In January 1839, the *Herald* noted that rents for houses and business properties were rising from their depressed levels of 1837 and 1838. Building operations were returning to a state of health. Construction workers' wages were rising, although not yet to the inflated levels of pre-Panic days. A house carpenter in 1840 received $1.25 to $1.50

a day, the same wage he had received in 1830 and a sad contrast to the $1.65 to $2.00 a day he earned in 1836. A mason's wages followed much the same pattern. A hod carrier, or common laborer, received $.75 to $.87 a day in 1840, as he had ten years before, though he had earned $1.00 to $1.25 a day in 1836.

By 1840 the *Mirror* again could rightly describe New York as "the city of modern ruins." "No sooner is a fine building erected than it is torn down to be put up a better . . . We have our misgivings as to the permanency of the Merchants' Exchange now going up in Wall Street. It is very much to be feared that it will be torn down and 'improved' before it can be fairly finished; so restless are the tastes and habitudes of the city . . . Oh, for the day when some portion of New York may be considered finished for a few years."

Bowling Green and lower Broadway were again caught up in the shift from residences to businesses, which had come to a halt during the Panic years. A few rich New Yorkers, however, still clung to their homes in the area. Although she lived uptown, Mrs. Harriet Douglas Cruger kept her girlhood home at 55 Broadway empty but entirely furnished and well maintained for years after her mother's death in the mid-1840s. Robert Ray still lived in his granite mansion at 17 Broadway, which Philip Hone, after attending a party there in 1834, pronounced the "finest" in the city. The Ray mansion was "furnished and fitted up in a style of utmost magnificence — painted ceilings, gilded moldings, rich satin ottomans, curtains in the last Parisian taste."

Most of Bowling Green's remaining residences were destroyed on July 19, 1845, when another fire swept the downtown business district, leveling 300 buildings, worth $6 million, including their contents. The area devastated was, ironically, almost the same as that destroyed by the 1835 fire. The fire started on New Street in the J. L. Van Doren sperm oil warehouse. Although the flames quickly spread to Exchange Place and Broad Street, the firemen reportedly had gotten it under control when there was an explosion that was felt in Brooklyn and Jersey City and heard as far away as Sandy Hook. The fire had reached Brocker & Warren's warehouse on Broad Street and ignited the saltpeter stored there.

That explosion "shook the house like an earthquake and must have blown me out of bed, I suppose, for I was at the window before the roar had fairly died away," wrote twenty-five-year-old George Templeton Strong in the diary he had been keeping since he was fifteen and a sophomore at Columbia College. As a still-sleepy Strong stood in his bedroom window in his parents' Greenwich Street home, he saw, rising into the sky half a mile to the southeast, "a broad column of intense red flame that made the moon look pale and covered everything with a glow and glare that passed every effect of artificial light which I'd ever witnessed."

Strong "didn't stop to analyze the phenomenon." He hurriedly put on his clothes, alerted his parents and family, and "rushed out of the house as fast as possible." The fire had gone completely out of control after the explosion. "The stores in Broad Street, some of the finest in the city . . . were instantly overthrown" by the blast, and "the flames were communicated in every direction," wrote Philip Hone in his diary. Strong, a fire buff, "hadn't far to go" to reach the conflagration. "Everything in New Street as I looked down from Wall seemed withering away and melting down in absolute white heat." Broad Street, from Wall Street down to the East River, was "one grand solid substantial flame, most glorious and terrible to look at." Strong then "pelted home very expeditiously to tell my father that the days of '35 had returned and that he'd better turn out and see the sport."

By the time Strong returned to the scene, the fire was "crawling down Beaver Street and Exchange Place . . . quite unchecked" toward lower Broadway and Bowling Green. The iron night shutters on several warehouses on Broadway, just below Exchange Place, soon began to grow hot, and the Waverly House was "beginning to disgorge occupants, furniture, and smoke from every convenient outlet." The hotel was already on fire in the rear, but Strong thought that "it could have been saved had anybody made much exertion to save it." Soon the Waverly House, "abandoned to its fate, was burning slowly down, story after story, beginning at the top."

The firemen had written off the eastern side of Broadway. They were trying to keep the fire from jumping Broadway and devastating the streets leading down to the Hudson. The east side of Bowling Green was soon in flames, and the Adelphi Hotel, at the corner of Beaver Street, was "a magnificent sight, blazing from roof to cellar," according to Strong. On the other side of Bowling Green, he saw "Whitney and Wilmerding and all those people" moving their possessions, and "cordons of police crossing Broadway to keep people off."

A while later, the wind rose from the east, and the fire unexpectedly leaped Broadway near Morris Street and started to destroy the buildings on the west side of Bowling Green. Panic now seized the city. If the fire could leap Broadway at its widest point, then it could go anywhere. Strong declared:

The fire will go from river to river, a sure thing in all men's mouths. Everybody in Water, Front, Pearl, and the other streets about those parts [are] moving out in frantic haste . . . The throngs of people in the streets [are] all working for their lives, hurrying back for fresh loads — the indications of desperate terror and haste in every store one passed seen in the boxes and barrels that were tumbling out of doors in such utter recklessness — the universal consternation that prevailed made even the streets that were yet untouched by fire most exciting and rather perilous places.

The "crowds, confusion, and panic" in the streets west of Broadway were "worse if possible than on the east side of the city." The wind was shifting around to the south and might drive the fire from the houses burning on the west side of Bowling Green toward fashionable lower Greenwich Street, about a block and a half away. "Everybody in Greenwich and Washington Streets as far up as Rector [is] moving out in hot haste," reported Strong, who was worrying about the fate of his family's home at 108 Greenwich Street, near Carlisle Street. Strong thought that the "crisis had come" when a house at the southeast corner of Greenwich and Morris streets " 'took' on the roof. But by dint of cutting off burning fragments and sending a stream into the building it was stopped."

The wind, fortunately, dropped at this point, and the fire gradually burned itself out. The next morning all Broad

Street below Wall Street was "a heap of undistinguishable ruins," according to Hone. The fire also destroyed Beaver Street from William Street to Bowling Green, and nearly all of New Street, Exchange Place, and South William Street. The warehouses on Pearl Street and near the East River, which had been emptied in such panic the night before, had been untouched by the fire. Along Bowling Green, Hone noted, the fire "burned all the houses from Morris Street, including Robert Ray's great granite edifice, Brevoort's house, Gardiner Howland's three houses, all down to Edward Prime's [1 Broadway], which is saved."

The fire burned for nearly a week before it was completely out. On July 22, the fourth day after the start of the conflagration, "the fire was blazing to the height of six or eight feet above the heap of ruins, in as many as twenty places," reported the *Evening Post*. Firemen were still pulling down the walls and chimneys of burned-out buildings. Even so, contractors had stacked brick and timber for new buildings along the still-smoldering streets. "There is such an abundance of capital now lying in wait for any opportunity of safe investment," wrote the same newspaper, and "the ground burnt over is so valuable, that we have no doubt, all the buildings consumed will be replaced by better ones in the course of six months."

Some New Yorkers hoped that the burned district could be rebuilt in a way that would eliminate, or at least reduce, the danger of fire in the future. On July 23, the *Evening Post* suggested that some of the streets within the area be widened and straightened. "If it be found practicable, it would be an improvement to close up altogether such generators of combustion as the narrow lanes of New Street and Marketfield Street." But two days later the *Evening Post* admitted that "the width of a street is of much less consequence as a protection against a large fire than is commonly supposed." The fire, after all, had crossed Broad Street against the wind, and, with the aid of the wind, had jumped Broadway at its widest point. The way to reduce the danger of these conflagrations, the *Evening Post* said, was to initiate changes in construction that would make "such buildings as are called fire-proof, worthy of the name [and to] let a little more

81

rigor be used in excluding from the crowded portion of the city of combustible and explosive materials, and in the prevention of danger from furnaces, engines, camphine manufactories and others." Contractors and property owners in the burned district, however, were not about to change their ways voluntarily. After walking through the area a week after the onset of the fire, the reporter from the *Evening Post* "could see no evidence of a better or more substantial masonry . . . Build quick and burn quicker seems to be our order of the day."

After the fire of 1845, almost all the wealthy families deserted Bowling Green and lower Broadway. The houses that still stood became offices for merchants, auctioneers, and brokers; and dry goods warehouses rose on the site of those buildings destroyed by the fire. One pleasant addition to the location was Delmonico's hotel and restaurant at 25 Broadway. The Delmonico brothers were among the first to introduce New Yorkers to fine Continental cuisine. In 1827 they had opened a "capacious and splendid establishment" at the corner of South William and Beaver streets, but New Yorkers were generally suspicious of European food, particularly when served in an elegant public place. Late in 1830 Philip Hone and two friends went to Delmonico's, which Hone "had heard was upon the Parisian plan and very good. We satisfied our curiosity but not our appetites," he complained. Four years later Hone had another meal there and apparently changed his mind. "Such a dinner! Every delicacy of meat. Game in the highest perfection of French cookery, and fine wines and libation." Hone, however, could not allow himself to enjoy this pleasure completely: "I begin to fear I am using myself up with high living."

The opening of the Delmonico brothers' hotel and restaurant in 1846 was proof that New Yorkers now welcomed fine European cuisine. The five-story building was the "most elegantly furnished and admirably adjusted boarding and eating establishment in this country," wrote the *Daily Tribune*, and it gave the proprietors "a new and indisputable claim to immortality." The hotel rooms, intended as long-term residences for single gentlemen, were "furnished in the most costly and magnificent style" and cost $10 to $60 a month,

82

Delmonico's restaurant, 25 Broadway

exclusive of meals. New Yorkers welcomed this establishment so enthusiastically that just the next year Delmonico's opened an addition next door, at 23 Broadway, with additional restaurant facilities and hotel rooms intended for families.

Another landmark on lower Broadway to be completed in 1846 was the new Trinity Church. The old church had been demolished in 1839, and New Yorkers occasionally grumbled that it was taking too long to build the new one. These complaints disappeared once the scaffolding was removed from the richly ornamented Gothic Revival brownstone façade and the even grander interior. "Every day brings forth some new beauties," wrote Hone several weeks before the church's consecration, "and crowds of spectators avail themselves of permits from some of the vestry to visit, admire, and wonder at the magnificent edifice." George Templeton Strong was one of those who visited the church before its completion. "It is the finest interior I ever saw, the only Gothic interior that ever seemed natural and genuine and not the work of yesterday."

83

Trinity's elaborate Gothic tracery, arched vaults, flying buttresses, medieval-style sculpture, and stained-glass windows were a surprise and a delight to New York. Nathaniel Parker Willis, editor of the *Home Journal*, pronounced Trinity Church an "exquisitely conceived piece of architecture . . . It will doubtless be the first Gothic structure in America." While the Gothic Revival inspiration won praise for its religious and medieval inspirations, some New Yorkers criticized the church's brownstone façade. Until then, brownstone, a red sandstone found in New Jersey or the Connecticut River valley, had been used as an inexpensive substitute for classically correct granite, limestone, or marble

Trinity Church

84

on row-house stoops and doors and window trim. When the *Herald* learned in 1839 that Trinity Church's vestry had decided to use brownstone for the new building, it asked why "the richest body in this country . . . intend to rebuild their church with the poorest stone in the world, ring red sandstone." Some New Yorkers suggested that the vestry had selected brownstone over the gray limestone proposed by the architect Richard Upjohn to save money. This saving was probably unimportant to so rich a congregation, which was holding on to its valuable plot of land downtown and was prepared to spend hundreds of thousands of dollars on the new church. More likely, the well-educated and well-heeled vestrymen were already familiar with the rising Romantic Movement and its architectural ideals, which called for setting aside light-colored building materials in favor of dark ones, the better to harmonize with the hues of the natural landscape.

Interior of A. T. Stewart's store (OVERLEAF)

The sight of the completed church, with its 284-foot tower, standing at the head of Wall Street silenced most criticism of its design. Trinity Church was consecrated on May 21, 1846, with the help of the bishop of the diocese, 150 clergymen in white robes, and a standing-room-only crowd of what Philip Hone called the "most dignified and respectable . . . laymen."

For New Yorkers who were not Episcopalians, the new Trinity was equaled, if not overshadowed, by another building nearing completion on Broadway, the A. T. Stewart & Company store. Some New Yorkers were already predicting that the large building, which stood at the southeast corner of Reade Street, would soon be known as "Stewart's Folly." For one thing, Stewart's store would be America's first department store, offering women the convenience of buying different kinds of merchandise under one roof. Other merchants did not expect women to change their custom of purchasing their fabrics, Parisian bonnets, furniture, and ready-made clothing at small specialty shops scattered along Broadway.

Stewart, however, planned to make shopping at his department store a more pleasant and luxurious experience than at any other store in the city. Aside from its dimensions, cer-

*A. T. Stewart's store, Broad-
way and Chambers Street*

tainly vast for its time, the store was built of white marble, quite a surprise in a city whose buildings still were almost entirely of wood or red brick. The store, furthermore, introduced to America the highly ornamented Italianate style, which would soon replace Greek Revival and become the reigning architectural mode in New York for houses and commercial structures for the next thirty years.

Stewart's store, critics also noted, was rising on the east side, the "shilling side," of Broadway rather than on the more prestigious west side, the "dollar side." Until the opening of Stewart's, all the finest shops and hotels carefully stayed on the dollar side of Broadway. This distinction, silly as it sounds, had some basis on common sense. The sun "falls here earliest in the morning, lighting up the shops and making all things gay," wrote Nathaniel Parker Willis in the mid-1850s. "It lingers longest at noon and afternoon, and is thus always cheerful. There is only a brief season during Summer when the sun is disagreeable." The women who could afford to patronize these shops usually spent the entire summer out of town at their country homes or a fashionable spa.

All the talk about "Stewart's Folly" and his error in building on the shilling side of Broadway vanished on the store's opening day, September 21, 1846. "Stewart's is a palace of a store," wrote James Fenimore Cooper to his country-bound wife, and Philip Hone thought that "there is nothing in Paris or London to compare with this dry goods palace." With one stroke, Stewart had dramatically changed retailing in New York and America, rid the east side of Broadway of its shilling-side stigma, and helped popularize a new style of architecture. The store soon made Stewart one of the richest men in the city, and in ten years Stewart would become, "next to the President, the best known man in America," according to George T. Borrett, a fellow at Cambridge University. The white marble store became a landmark so well known across America that Stewart never had to put a sign on the building.

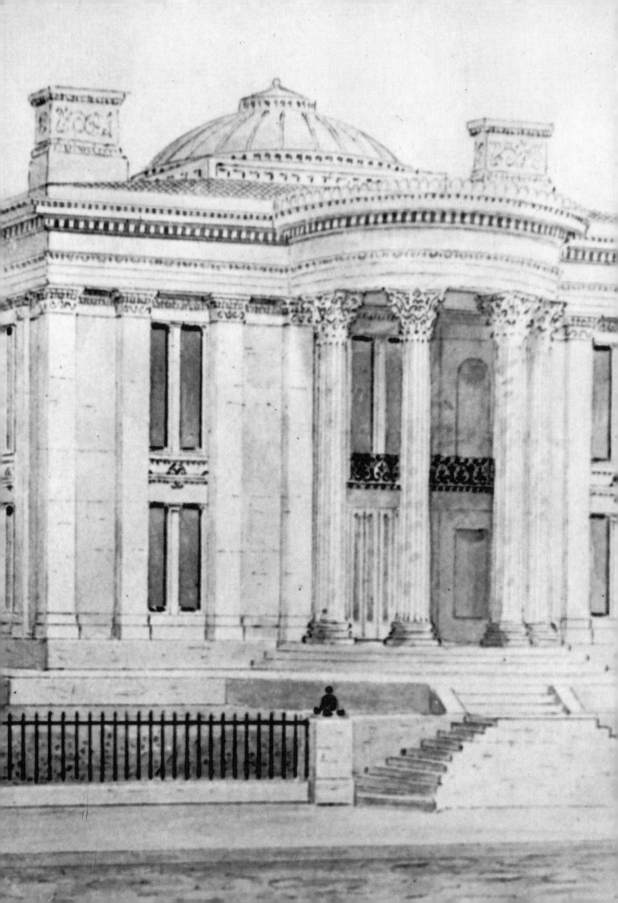

6

As A. T. Stewart opened his department
store in September 1846, another prominent New Yorker,
John Cox Stevens, was erecting another white marble building just a few blocks away. It, too, would become a city
landmark. John Cox Stevens, a millionaire property owner in
Hoboken, New Jersey, was building a mansion at the southeast corner of College Place and Murray Street. Stevens' residence was one of the first mansions in nineteenth-century
New York and typified the most extravagant houses in the
city until the 1880s. The mansion, called "Stevens' Palace,"
occupied one corner of the Columbia College campus, which
he had leased from the financially hard-pressed institution.
The house, designed by Alexander Jackson Davis, boasted
lovely landscaped grounds, a daring semicircular portico supported by Corinthian columns two stories tall, richly decorated parlors and a ballroom, and a sweeping circular
stairway and central reception hall beneath a dome. The
Stevens mansion, wrote *Putnam's Monthly*, is "the most elegant Grecian mansion in New York . . . without doubt."
Hone, reveling in the expertise gained in his travels abroad,
wrote: "The house is, indeed, a palace. The Palais Bourbon
in Paris, Buckingham Palace in London, and Sans Souci at
Berlin are little grander than this residence of a simple citizen
of our republican city."

Stevens' College Place mansion, grand as it was, was
strangely out of touch with the times. It was the last great
Greek Revival house built in New York. Several of Stevens'

peers were already building their houses in the Italianate style. Stevens' real mistake, however, was putting his mansion where he did. The surrounding neighborhood, though still the home of rich and fashionable families, was definitely on the decline during the mid-1840s. Church Street, running parallel to Broadway, one block to the west, had become "a vast sink of infamy and degradation," best known for its handsome brothels.

The proximity of costly residences and brothels was not uncommon in nineteenth-century New York. Vice at its most elevated was usually found just a block or two from the best hotels and restaurants. The incursion of brothels and gambling houses into Church Street followed that of large hotels into Broadway in the Park Place vicinity, beginning with the Astor House in 1836. These Church Street establishments were, for the most part, discreet, but by the mid-1840s the decaying street had also begun to attract drunks and rowdies

John Cox Stevens' residence

at night. The parents of young men attending Columbia College began to complain about the immoral sites and unpleasant sights their sons had to pass on their way to school.

College Place, the next north-to-south street to the west, was another threat to the Park Place neighborhood. Just a few blocks north of Stevens' "palace," College Place turned into a black and Irish-immigrant slum. About 10,000 of New York's 850,000 residents in 1855 were black, a large portion of that number living on or near College Place, "crowded into broken down, dilapidated houses of the most unhealthy description," according to the *Herald*.

Some New Yorkers tried to improve the lives of the city's black poor through their own efforts and charities. Robert B. Minturn, a merchant, built a model tenement for a hundred black families on Mott Street, just off Canal Street. Although the building looked somber and gloomy, it was fireproof and well ventilated, and each apartment had a sitting room, kitchen, and two or three bedrooms. Minturn's tenement, "doubtless . . . a profitable investment," in the *Herald's* opinion, "succeeded to some extent . . . to improve the condition of the poorer class of the colored population by furnishing them with better habitations."

Although the *Herald* supported the prevailing idea that decent housing would solve the problems of the poor in the city, it also acknowledged that the lack of decent jobs for blacks led to their poverty and some of their social problems. Over one third of the black population, according to one survey, was dependent on private or public charity. The men were usually laborers, and the women did washing, cleaning, and "such like house work, at which they earn a very precarious subsistence." In the late eighteenth and early nineteenth centuries, black citizens of New York enjoyed what the *Herald* called "independent circumstances." The men were waiters, bootblacks, and barbers, as well as laborers, and the women were cooks or maids in private homes. Those days were long gone by the 1840s. Immigrants from Ireland and Germany were flooding into New York and gladly filling these jobs, which native-born Americans had left to the blacks in earlier years.

93

Residents of the Park Place area were worried that the black slums of College Place, north of Chambers Street, would spread south and ruin their neighborhood. Instead, the first serious blow to the neighborhood came from fashionable Greenwich Street, the north-to-south street immediately to the west of College Place. Suddenly, in 1844 or 1845, Greenwich Street began turning into an immigrant slum district. "In taking a stroll through the lower part of our city, after an absence of scarcely a year, I could not but observe the changed character of many of my old haunts and familiar rambling places," commented a writer for the *Evening Post* in 1845. "Greenwich Street, where erst the nabobs of our town held dominion, has changed but with a few exceptions to boarding houses and lofty stores."

One night in the same year, George Templeton Strong, living with his parents at 108 Greenwich Street, three blocks north of the Battery, wrote in his diary: "This section of the metropolis is beginning to pass all toleration, and I think we shall be forced to become emigrants before we're much older." That evening, a Sunday, the Strongs' neighbors to the rear, in buildings facing Washington Street, had been "comparatively quiet — there's only the average choir of cats, a pulmonary horse (stabled within twenty-five feet of this room) afflicted with a periodic cough of great severity at regular intervals of about fifteen minutes, and a few drunken Dutch [German] emigrants singing what I've no doubt's a highly indecent low Dutch canticle, fortunately unintelligible, with a chorus like a house on fire." All this noise was just the "Sabbath stillness" compared to the rest of the week, according to Strong. Then, the family was bothered by "two Dutch lust-houses in Washington Street that keep an orchestra apiece — one has nothing but some kind of tum-tuming instrument and a cracked clarinet, but t'other exults in a very violent cantatrice accompanied by a piano and two trumpets."

Oddly enough, Strong never complained about Madame Restell, the notorious abortionist, who lived and practiced her trade at 148 Greenwich Street, just a few blocks from his family's home. Madame Restell, the professional name of Ann Trow Lohman, advertised her services as a "female physician" and "professor of midwifery" in New York newspapers like the *Herald*. The staid *Daily Tribune* and *Evening Post* refused to carry her advertisements. Besides performing abortions, Restell sold patent medicines, such as her "celebrated Preventative Powders for married ladies, whose health forbids a too rapid increase of family."

The convenience and seedy gentility of the Park Place district had attracted other "peculiar physicians" besides Restell. In 1840 Dr. de Angelis, at 46 Robinson Street, promised to cure "obstructions, chronic afflictions, physical complaints, ulcers in the throat, eruptions of the skin, stiffness of the joints, and pains in the limbs" with his "incredible . . . Vegetable Syrup of Sabza and other appropriate remedies." In the same year, a Dr. Ralph at 38 Cortlandt Street advertised in the *Herald* that he could cure "certain delicate diseases," namely syphilis, gonorrhea, and masturbation.

In 1848 the Strongs finally left Greenwich Street for developing Gramercy Park. George Templeton Strong felt that "in all the happiness of this time there's now and then something like a feeling of self-reproach." Like so many other New Yorkers leaving their homes downtown in the 1830s and 1840s, he asked: "How *can* I abandon all these old usages and leave this dirty, rat-infested loaferine Greenwich Street and everything that I've grown up among and got used to, and yet feel no sorrow about it; give up all my old friends here, the row of houses on the opposite side of the way I've known so long, the lookout on shabby brick walls from the windows of this room, this inconvenient old house where alone I can remember living, and yet change cheerfully." Indeed, Strong so often said that "somehow I a'nt a bit . . . unhappy" about moving uptown that one suspects he protested too much.

The immigrant boardinghouses, as would be expected, turned the corner from Greenwich Street onto the adjacent east-to-west sidestreets. These blocks down by Greenwich Street had never been quite as desirable as those just off Broadway. They were several blocks west of Broadway, with its fashionable shops and afternoon promenade, just a block or two east of the Hudson River waterfront, with its shipping and crowds of common workmen, and the houses occasionally had structural problems because of the high water table here. But it was not the onslaught of roominghouses from the waterfront and Greenwich Street that caused the final collapse of the Park Place district as a fashionable residential area.

It was, instead, the dry goods trade, which suddenly overwhelmed the neighborhood in the early 1850s. "Calico is omnipotent, and whole streets melt away at her approach," wrote *Putnam's Monthly* in 1853. This "great business . . . spread with . . . astonishing rapidity over the whole lower part of the city, prostrating and utterly obliterating everything that is old and venerable, and leaving not a single landmark, in token of the former position of dwelling houses of our ancestors." Dry goods wholesaling, which had been centered on Pearl Street and the East River since the eighteenth century, was the most profitable business in mid-nineteenth-century New York. Dry goods merchants could, and did, pay more for their buildings than any other businessmen, except for the few banks and insurance companies seeking an impressive Wall Street location. The dry goods trade, wrote the *Herald*, "enhances inordinately any property it uses."

The trade found enough space for expansion in the traditional Pearl Street district in the 1830s, but once New York recovered from the Panic of 1837 the merchants began searching for a new area for their warehouses. Some merchants and real estate speculators looked to Broadway between Bowling Green and Trinity Church, and handsome warehouses rose there in the late 1840s. The land, however, was prohibitively expensive, even for the prosperous dry goods trade. The old row houses along lower Broadway sold for $40,000 to $50,000 in the 1840s. When Grace Church decided to move uptown in 1845, the congregation sold the old church at Broadway and Rector Street for $65,000. That same year row houses standing on the standard 25-by-100-foot lot in the Park Place district were selling for $7000 to $9000.

Yet these low prices did not set off a stampede of dry goods merchants and real estate speculators into the Park Place area. "There were few capitalists who believed that the 'North Side' would ever become a favorite locality for business, much less that they should live to find it the successful rival of South, Water, Front, and Pearl Streets, for the immense wholesale trade of the metropolis," recalled the *Daily Tribune*. The area instead conjured up images of "narrow and filthy streets, murderous-looking old rookeries, dilapidated dwellings, old mansions abandoned by the aristocracy, and reeking with the dirt and wretchedness of a densely packed population."

Still, the Park Place district had several advantages for the dry goods trade other than the reasonably priced real estate.

Rebuilding of Liberty Street, 1854

97

The ferries between New York and Jersey City stopped at the foot of several streets in the area. In addition to carrying the growing numbers of commuters from suburban New Jersey, the ferries transported all the freight and passengers bound for New York by railroad from points to the South and West. No tunnel or bridge crossed the Hudson River, and all trains coming to New York, except those from New England or the Hudson River valley, stopped at the sprawling rail yards of Jersey City. One busy ferry stopped at the foot of Cortlandt Street, and by 1845 that street had seven hotels, largely patronized by travelers getting off the ferry.

As railroads carried more and more freight in the 1840s, dry goods merchants realized that the Hudson River waterfront might be more convenient for their warehouses than the streets along the East River. All day long the wagons of the wholesale firms filled the crowded downtown streets, bringing merchandise to the firms' warehouses from the Jersey City ferry stop or taking goods there for shipment to customers in the South or Midwest. Furthermore, Pearl Street's proximity to the East River was no longer the great advantage it once had been. Although New York thrilled to the stories of the clipper ships racing around Cape Horn to California or China in the late 1840s and early 1850s, the clipper ship actually was the magnificent end of the sailing ship era. Steam-powered vessels were carrying more passengers and freight every year between American ports and between New York and Europe. These ships docked along the Hudson River rather than the crowded East River waterfront, again sending the wholesale firms' wagons on the difficult crosstown journeys.

By 1850, though, the dry goods trade still had not begun moving into the Park Place district, except for several warehouses erected the year before on Dey and Cortlandt streets. However, several cases of cholera, discovered on Greenwich Street in 1850, proved to be the catalyst that led the city government to encourage the growth of this vital business by giving it room for expansion. Realizing that wholesale trade would displace immigrants from the crowded and unsanitary old houses, in 1851 the city widened Dey and Cortlandt streets ten feet each between Broadway and Greenwich

Street, demolishing all the buildings on the south side of each street. This left vast tracts of land cleared for real estate speculators and builders, who were relieved of the usual problem of buying out residents and businessmen one by one.

That year the *Daily Tribune* declared that Dey Street, like neighboring Cortlandt Street, "has undergone a most complete revolution within the last two years. It was then a narrow street, occupied by groggeries and low boarding houses; it has since been widened ten feet, splendid stores are being erected, and it bids fair to become one of the most beautiful little streets in the city." Rents and sale prices began to climb sharply on the two streets even before the debris of the street-widening was carted away and many of the new warehouses completed. "There has been of late a great rise in the value of real estate, especially in business situations downtown in streets communicating with Broadway westerly," wrote Hone in February 1851. "My house in Cortlandt Street which I built in 1813, and occupied many years before I removed to Broadway, has never rented for more than $900, and that sometimes badly paid, until I leased it four years

99

ago to Mr. Lucky for $1,300. There is one year unexpired, and I have now leased it for $3,000 per annum." The influx of dry goods firms into Dey and Cortlandt streets and the subsequent rise in real estate values there led the *Daily Tribune* to declare in 1850, "Cortlandt Street has proved such a wise investment and such a good stand for business that contiguous streets leading to the North River will soon undergo the same transformation. Barclay and Dey Streets are fated."

In 1851 several dry goods warehouses rose on Park Place, Vesey Street, and College Place, and, according to the same newspaper, "forthwith commenced a most astonishing migration. [The] whole mercantile community seemed to have woke from a long sleep." Suddenly the dry goods merchants decided that Pearl Street was inconvenient, the streets too narrow and crowded, the rents too high, and their countinghouses and warehouses impractical and old-fashioned. Merchants and real estate speculators were so eager to purchase property in the Park Place district that prices there doubled in a three-month period in 1851. By 1853 and 1854 the old dwelling houses, which had cost $7000 to $9000 in 1845, quickly sold for $25,000, sometimes more for a corner property.

Some New Yorkers wondered how real estate speculators could make money around Park Place when they paid so much for sound houses only to rip them down and build warehouses in their place. The answer lay in the growth and prosperity of the dry goods trade. Just twenty or thirty years earlier, merchants along Pearl Street or the East River had been content to open their countinghouses and warehouses in former residences. By the 1850s business was so good that space in the dry goods district was at a premium. Now warehouses in the center of this district covered virtually the entire 100-foot-deep lot, had two cellars below the street, and were five, sometimes six, stories tall. Some warehouses did not even stop at the back lot line but ran the full 200 feet through the block to the next street.

By 1855, over 200 warehouses had risen in the area, and the building boom was showing no signs of slowing down. The warehouses in the Park Place district were some of the handsomest buildings in the city. Architects working in the

Worth Street: typical warehouses of the 1850s and 1860s

area included Trench and Snook, Samuel Warner, Thomas Thomas, and Richard Upjohn, all of whom were designing fashionable mansions, hotels, and churches at the same time. The warehouses had white marble or brownstone Italianate façades. The once-decaying neighborhood, observed the *Daily Tribune*, was "in the chrysalis state of change, and from the old worm of Decay flutters forth the gorgeous butterfly of Wealth and Beauty."

The transformation of the area had "a moral influence" on the area. "The movement of trade," noted the *Herald*, "has almost entirely depopulated Church Street, once noted for its houses of prostitution." The rebuilding mania next affected Greenwich Street, and, to the delight of many New Yorkers, warehouses replaced a large number of the run-down houses along with their immigrant tenants. The city government speeded the rebuilding of Greenwich Street by raising the level of the street from two to six feet from the Battery to Cortlandt Street. The city said that this work, which took over 66,000 cartloads of dirt, was necessary to flatten out a hill at Morris Street, which might have caused trouble for heavily laden wagons from the wholesale firms. The hill, however, was "not all that difficult for wagons," wrote the *Daily Tribune*. "It seems like a piece of folly to spoil three or four blocks of buildings . . . but we suppose Corporate wisdom knows best."

The regrading of the street did indeed diminish the value of the old houses as residences, which appears to have been the intent of the city all along. The houses no longer stood several feet above the curb. The work, according to the *Home Journal*, had "sent first floors to lower regions, and shut up the inhabitants of cellars in utter darkness." These houses no longer fetched the $500 to $700 rents they had before the regrading. Now they could be torn down, and warehouses built on the site could easily command $4000 to $5000 a year. Once the regrading was finished, the *Herald* reported that "great improvements are just now being made in Greenwich Street," and the *Home Journal* predicted that "a few years will see it another Water Street, an avenue of massive wholesale stores."

The rebuilding of the Park Place district was not without its inconveniences. The widening of a street filled it with debris, which forced traffic into nearby, already crowded streets. Before the work was completed, the wholesale merchants and real estate investors began to build their warehouses, and, according to the *Daily Tribune*, "there is no other city in the world where builders are allowed such a perfect monopoly of the streets." Builders left piles of brick, stone, lumber, sand, and lime along the curb and sidewalks for months at a time. At some sites they even mixed the mortar in the street, and not in the building's cellar, to save a few steps for the hod carrier. Church Street, wrote the *Daily Tribune*, was "entirely broken up," its omnibus tracks half destroyed, "all other vehicles shut out"; and "even foot passengers have to get along as best they can at the risk of their necks."

The speed and carelessness with which the Park Place area was rebuilt jeopardized the health of the entire city. In June 1853, the city ordered that all the old privy vaults in the area be emptied that summer. There were twenty-five hundred vaults in the area, each one filling ten carts, according to the calculations of the *Daily Tribune*. So "25,000 loads of disease-creating, death-producing filth [will be] carted through the streets and dumped off the pier heads in two of the hottest months of the year, without using one single pound of any disinfecting agent. And every one of these vaults might have been emptied in mid-winter as mid-summer."

Although New York prided itself on its growth and what the newspapers called the "go-ahead" spirit of the age, some people wondered if progress were always an unquestionably desirable thing, particularly in the Park Place district. Besides the real dangers to public health and the virtual blocking of the streets that accompanied the rebuilding, some New Yorkers missed the "traditions and associations" and "scenes of by-gone dignity and elegance" that the old houses and streets held for them. All those memories, wrote the *Home Journal*, "are sacrificed, absorbed in the tide of business, which is forever spreading, and swelling onward, going round nothing, but taking all in its course."

In 1856 the Park Place district lost one of its last landmarks when Columbia College left its campus and moved uptown to East Forty-ninth Street. Columbia had occupied its original site since 1760, when it was known as King's College. At that time, according to an account of the late 1760s, the neighborhood was "totally unencumbered by adjacent buildings, and admitting the purest circulation of air from the river and every other quarter, it has the benefit of as agreeable and healthy a situation as can possibly be conceived." By the mid-1850s "the encroachment of business," reported the *Daily Tribune*, "[has] rendered the present site of the institution far more valuable for purposes of trade than of education."

In 1855 the city cut Park Place through the old campus, leaving the forlorn college buildings on the remnants of the sycamore-shaded hill, surrounded by the marble and brownstone warehouses rising on all sides. They were not left standing for long. In May 1857, the *Daily Tribune* reported that "a strong force of workmen were employed in tearing off the roofing and undermining the walls." Before the year was over, the old college had disappeared without a trace, and warehouses were already rising on that newly opened stretch of Park Place.

Progress reserved its cruelest fate for the John Cox Stevens mansion. After the death of his wife in 1855, Stevens moved back to the family home in Hoboken and rented the College Place mansion as office space to the U.S. District Attorney, the U.S. Marshall, and U.S. Commissioner for $16,000. A year later the mansion stood empty, "its fine frescoes and tasteful decorations . . . undergoing a process of rapid defacement and ruin," according to the *Home Journal*, while Stevens decided what to do with the property. Stevens, already active in the redevelopment of his old neighborhood, decided to tear down his own "palace" and build warehouses on the site. In May 1856, the *Daily Tribune* sadly wrote: "We saw the busy hands of the ruthless destroyer pulling out its vitals and scattering its costly walls." Stevens, who survived his home by just one year, was simply acting in accordance with the "go-ahead" spirit. "Little do those who are pulling down old landmarks to build up a new one," observed the *Daily Tribune,* "think of the day when another generation will also be engaged in this great work of pulling down."

7

As the dry goods trade overran the Park Place district in the 1850s, the *Herald* boasted: "Extravagance in living, extravagance in style, extravagance in habitations, extravagance in everything prevail in New York to even a greater extent than in 1834, 1835, or 1836." One result of the transformation of the Park Place area and lower Greenwich Street, noted a reporter, was the "German and Irish boarding houses . . . being driven into some out-of-the-way quarter." He did not see poverty as a problem of New York in the 1850s; it was simply a nuisance that wasn't all that harmful to the city, and should be hidden away from polite society's view. That opinion might have been practical, though no less defensible, twenty or thirty years earlier, when outright destitution was uncommon and sprawling slum districts unknown in New York. Frances Wright D'Arusmont, social reformer, early proponent of women's rights, and successful advocate of free public schools, recalled, of the New York she visited in the 1820s, "no dark alleys, whose confined and noisesome atmosphere marks the presence of a dense and suffering population; no hovels, in whose ruined garrets, or dank and gloomy cellars, crowd the victims of vice and disease, whom penury drives to despair."

Things had changed by the 1850s. Less than one year after the *Herald* applauded the removal of slum dwellings from Greenwich Street and vaunted the city's extravagance, the *Daily Tribune* saw that "underneath this gay varnish of wealth, luxury, and prosperity, there is an abyss of poverty and destitution, whence issue ominous though subdued moanings of discontent and misery." Visitors to New York in the 1840s asked to see two sights first: the mansions of Washington Square and the hovels of the Five Points, the city's worst slum. As early as 1829, the Five Points, a five- or ten-minute walk north and east of City Hall, was "the most dangerous place in our city," according to the *Evening Post*. Crimes and other outrages were occurring there "almost daily."

The situation was far worse by the 1840s. The Five Points, wrote the *Daily Tribune* in 1848, "would strike even the practiced eye and hardened olfactories of a veteran New Yorker as particularly foul and loathsome." The area was "the great center ulcer of wretchedness — the very rotting skeleton of civilization." George Foster, a journalist who wrote *New York in Slices* in 1849, described what visitors saw in the Five Points:

The buildings in all that neighborhood are nearly all of wood, and are so old and rotten that they seem ready to tumble together into a vast rubbish heap. Nearly every house and cellar is a groggery below and a brothel above. In the doors and at the windows may be seen at any hour of the afternoon or evening, scores of sluttishly-dressed women, in whose faces drunkenness and debauchery have destroyed every vestige of all we expect in the countenance of women, and even almost every trace of human expression.

Like most observers of the period, Foster was particularly appalled at the condition of the children, barefoot and dressed in dirty ragged clothing, playing in the garbage-strewn gutters or drinking the last few drops from a discarded whiskey bottle. "Here and there, digging in the foul gutters, or basking in filthy nakedness upon the cellar doors," he wrote, "may be seen groups of children . . . some seeming pretty, some deformed and idiotic, and others horribly ulcerated from head to foot with that hereditary leprosy which debauchery and licentiousness entail as their curse upon their innocent offspring."

The best-known sight in the Five Points was the "Old Brewery," a rambling, decaying frame building, several stories high, reputed to house twelve hundred people. The Old Brewery, which was the hiding place for stolen goods and criminals, was "everywhere recognized as the headquarters of crime in the metropolis," recalled James McCabe in the 1860s. The narrow streets around the building were known as "Murderers' Alley" and "The Den of Thieves," and the police would enter the Old Brewery only in the day and then only in pairs. These visits usually yielded them nothing. The building abounded in secret passages and hid-

Five Points, ca. 1870

den rooms, and a number of tunnels, known only to its residents, ran under the streets from the Old Brewery to other buildings in the vicinity.

Throughout the 1840s and 1850s the newspapers and civic-minded New Yorkers appealed to the city government to do something about the Five Points, but the area became, if anything, more vile and more dangerous during these decades, and the decaying housing spread north and east, forming new slum districts. In 1852 the Ladies' Home Missionary Society purchased the Old Brewery "in order to change it from a pest-house of sin to a school of virtue." The Society replaced the Old Brewery with the Five Points Mission — an employment bureau, day school, and Sunday school.

Before the start of the Brewery's demolition, the Society opened the building to New Yorkers eager enough to see the "haunts of vice" to make small contributions. During the one week of viewing, hundreds of citizens flocked to the Brewery, and, each taking a candle in hand, explored the long, dark, winding halls, saw the squalor of the rooms recently abandoned by their residents, and looked for the secret tunnels and passageways. The Brewery's "narrow passages were crowded and its old staircases creaked as the visitors ascended them," reported the *Daily Tribune*. "The company thronged several of the apartments where miserable men, women, and children yet remain, and moodily submitted to the gaze of the strangers in that community of degraded outcasts."

The showing of the Old Brewery was a brilliant publicity gimmick for the Missionary Society. For the first time, thousands of middle-class New Yorkers saw just how badly the poor were living in their city. Most genteel New Yorkers, particularly the women, never ventured into the city's slum districts, much less into the tenements. The viewing of the Brewery coincided with, and indeed encouraged, the growing realization that poverty had become a problem in New York and that things had to be done to improve the lives of the poor, especially their housing.

Around 1850, New York newspapers began to publish accounts of tenement conditions gathered by their own reporters, charity organizations, or newly formed city government committees. Some poor families lived in one or two rooms of what had once been a single-family residence. The poor of the late eighteenth and early nineteenth centuries, less numerous, had lived in this manner, and the old houses, though run-down, still offered the best housing available to needy families in the 1850s. The rooms after all, had the high ceilings, abundant light, and good ventilation associated with housing for the middle or upper class. But the old houses had become overcrowded. Some of the families that lived in one room took in boarders to help pay the rent.

In 1853 the *Courier and Enquirer* visited a number of the houses along the East River. In one building, a twelve-by-twelve-foot room housed five families, a total of twenty people. Two beds made up the entire furnishings; there were no chairs, tables, rugs, or partitions for privacy. These people made their living by gathering chips, that is, dried pieces of manure, from the streets and selling them at four cents a bucket. One family just down the hall had a room all to itself. Too poor to pay the rent of several dollars a month, it made money, according to the newspaper, "by permitting the room to be used as a rendezvous by the abandoned women of the street." In one large room the *Courier and Enquirer* saw no source of heat other than a "tin pail of lighted charcoal placed in the center of the room, over which bent a blind man endeavoring to warm himself; around him three or four men and women swearing and quarreling; on one corner of the floor a woman, who had died the day previous of disease, and in another two or three children sleeping on a pile of rags." The scenes in this building were so awful that the *Courier and Enquirer* thought that words did not adequately convey the "gaunt and shivering forms and wild ghastly faces" living in the "hideous squalor and the deadly effluvia, the dim undrained courts oozing with pollution, the dark narrow stairways decayed with age, reeking with filth and overrun with vermin, the rotted floors . . . and windows stuffed with rags."

In the 1840s, tenement landlords found a way to make money from these old residences other than by putting several families in each room. They built so-called "rear buildings" in the back yards. Until then, the rear windows of the

A rear building on Roosevelt Street

old houses had enjoyed plenty of light and air and perhaps the sight of a shade tree or two. Now these windows looked out on a brick wall and the windows of other peoples' rooms just ten or fifteen feet away. The rear building was five or six stories tall and loomed over the front house, which was three, possibly four, stories tall. The courtyard between the front and rear buildings was usually filled with garbage.

Another way to get more money out of an old house was to rent the cellar as living quarters. In 1850 the Chief of Police reported that 18,456 of New York's half-million people lived in cellars. These quarters were the most miserable in the city: totally dark, without a candle or oil lamp; unventilated; damp; foul-smelling. The floors were generally dirt, which turned to mud during heavy rains, and the ceilings were so low that a grown man could not stand upright. If the building had indoor toilets and running water, the pipes ran through the cellar and sometimes leaked or burst, emptying their contents upon the unfortunate residents.

Slum housing was so profitable that, beginning in the 1840s, real estate investors started to erect buildings intended specifically as tenements for the poor. The "Barracks," at 64–72 Goerck Street, were several adjacent buildings, four stories tall, which extended 125 feet along Goerck Street and stretched 300 feet through the block to Mangin Street. Several narrow, trash-filled courts ran through this sprawling complex. The apartments, which rented for $3 to $6 a month, each had a small sitting room with a window on the street or a courtyard, a kitchen, and one or two bedrooms without any windows at all. Over eleven hundred people lived here, less than twenty of them native-born Americans.

These tenements and the growing slum districts threatened the well-being of the city and its entire population. As early as 1842 Dr. John H. Griscom, a city inspector, reported to the Board of Aldermen that filthy, overcrowded tenements contributed to much of the disease and many of the deaths in the city. The cholera and yellow fever epidemics of the 1820s and 1830s had broken out in the run-down streets along the East River, and when Greenwich Street became an immigrant quarter in the 1840s, the city inspectors began to find cholera cases there, too. The residents of the Five Points

Tenement district, ca. 1860

suffered the worst health in the city. Cholera was discovered there even after the Civil War. In one of his less charitable moments, Philip Hone wrote that Five Points residents were so filthy, poor, and intemperate that the pigs, which roamed the streets there, "were contaminated by the contact of the children."

New Yorkers also realized that the assaults and burglaries that began to plague the city in the 1830s and 1840s originated, in part, in the misery of the slums. After a number of well-publicized stabbings on the streets late in 1839, Philip Hone wrote that "the city is infested by gangs of hardened wretches, born in the haunts of infamy, brought up in taverns . . . [who] patrol the streets making night hideous and

114

Slum dwellers, ca. 1860

Slum dwellers, ca. 1860

Garbage on East Fifth Street

insulting to all who are not strong enough to defend themselves." By the early 1850s Isabella Lucy Bird, a young English writer, later to become the first woman member of the Royal Geographical Society, reported that "the existence of a 'dangerous class' at New York is now no longer denied." She stayed in New York for a month and probably echoed the feelings of the several rich families with whom she lived when she wrote that "probably in no city in the civilized world is life so fearfully insecure" as New York. "The practice of carrying concealed arms, in the shape of stilettoes for attack, and swordsticks for defense, if illegal, is perfectly common . . . and terrible outrages and murderous assaults are matters of such nightly occurrence as to be thought hardly worthy of notice."

In 1850 Silas Wood, a Quaker who wanted to improve the lives of the poor, built a "model tenement" at 36–38 Cherry Street, between Roosevelt Street and Franklin Square, "with the design of supplying the laboring people with cheap lodgings," according to the *Evening Post*. This tenement, known as Gotham Court, was built of brick, painted a slate gray, and was five stories tall. It was just 35 feet wide on Cherry Street but ran 240 feet through the block to the next street. Gotham Court had 144 apartments, or nearly 30 on each floor. Each apartment had two rooms, a living room 14 by 10 feet and a bedroom 14 by 7 feet. The *Evening Post* believed that "this is a praiseworthy enterprise and well worthy of imitation."

Gotham Court was not the salvation of the poor that its sponsor had hoped it would be. Just six years after its completion, a legislative committee headed by the city's Superintendent of Sanitary Inspection pronounced Gotham Court one of the worst tenements it had visited in the streets along the East River. Nearly half the apartments contained two families, not one as originally planned, thereby raising Gotham Court's population from 600 at its opening to well over a thousand. "The basement is a general receptacle of every kind of filth," reported the *Herald*, and when "the committee attempted a partial exploration of its recesses [it] . . . had to retreat from the sickening task . . . A look into the apartments and breathing their unwholesome air proved indeed a severe test to the untried sensibilities of the committee."

Decent housing alone would not raise the poor from their misery. Other New Yorkers already believed that the poor also needed good jobs, free public schools, even advice on personal hygiene and family matters. The stretch of Cherry Street where Wood had built Gotham Court was in such bad repair and was so dangerous that no single building, no matter how large or well managed, could remain immune from the surrounding vice and squalor.

Cherry Street, like all the streets along the East River north of Franklin Square (now the site of the Brooklyn Bridge), had once been an intensely respectable address. Around 1809 or 1810, John Melish, a Glasgow textile manufacturer visiting New York, thought that this area, whose streets had just been opened, was "constructed on a handsome plan." Rather than the jumbled streets of the Pearl Street district just to the south, he found the "streets crossing one another at right angles" and plans for several parks, of which "there are by far too few in the city." The public squares were never laid out, but Caroline Gilman, the author, described the area in 1836 as "all handsomely built up with private residences." Shopkeepers, skilled craftsmen, countinghouse clerks, and workmen from the nearby shipyards along the East River lived in the area in modest frame and red brick Federal row houses, similar to those being built in the western reaches of Greenwich Village. East Broadway, thought Mrs. Gilman, was "a spacious and elegant street." Here were the homes of merchants and ships' captains — large, elegantly decorated Federal and Greek Revival row houses, much like those on Bond Street or St. Mark's Place.

Several eighteenth-century mansions stood on Cherry Street, reminders of the time when the area was pasture and farmland leading down to the East River. George Washington had lived at 3 Cherry Street, just a few doors from Franklin Square, between his election as President in 1789 and the moving of the capital to Philadelphia in 1790. The mansion, built in 1770 by Walter Franklin, a merchant, was square, three stories tall, and five windows wide; it sat back from the street on modest grounds. Though known, as

117

Stevens' house it would be known some years later, as the "palace," the house was not especially spacious or well appointed, and the ceilings on the main floor were so low that on more than one occasion the ostrich feather headdresses of ladies attending Martha Washington's receptions brushed past one of the chandeliers and caught fire. After the capital moved to Philadelphia, 3 Cherry Street was, in its several incarnations, a genteel boardinghouse, a music store, and the Franklin Bank. It was demolished in 1856.

Another mansion on Cherry Street, the Hendrick Rutgers house, saw much more of the neighborhood's growth and decline than the more famous Number 3. Rutgers built the house in 1754 as a country residence, and an engraving made forty years afterward shows that meadows, shade trees, and several mansions, all widely separated from each other, still dominated this stretch of the East River. When city growth reached the area soon after 1800, the Rutgers family sold most of its estate to builders and real estate speculators. The house, however, still stood on a full city block, bounded by Cherry, Jefferson, Monroe, and Clinton streets.

In 1830 William Crosby inherited the mansion from Henry Rutgers, a descendant of the original builder. Years later the *Times* recalled that "he not liking the ancient aspect of the old mansion, undertook to modernize it, which he did with a vengeance." Rutgers built a Doric portico on the house and added a small wing on each side. He updated the interior of the mansion with marble mantels, paneling in rare woods, and elaborate plasterwork with classic motifs. The surrounding neighborhood started going downhill in the 1840s, but Crosby continued to live in the mansion, with its square block of gardens. The newspapers delighted in reporting just how bad the area had become. "What is needed here," wrote the *Herald*, "[is] the reconstructive influence of a good fire." Crosby, however, was not the only prosperous gentleman who chose to stay. Six men on the *Daily Tribune's* 1851 list of the 200 richest men in New York were other residents of the neighborhood; one lived on Madison Street, another on Rivington Street, and four on East Broadway.

These men represented the end of an era for the area that was soon known as the Lower East Side. As the immigrant poor moved in, middle-class families fled their homes, which were turned into boardinghouses or torn down for tenements. Shops for the local population took over many of the former captains' mansions on East Broadway. By 1850 the *Daily Tribune* reported that local hoodlums, who had once stayed on the narrow sidestreets off East Broadway, were now gathering on that bustling thoroughfare itself. "Gangs of rowdy boys, in numbers from fifteen to sixty," wrote the newspaper, "are continually hanging about these corners, seeking all occasions for fights, yells, and general disturbances, much to the annoyance of respectable dwellers thereabouts." Ten years later the *Daily Tribune* noted that the remaining single-family houses on East Broadway sold for one-fourth the price they had fetched in the 1820s and 1830s.

When William Crosby died in 1860, none of his sons wanted to live in the Rutgers mansion. "By this time the neighborhood was greatly altered," wrote the *Times*, "and was, in fact, an unpleasant one for people of his standing in society." So Crosby's heirs sold the mansion to a cooper named Briggs for $80,000. Briggs moved into the old house and filled the gardens with used barrels and sugar boxes, which he sold to local residents for firewood. "Mounds of these seventy feet high were soon reared in every direction, and the whole place was obscured by them, narrow labyrinthine paths being left through which the workmen might pass," wrote the *Times*. After a year or two, Briggs moved out and rented the middle section of the building to a children's refuge called the Chapel of the Holy Rest. The organization stayed there only a few months. When it left the house, Briggs sold off the marble mantels and wood paneling and then gutted the interior for more storage space for barrels. The Rutgers mansion "was now a forlorn sight," according to the *Times*. "A rough wooden staircase, more like a ladder than anything else, enabled workmen to reach the top of the barrels, but below it was impossible to move, for there was no space. But the visitor, casting his eyes upward, can still see, solid vestige of ancient grandeur amid all the squalor, a superb molding on the ceiling next to the roof, which was difficult to remove and was therefore left." In 1872 Briggs sold the property for $120,000. The battered shell of the old mansion was demolished in 1875, and tenements and sweatshop lofts rose on the site.

As New York swept up Manhattan Island in the 1840s and 1850s, the slum district, once centered on the Five Points and Cherry Street, also moved rapidly northward, first past Grand Street and into Delancey, Rivington, and Stanton streets, then past Houston Street and into the numbered streets around Tompkins Square. In 1857 the *Herald* observed that "the destiny of all the east side of the island seems to be as an abiding place for the poor."

Just as life for upper- and middle-class New Yorkers focused on Broadway, so the inhabitants of this sprawling boardinghouse and tenement district had their own shopping and entertainment street, the Bowery, which begins at Chatham Square and ends two miles uptown at Eighth Street, where it becomes Third Avenue. In the seventeenth and eighteenth centuries such prominent Dutch families as the Dyckmans, Brevoorts, Bayards, Rutgerses, and Van Cortlandts owned estates along the country road. Once the farms disappeared and this section of Manhattan was built up, however, the Bowery, "commenced to lose caste," reported James McCabe. "Decent people forsook it, and the poorer and more disreputable classes took possession. Finally, it became notorious."

This reputation did not stop New York's citizens from crowding the Bowery's sidewalks throughout the day and long into the night or patronizing its clothing stores, hotels, theaters, pawnshops, restaurants, bars, dance halls, and brothels. In 1836 George Templeton Strong, then sixteen years old, and several of his friends were walking through the east side of town and, "being two-thirds famished, we stopped to get some grub in the Bowery. Found it to be a very loaferish place — pie tasted of potato peeling and coffee was a dirty infusion of tobacco — accommodations to correspond." So Strong and his companions "cleared out in a hurry, leaving pie and coffee to take care of themselves. Minus eighteen pence for this speculation."

Food along the Bowery may not have been very good, if we believe Strong, but the theaters were some of the best in the city and seemed to be on every block of the street. In the mid-1820s, Peter Neilson declared that "the inhabitants of New York are very fond of theatrical entertainments." He knew "instances, in no very exalted rank of life, wherein the lady considered herself as being ill-used by her husband, if not conveyed at least once a week to a play-house." This taste of the local population and of the thousands of tourists in the city made "theaters . . . probably more numerous in New-York than in any other city in the world with the same population," according to the *Knickerbocker*. In 1850 the *Home Journal* estimated that at least ten thousand people attended "places of amusement" in the city every night, the most popular being the theaters.

To some New Yorkers, the popularity of the theater was a sign of moral decline in the city. The *Daily Tribune*, which discouraged all theater advertisements in its pages in the 1840s and 1850s, believed that "the stage, as it is, is more an injury than a benefit to the community — vicious, licentious, degrading, demoralizing." Even the *Herald* declared that too many plays glorified "murder, adultery, fornication, arson, lying, robbery, and a few other choice crimes, without names." Newspapers and clergymen also criticized actors and actresses for their "notorious moral character." It is a "notorious fact [the adjective seemed indispensable to those passing judgment] that a large proportion of those connected with the stage are libertines or courtezans — a proportion much larger, we are confident, than can be found in any other tolerated profession," declared the *Daily Tribune*.

Most theater in New York was just a few hours of entertainment, neither particularly bawdy nor violent. But in 1847 and 1848 those who thought theater was immoral actually had something to talk about. Hiram Powers' statue, the *Greek Slave*, was the rage of the city, and thousands of New Yorkers were buying tickets to see the scantily clad figure. So a self-entitled Dr. Collyser decided to go the *Greek Slave* one better, and rented Palmo's Opera House on Chambers Street to show "living men and women in almost the same state in which Gabriel saw them in the Garden of Eden in the first morning of creation." Soon a number of model-artist shows around town were showing their own version of the Garden of Eden, each with a different idea of just how much clothing Adam and Eve wore that morning. As more and more theaters put on model-artist shows, they added other scenes, such as Neptune rising from the sea or Esther in the Persian bath.

The police left these shows alone until the Odeon Theater opened one Sunday, in direct violation of the blue laws. Everything went smoothly until the tableau called *Jacob in the House of Laban*, "with three well-formed females attired in short skirts." At that moment a score of policemen, led by the Chief of Police and several Aldermen, entered the Odeon to end "this curious idea." The members of the audience, already excited by what was on the stage, erupted into a cheering, booing mob, running about the theater, throwing whatever they could find at the police and at each other. The scene in front of the stage was nothing compared to what reputedly happened in the backstage dressing rooms: Some five or six well-formed females were in the act of preparing for the next tableau. In one corner was seen a very fleshy lady dressed as Bacchus, studying her position on a barrel. Another beautifully formed creature, just drawing on her tights for the Greek Slave, and some of the others, were so dreadfully alarmed at the sight of the police with their clubs in hand that they seized up a portion of their garments in order to hide their faces, forgetting their lower extremities, thus making a scene mixed up with the sublime and ridiculous.

The newspapers carried the story of the police at the Odeon Theater, and now all New York knew about "the whole world of the under crust of fashion." Hereafter, the Odeon, which reopened the next night, the Thiers Concert Hall, the Temple of the Muses, Novelty Hall, the Anatomical Museum, and other theaters were filled to the rafters night after night. The shows were becoming more and more indecent — "more nakedness and less drapery," as one newspaper put it. At one theater, patrons paid a dollar apiece to see several naked ladies through a doorway that had been covered by a "large gauze." At another theater, unclad men and women danced the polka and minuet on the stage. "Only think of the indecency now indulged in," exclaimed the *Herald*. Then one night a gang of thugs invaded a theater, breaking up funiture, terrifying the audience, and chasing the exiguously garbed performers down the Bowery. Early in 1848, one year after the beginning of this frenzy, the city closed all the model-artist shows for good.

Proper New Yorkers might be too timid to venture into one of the Bowery's crowded bars or theaters, but they could see two of the area's greatest attractions, the "Bowery B'hoys" and "Bowery Girls," just by walking down the street. "None was so ready as he for a fight, none so quick to resent the intrusion of a respectable man into his haunts," recalled James McCabe. It was a gang of Bowery B'hoys that broke up the model-artist show in 1847. "You might see him," continued McCabe, "strutting along like a king with his breeches stuck in his boots, his coat on his arm, his flaming red shirt tied at the collar with a cravat such as could be seen nowhere else; with crape on his hat, the hat set deftly on the side of his head, his hair evenly plastered down to his skull, and a cigar in his mouth." The Bowery Girl was as femininely dressed and coquettish as her B'hoy was manly and fierce. "Her bonnet was a perfect museum of ribbons and ornaments, and it sat jauntily on the side of her head. Her skirts came to the shoe tops and displayed her pretty feet and well-turned ankles, equipped with irreproachable gaiters and the most stunning of stockings. One arm swung loosely to the motion of her body as she passed along with a quick, lithe step, and the other held just over her nose, her parasol, which was sometimes swung over her right shoulder."

Another newspaperman, Henri Junius Browne, was just as fascinated by the Bowery as McCabe. The street was "one of the most peculiar and striking quarters of the metropolis." But for all its crowds and excitement, this "city in itself" was removed from the activity and spirit of the rest of New York. Although the Bowery, in places, was no more than a ten-minute walk from Broadway, Henri Junius Browne knew that the few blocks between the streets were as impenetrable "as a Chinese wall."

_8_

Broadway was "altogether the most showy,
the most crowded, and the richest thoroughfare in America,"
declared _Putnam's Monthly_ in 1854. It was "the most famous
and oftenest-borrowed name of any street in the United
States, and perhaps the only one that has any European
name and celebrity." But "the peculiarity of Broadway," continued the magazine, "consists in its being not only the main
artery of the city, not only the focus [but also] the agglomera-
tion of trade and fashion, business and amusement, public
and private abodes, churches and theaters, barrooms and
exhibitions, all collected into one promiscuous channel of
activity and dissipation."

Even twenty years earlier, when Broadway came to an
abrupt halt in the pastures north of Houston Street, it had
been the setting of all the city's different activities. The
banks, countinghouses, and dry goods warehouses had just
appeared on Broadway between Bowling Green and Trinity
Church. The city's finest shops, hotels, and theaters filled the
stretch between Trinity and City Hall. Beyond that were the
large red brick homes of the city's richest and most prominent families.

By the mid-1840s, the built-up portion of Broadway, like
New York as a whole, had progressed a mile farther north up
Manhattan, as far north as Union Square at Fourteenth
Street. Broadway was still divided into three separate areas,
each representing a different function, but they had all
moved north in the passing years. The banks and counting-

Broadway: view north from
Spring Street, 1867

houses had taken over the blocks from Bowling Green to the beginning of City Hall Park. The shopping and hotel district now began around City Hall and continued a few blocks past Canal Street, and the residential portion of Broadway filled the next mile leading to Union Square. Just ten years later, around 1855, Broadway changed again, with business now reaching Canal Street, shops and hotels between there and Union Square, and residences gone from the street entirely.

No other street in America compared with Broadway in activity or elegance. "Washington Street in Boston, Chestnut Street of Philadelphia, and Chartres Street of New Orleans, although each attractive in its way, would not altogether make a fair match for Broadway, either in costliness or appearance," boasted George Foster in 1849, "and, as for business, you could pour all three of them into Broadway at any hour of the day, without perceptibly swelling its current." Even British visitors, who had found Broadway's shops and hotels distinctly inferior to those of London in the 1820s and 1830s, now praised the street as one of the finest in the world. Charles Mackay, editor of the *Illustrated London News*, wrote in the late 1850s that "there is not street in London that can be declared superior, or even equal, all things considered, to Broadway," and youthful Isabella Lucy Bird found Broadway "at once the Corso, Toledo, Regent Street, and Princes Street of New York."

Except for a few residents of Boston or Philadelphia, most Americans admired Broadway as evidence of America's rising power and wealth. "Broadway is New York intensified — the reflex of the Republic," wrote Henri Junius Browne. "No thoroughfare in the country so completely represents its wealth, its enterprise, its fluctuations, and its progress. Not all European visitors shared upstart America's pride in Broadway. "Now if you have ever met an American in England or on the Continent," wrote George Borrett, "you will have been informed by him before you have had five minute's conversation with him, that no street in the world is worth looking at after Broadway . . . If you are talking of shops, he will take the opportunity of telling you that there is nothing like 'our stores down Broadway.' If you observe upon the points of some passing beauty, he will 'guess, sir, you've never seen our gals on Broadway.' In short, Broadway licks cre-ation."

It was, indeed, best known for its shops. "The shops are more numerous, more extensive, and are filled with more expensive and rarer assortments of goods than those of any other street in American," declared George Foster. "This superiority is so unquestionable that all other cities involuntarily accept the cue from the dealers in Broadway." From eleven o'clock in the morning until three o'clock in the afternoon, stylish carriages jammed that part of Broadway devoted to shopping — slowly moving up and down the pavement, dropping off several ladies for a shopping foray, or patiently waiting along the curb for the trip home or yet another stop at a fine shop.

On pleasant spring and fall afternoons, so many smartly dressed women strolled along the sidewalks or hurried from one shop to another that from a distance both sides of the street appeared to be "one sheet of bright, quivering colors." The ladies along Broadway were "almost uniformly good-looking . . . much handsomer than the men," wrote James Silk Buckingham, an English author of travel books, around 1840 — and "evidently fond of dress," added Charles Mackay. Charles Dickens was not so reticent about the women promenading along Broadway as these two gentlemen; he exclaimed, "Heaven save the ladies, how they dress!" The *Daily Tribune* agreed that the ladies were "peripatetic and vitalized museums of feminine display" with "brocades, poplins, and all imaginable unutterables, lashed in oriental gorgeousness . . . bonnets saucy as a hummingbird's nest in a rosebush; plumes, laces, diamonds even; gloves cut from a rainbow; shoes insolently piquant."

Only the famed Broadway dandies, that street's better-mannered answer to the "Bowery B'hoys," challenged the splendor of the ladies. "It is impossible to meet a more finished coxcomb than a Broadway dandy," reported Alexander Mackay in the 1850s. "The Broadway dandy — here he is, in radiant perfection!" wrote *Life Illustrated*. "What horn-like moustaches! What hyacinthine curls! What delicately kidded little hands! . . . Who else can squeeze his feet into such astoundingly *little* sections of patent leather? Who else wears such superfine broadcloth? . . . Who else can boast of such glossy hair, with such a very small quantity of brains beneath it?"

The fine clothing of the dandies and promenading ladies was better suited to gas-lit drawing rooms and ballrooms than to the Broadway *trottoir.* In summer, the street and sidewalks, according to the *Daily Tribune,* were covered with dust — a "horrible, intolerable, eye-filling, teeth-gritting, breath-choking, patience-destroying, anger-provoking dust." Miss Bird thought it "rather repugnant to one's feelings to behold costly silks and rich brocades sweeping the pavement of Broadway with more effect than is produced by the dustman." In winter and rainy weather at any time of the year, the street was ankle-deep in mud and filth, and, according to

A New York belle

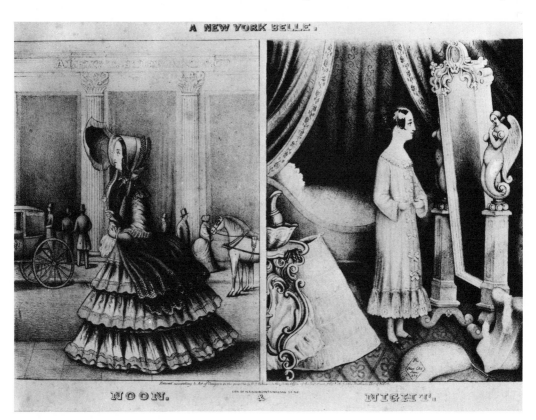

A NEW YORK BELLE.

NOON.   NIGHT.

the *Daily Tribune,* "everything goes on sloppishly, and be-draggledness is the general condition of all things."

The garbage, which filled the gutters, was a year-round problem. The city's trash collection was erratic, so Broadway's shopkeepers kept their sidewalks and street clean by hiring private trash collectors. "Broadway was dazzling," reported William Chambers, a Scottish journalist, in the early 1850s, but the sidestreets were filled with "boxes, buckets, lid-less flour barrels, baskets, decayed tea chests, rusty iron pans and earthenware jars full of coal ashes." The pigs rooted among the garbage on the sidestreets and, according to Dickens, sometimes joined the promenade along Broadway's sidewalks. They did not even look like proper farmyard pigs, thought the author; they were "ugly brutes, having, for the most part, scanty brown backs like the lids of old horsehair trunks, spotted with unwholesome black blotches [and] long, gaunt legs."

Conversation along Broadway was often difficult because of the roar of traffic. Some fifteen thousand vehicles passed St. Paul's Chapel at the corner of Broadway and Fulton Street on a weekday in the 1850s. "Pack the traffic of the Strand and Cheapside into Oxford Street, and still you will not have an idea of the crush in Broadway," wrote Isabella Lucy Bird. "There are streams of scarlet and yellow omnibuses, racing in the more open parts, and locking each other's wheels in the narrower . . . There are loaded stages hastening to and from the huge hotels . . . carts and wagons laden with merchandise, and 'Young America' driving fast-trotting horses, edging in and out among the crowd."

The rumbling noise of the omnibuses' wheels along the iron rails, the shouts and curses of their drivers, the sharp sounds of hundreds of iron horseshoes striking the stone pavement, and the rattling of boxes and building materials in the wagons made Broadway "less inviting than it otherwise would be to promenaders who love to chat, as well as walk," complained a visitor. Walt Whitman probably was thinking of the tumult of Broadway when he asked in 1842: "What can New York — noisy, roaring, rumbling, tumbling, bustling, stormy, turbulent New York — have to do with silence?"

A Broadway stage

Broadway, despite its name, was no more than eighty feet wide in most places, and sometimes the traffic simply ground to a halt. The year 1852 was particularly bad for traffic; the Park Place district was in the throes of its commercial transformation, and Church Street, College Place, and the sidestreets leading down to the Hudson River were virtually impassable because of street-widenings and building operations. Greenwich and Washington streets were also closed because of the regrading work. The traffic that normally used all these streets poured into an already overcrowded Broadway.

A traffic jam was an unexpected boon to pedestrians: they could cross the street without dashing for their lives among the carriages and omnibuses. "I merely think of getting across the street alive," wrote Fredrika Bremer, the Swedish novelist and feminist. Just walking down the sidewalks presented dangers from buildings under demolition or construction. Because of careless builders and their workmen, "we must consent to be smothered in dust, thumped by falling bricks, driven into the mud by piles of rubbish," complained Philip Hone. Some New Yorkers crossed the street rather than walk past building sites. There were perils, however, that no one could avoid during a walk along Broadway. "Crash comes something across our path," wrote a contributor to *Leslie's Illustrated*. It sounded as if two vehicles had collided in the street or an onmibus had tipped over. "No such thing. It is simply one of our merchant princes . . . who is getting in or getting out stock. A score or two of huge boxes litter the pavement, and the small aperture that is left, is scarce wide enough for a fearfully thin man to push through."

Most women who were going from one shop to another or enjoying an afternoon promenade overlooked or did not even notice the nuisances that troubled visitors. "Sights to which we are daily accustomed, make but little impression upon us," wrote Alexander Mackay, "and therefore it is that New Yorkers frequently express an honest surprise at the discoveries in this respect, made by strangers." Then, too, the Broadway shopkeepers insulated the lady shoppers from reality with their luxurious establishments, pleasant clerks,

Broadway traffic, 1854

and tempting array of merchandise. "The lady who goes in a graceful mortal comes out a divinity," observed the *Home Journal*. So Broadway was filled with women, according to Englishman James Robertson, "whose chief occupation seems to be, to admire the tempting wares which are exhibited in the shop windows, and to spend the money, which their husbands and other relatives strive to make at the lower end of the street."

The most numerous establishments were the department stores and the dressmakers, because, as the *Herald* observed, "American women indulge in . . . the love of dress to a greater degree than those of any other country." In 1850 James Fenimore Cooper thought that New York was "a great arena for the women to show off their fine feathers in," and William Makepeace Thackeray, on a lecture tour of America in 1852–1853, was amazed by the prodigious expenditures for clothing. "I watched one young lady at four balls in as many dresses, and each dress of the most 'stunning description.' " But what was extravagant in women's clothing in the 1840s and 1850s was not at all extraordinary by the 1860s. It was "nothing uncommon to meet . . . society ladies who have on dry goods and jewelry to the value of from $30,000 to $50,000," wrote James McCabe after the Civil War. With walking dresses costing $50 to $300, ball gowns $500 to $2500, bonnets $200, and shawls as much as $1000, a lady's wardrobe could easily cost over $100,000.

Although A. T. Stewart & Company was New York's first department store, there were several equally fashionable competitors, including one whose name is well known today. Lord & Taylor was founded on Catherine Street by Samuel Lord, a native of England, and George W. Taylor, a New Yorker. The firm prospered, and in 1852 opened its first luxurious building at Grand and Chrystie streets, one block east of Broadway. That store proved so popular that an addition was built in 1856. Still Lord & Taylor could not accommodate the crowds of ladies, and in 1859 opened yet another store at the northwest corner of Broadway and Grand Street. The five-story white marble building looked "more like an Italian palace than a place for the sale of broadcloth," declared the *Times* on the opening day. The ornamentation,

Lord & Taylor, Broadway and Grand Street, 1860

inside and outside, was so grand that the *Times* thought "it would be regarded as faulty by persons of more moderate taste than New Yorkers."

The Broadway shopkeepers were some of the first businessmen in American to promote their merchandise and attract customers with frequent, carefully planned advertising. Even the best shops advertised a sale or the arrival of the latest shipment of dry goods from Paris in the newspapers or ladies' parlor magazines like the *Home Journal* or *Godey's Lady's Book*. Most shops, though not the tasteful A. T. Stewart's and Lord & Taylor, hung colorful advertising placards on poles protruding from the building or stuck to the post that supported the outer edge of the awnings. Some shopkeepers painted or chiseled their names and addresses on the slate sidewalk at the front door, to catch the pedestrians who walked with their eyes downcast. No one could miss the occasional corner building that had been covered from sidewalk to roof with various advertisements — "written, painted, printed, or drawn in every conceivable style, the favorite being that which is the most ugly of conception and disfiguring in effect," wrote the *Daily Tribune*. Armed with his wooden ladder, pot of paste, wide brush, and notices, the hard-working bill-poster often destroyed the architectural pretensions of many buildings and, sometimes, turned the advertisements into jokes by unwittingly pasting up a notice in such a way that a corner or a line of an earlier one still showed. One day the *Daily Tribune* reported that one much-covered wall read:

George Christy and Wood's Minstrels
Will be sold at auction without reserve
Laura Keene's
Inflammatory rheumatism positively cured by
    three applications of
Journeymen gas fitters and plumbers
No cure, no pay
Scrofula, gout, neuralgia
Country orders supplied with dispatch
Children under ten years of age half price
A rhinoceros, a boa constrictor, two camels, a pair of lions,
    and a zebra
All take Hobensack's liver pills.

The single most important thing a clothing advertisement could say was that the items were imported from France. By the 1840s, Paris was the supreme fashion authority for Americans, and the Broadway shops imported boatloads of exquisite fabrics, which the *modistes* made into gowns, and ready-made French shoes, gloves, and bonnets. The French styles in clothing, of course, had their enemies. "The rage for foreign materials and workmanship of every kind is as ludicrous . . . as in England," wrote Isabella Lucy Bird, never backward with an opinion. "No dressmaker is now considered orthodox who cannot show a prefix of *Madame* . . . Large numbers of the caps, bonnets, mantles, and other articles of dress, which are marked ostentatiously with the name of some *Rue* in Paris, have never incurred the risk of an Atlantic voyage."

Jewelers were among the most popular shops along Broadway. Isabella had come to New York knowing that "American ladies wear very costly jewelry," but she was "perfectly amazed" at the luxury of the Broadway jewelry shops and "at the prices of some of the articles displayed." At one jeweler's, she saw a diamond bracelet for $25,000 and asked the clerk who would buy such an item. "I guess some Southerner will buy it for his wife," he replied. But New Yorkers were also buying costly jewelry. On one day before Christmas in the 1860s, the city's two leading jewelers, Tiffany & Company and Ball, Black & Company, did over $150,000 of business. That day, Ball, Black's "gorgeous palace of the jewel trade" was jammed until 10:00 P.M. with "eager purchasers, who paid their greenbacks to the obsequious clerks with a nonchalance that made money dross [and] condemned thousands of dollars to . . . a mere bagatelle."

Tiffany's was so impressive that the *Herald*, in 1850, thought it was "as deep and rich as the gemmed cavern of Aladdin, and every step brings the visitor in the face of new wonders in the jeweler's art." The company was founded in 1837, hardly an auspicious year for a shop dealing in luxury goods. It weathered the Panic, however, and won national prominence in 1845 by producing the first standard gold and gem jewelry in the nation. Two years later it moved to 271 Broadway, just across the street from A. T. Stewart's. The fashionable retail trade was steadily moving uptown, and in 1852 Tiffany's sold its building for $100,000 to D. Devlin & Company, who manufactured the first stylish ready-made clothing in America.

Tiffany's new store, at 550 Broadway, just north of Prince Street, was "hardly surpassed in beauty by any building of the kind in the world," according to the *Herald*. The thirty-five-foot-wide, five-story building, designed by R. G. Hatfield, had a white marble Italianate façade. Over the front door stood the familiar statue of Atlas holding a clock on his shoulder that has graced all subsequent Tiffany buildings. Willis of the *Home Journal* thought that "there is nothing that compares with it in any of the great European capitals."

Once past the front door, even the most stalwart lady shoppers fell captive to the "brilliant *bijouterie*," the "blaze of glittering temptations" on all sides. The first floor was a single room one hundred feet deep with sixteen-foot ceilings. Lofty arched mirrors, alternating with frescoes, adorned the wall on the left. The silver-trimmed jewelry case, which stood a few feet out from this wall, stretched forty-eight feet back into the store, beneath the light of six gas chandeliers. The opposite wall was a row of intricately decorated arches and more display cases, which reached halfway back into the store, where there was a stairway to the second floor. Behind the stairway were the firm's offices, "perfectly retired and secluded." Another line of display

*Tiffany & Co., 550
Broadway, 1855*

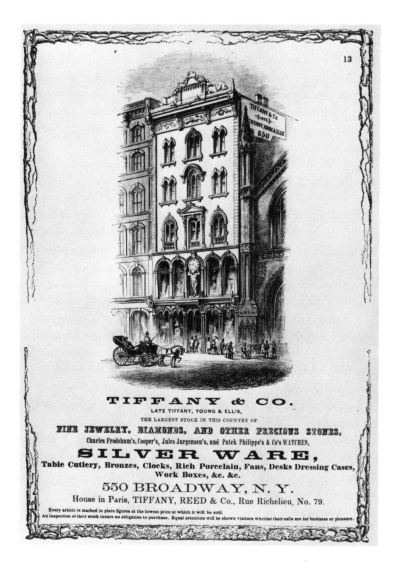

cases ran down the center of this room and contained "entire sets of elaborately worked silver." These arrangements of silver, like everything at Tiffany's, were "so arranged that they remind you rather of the artistic distribution of a magnificent palace, than the tawdry and overloaded display of a cluttered bazaar," wrote the *Herald*.

The second floor was painted pure white, "without any ornament around the walls or on the ceiling," to show off the chandeliers, bronzes, and "infinite variety of exquisite work" to their best advantage. Glass, china, and porcelain filled the third floor, and the fourth floor was given over to the manufacture of jewelry. The silversmiths had their own factory a few blocks away, on Centre Street. Tiffany's occasionally sold novelties as well as jewelry and silver. In 1858 the firm bought several miles of unused cable, left over after the laying of the Atlantic Cable. America was agog over the first telegraph communication with Great Britain, and the shop sold souvenir pieces of the cable, each several inches long.

Shopping and promenading along Broadway was a pleasant but tiring way to pass the afternoon. The ladies needed a place to rest, talk with their friends, and enjoy a light meal. But women without a gentleman escort were unwelcome or on questionable social ground in mid-nineteenth-century New York. So a number of "ladies' saloons," restaurants for women, opened on Broadway in the 1840s and 1850s. The most famous was Taylor's restaurant, at 365 Broadway at the corner of Franklin Street. Taylor's, however, was more than just a place for women to snack and talk during their shopping forays. It was the "largest and most elegant restaurant in the world," according to *Putnam's Monthly*, having grown "from a humble ice-creamery and confectionary to its present magnificent dimensions."

Taylor's served three thousand people on an average weekday, and on Sunday afternoons and evenings people waited on line outside for an hour or more before getting a table. People often cried out with delight the first time they walked into Taylor's. Just a glance was "bewildering," according to one guidebook to the city. "The glory of the arts seem to flash in concentrated beauty." The 50-by-100-foot grand saloon was "a perfect blaze of decoration . . . a complete maze of frescoes, mirrors, carving, gilding, and marble," according to the *Daily Tribune*. Nine lofty, richly draped windows on the left overlooked Franklin Street; the opposite wall was all mirrors. Corinthian columns, painted crimson with gilt trim, rose to the frescoed and gilt ceiling twenty-two feet above. A stained-glass window occupied the back wall and, on each side, was a fountain rising among flowers. A curved mirror rose in back of the fountain, thereby multiplying the scene indefinitely.

By day lady shoppers filled the more than a hundred black walnut tables in this room. Twenty to thirty uniformed

Ball, Black & Co., 247 Broadway: interior of the jewelry store, 1850

waiters hurried among the crowds, serving oysters, ome-lettes, sandwiches, eggs, coffee, hot chocolate, and ice cream. The curtains and mahogany shutters in the windows along Franklin Street were partly closed during the day, to keep the room dimly lit. "Ladies love such subdued atmos-phere," declared one New Yorker. At night, however, the room was "perfectly dazzling." The "imagination could scarcely conceive anything to go beyond it," according to the *New York Journal*. The room was ablaze with hundreds of gas lights in the chandeliers, wall sconces, and torches held aloft by the classical bronze statues scattered around the room.

Taylor's restaurant,
365 Broadway

Now Taylor's was jammed with people out for dinner or a late snack after the theater.

Taylor's had another dining room on the floor below, where gentlemen guests dined on heartier fare than the omelettes and sandwiches favored upstairs. At the foot of the stairway leading to this dining room stood the decorative triumph of the establishment, a crystal fountain. Rising from a marble basin nine feet wide, the sparkling structure of silver-colored pipes, crystal basins, and splashing water rose twenty-one feet in the stairwell, the top portion being visible in the dining room on the main floor. A stream of water fed from a pipe into the topmost crystal basin and from there fell by gravity from basin to basin, lower and lower, forming a gently splashing twenty-one-foot "pyramid of water," which sparkled at a hundred different spots in the glare of the gas lights. After this shimmering descent, the water finally emptied into the marble basin, where six glass dolphins, each two and a half feet long, spouted streams of water from their snouts.

Taylor's restaurant, according to the *Herald*, was "the restaurant of the age." It was the most extravagant restaurant in the city and the undeniable favorite of rich uptown ladies, middle-class families out for a splurge on Sunday evening, and the street urchins standing on the sidewalks, peering through the plate-glass windows. It was one of the sights "strangers are always expected to visit," declared Isabella Lucy Bird. But Taylor's was not the "epicurean temple" so many claimed it to be. The meals "rank between a fifth-rate Palais Royal restaurant and a second-rate Vienna cream shop," wrote Willis. Other guests found fault with the service. "Intolerable, surly, inattentive, and careless," fumed the *New York Journal*. The discrepancy between ordinary food and an extraordinary setting did not trouble most New Yorkers, who were used to such startling contrasts in their city. Taylor's restaurant reflected a Broadway lined with white marble department stores and jewelry stores, still littered with garbage and visited by scavenging pigs.

9

Broadway by night was far different from
Broadway by day. The promenade of beautifully dressed
women ended around three o'clock, when they returned to
their homes uptown in the carriages that had filled Broadway
throughout the day. Around five, men from countinghouses,
the waterfront, and Wall Street offices thronged the sidewalks and filled the omnibuses on their way home. This
homeward rush ended around eight, but by then Broadway
was filled with New Yorkers and tourists on their way to the
theaters, saloons, restaurants, and hotels.

As night fell on the city, Broadway became a brilliantly lit,
almost magical sight. Every carriage or omnibus on the street
carried at least one pair of lamps, in a variety of colors, which
went "dancing down the long vista like so many fire-flies,"
in James McCabe's words. The store windows were fully
illuminated, to lure the nighttime window shoppers, and the
entrances and first-floor façades of all the hotels were always
bright with light. The stores and hotels loomed high above
the street, their topmost floors and elaborate ornamentation
hidden from view on moonless or cloudy nights. But on a
clear night, Charles Mackay remembered, "The rays of the
moon fell upon the marble edifices with a brilliancy as if they
had fallen upon icebergs or the snowy summits of hills."

The sounds of Broadway changed with nightfall, too. The
thundering roar of the daytime traffic was gone because the
business wagons disappeared with the end of the workday,
and the number of omnibuses on the Broadway run dropped

as the night wore on. Now the relaxed voices and occasional drunken songs of the crowds on the sidewalks filled the air. Laughter and applause and music floated out into the street near the theaters and saloons. And there were the sidewalk musicians, who entertained crowds at some of the busier street corners.

Not every amusement on Broadway at night was as innocent as the theaters or restaurants. Saucily dressed streetwalkers were a frequent sight, as they strolled past the hotels, casually pausing in front of the glittering shop windows, or waited outside the theater entrances beneath the glare of a hundred gas lights. These women were a magnificent sight by any standard. "Their complexions are pure white and red, and their dresses are of the most expensive material, and an ultra-fashionable make," reported George Foster. "Diamonds and bracelets flash from their bosoms and bare arms, and heavily-wrought India shawls, of that gorgeous scarlet whose beaming hue intoxicates the eye, hang carelessly from their superb shoulders, almost trailing on the walk." Their "free and sweeping gait" gave away these women's true reason for being on the streets at night. They glanced quickly but searchingly at each man they passed on the sidewalk. "How do you do, my dear? Come, won't you go home with me?" was their familiar greeting.

By 1850, roughly ten thousand women in a New York of a half-millon people were prostitutes, according to Foster. This figure increased in the next twenty or thirty years, growing even faster than the city's population. No more than one tenth of these women were actually streetwalkers, the "noctivagous strumpetocracy," as George Templeton Strong described them in his diary. Most prostitutes worked in brothels. In the 1840s the city's most stylish brothels favored Church Street in the Park Place area, just a block from the largest and best hotels of the time. By the early 1850s the most fashionable hotels began to open on Broadway between Canal and Houston streets, and trade overwhelmed the once-residential Park Place district. So the most elegant brothels moved to Greene and Mercer streets, the first two north-to-south streets west of Broadway.

In the daytime these streets were silent, virtually empty; the red brick Federal row houses looked a bit run-down but still respectable. At night, however, red lights above the front doors of these houses twinkled from one end of Greene and Mercer streets to the other, and the sidewalks were filled with men getting out of hired carriages or walking over from Broadway. The houses were finely furnished and, in general, were a safe and discreet pleasure for their customers.

All New York knew what was happening on Greene and Mercer streets, but the madams paid off the police regularly so that they could operate without interference. When the Mayor announced a drive against prostitution in 1855, Strong realized that "what the Mayor seeks to abolish or abate is not the terrible evil of prostitution, but simply the scandal and offense of the peripatetic whorearchy. The great notorious 'ladies' boarding houses' of Leonard and Mercer Streets are left in peace."

Occasionally the police did raid and close one of the brothels, an anything but pleasant experience for the clients. After such a raid in 1838, the *Herald* reported: "Clerks of respectable mercantile houses were found in this pious place in the embraces of the most depraved and abandoned denizens of the notorious spot. They were compelled to give their names and the names of their employers. They were then suffered to go home, covered with shame and mortification." In 1845 Hone recorded in his diary that John B. Gough, "an itinerant who has been going about the country delivering temperance lectures, and proclaiming his own shame in having been formerly a drunkard," was discovered in a Walker Street brothel. Gough protested his innocence, saying that he had been drugged by an acquaintance and carried senseless to the low establishment.

Another popular place to meet available young women was one of the several hundred concert saloons. By day, these establishments were closed or almost empty. With nightfall, "the concert saloons reveal their fascinations for the idle and unwary," wrote Henri Junius Browne. Lighted signs and sidewalk barkers promised free music all night, every kind of liquor, and, naturally, "the prettiest waiter girls in town," who were "most attentive and complaisant upon the wishes of visitors."

Walking through the front door of a typical concert saloon, the visitor entered a noisy and smoky room filled with small tables where men and women sat talking and drinking, a shining mahogany bar along one wall with eight or ten busy bartenders, and a noisy band in one corner, whose music became even noisier as the night passed. A waiter girl would emerge from the bustling scene and "tell you that so good-looking and nice a gentleman ought not to be alone, or go without a drink. Then she informs you she will take something with you, and keep you company. Without more words, she brings from the bar a glass of beer or liquor, and places herself at your side; asks if you like women; invites you to visit her when she is at home; perhaps grants you permission to escort her from the saloon."

Such an invitation was a safe offer to accept from most of the women in the concert saloons along Broadway. But visiting one of the brothels or bars along the waterfront or in the Five Points was foolhardy for middle-class New Yorkers or tourists unaware in the ways of the city. In these places, "the men swear and talk obscenely in loud voices," reported James McCabe, "drink to excess; leer, and roar, and stagger, and bestow rude caresses on the women, and are thrust violently into the street when they have lost their senses and spent their money."

Sometimes the customs of the Five Points spilled onto Broadway. In 1857 the newspapers were filled with accounts of a clever gang of "juvenile prostitutes," ranging in age from six to sixteen years. "Words can hardly be found to depict the true character of this class of — we hardly know what to call them," declared the *Herald.* In the guise of poor little match-sellers, the girls stood around the saloons and hotels frequented by tourists. After finding a customer, a girl would take him back to a sidestreet brothel, where he struck his bargain with the mother. Other times, a girl might take her customer directly to her own room, where an outraged "father" would "surprise" the pair soon after their arrival. Rather than risk the wrath of the father and his inevitable brawny friend, the victim paid more money and escaped into the street.

Charitable groups tried to rescue these "fallen angels" from their lives of sin. Around 1840 a Reverend McDowell

147

appeared in New York and began to publish a small weekly newspaper, *McDowell's Journal*, under the patronage of several church charities. This newspaper supposedly was "devoted to the cause of reforming women who had lost their virtue." Actually it was nothing more than a "weekly directory of the houses of prostitution in the city," according to the *Herald*. Besides giving the names and addresses of the city's brothels, *McDowell's Journal* included a list of the girls in each establishment along with "a *catalogue raisonné* of their charms — eyes, hair, busts, carriage, age, accomplishments, etc." Before his untimely exposé, the Reverend McDowell even opened a charity home for repentant prostitutes, again with church support. The home was nothing more than another whorehouse.

Although prostitution was an openly talked-about part of life in New York, some sexual behavior, particularly homosexuality, was so threatening to the prevailing moral ethic that there was almost no mention of it in the newspapers of the day. The arrest of a man for propositioning another on the street or in a park was rarely written up in a direct manner. In 1846 the *Herald*, quite typically, reported the arrest of a "young man who considers himself somewhat respectable in this community, keeping store in Warren Street," for participating "in one of those revolting and disgraceful acts which are nightly practiced on the Battery or in the vicinity of the City Hall." Men did meet each other more safely in some of the bathhouses, found near the Broadway hotels, which were open until well after midnight, or in bars, such as Pfaff's, at 647 Broadway, just north of Bleecker Street.

Pornography was another unacknowledged fact of life in mid-nineteenth-century New York. In broad daylight young boys stood in front of Broadway hotels and "exposed for sale, works of the most indecent and immoral character," according to the *Herald* in 1845. The books "are laid open, especial care being taken to display the engravings, which are generally unfit for a person of any refinement of taste to look upon, and much less for the boys and young men who gathered around them."

This "bawdy yellow-covered literature" was big business by the 1850s. Even some of the Broadway bookstores sold obscene books and photographs or prints, though they did so as unobtrusively as possible. Then there was the *Venus Miscellany*, a national magazine whose articles were "worthy of the most vigorous intellect that could be found in the lower regions" and its illustrations "fouler than the most morbid imagination could conceive," according to the *Herald*. When the police raided its offices on Frankfort Street, near City Hall, they found forty thousand copies of newspapers and booklets, and the account book indicated that over $60,000 worth of these items had been sold in the past year. Every day *Venus Miscellany* received at its post office box 150 orders for such material "from young men and women . . . of every town and village in the Union."

Although prostitution and other frowned-upon activities thrived on Broadway, they did not diminish the street's international reputation for fashion and excitement. Women of high social standing relished their afternoon promenades along Broadway, even though they passed the daring daytime streetwalkers along the way, and they patronized the stylish shops and restaurants that counted courtesans and madams among their best customers. The Broadway hotels, which might have been expected to become involved in these vices, remained free of any public scandal.

By most accounts, the hotels were the greatest and most awe-inspiring buildings in New York. William Chambers, the Scottish newspaperman, thought that the city's mansions, churches, and public buildings were generally magnificent but that "the edifices most worthy of attention are the hotels." In 1859 Charles Mackay wrote that American hotels were "very comfortable, very luxurious, very cheap, and very lively . . . the finest, most convenient, and best administered establishments in the world."

The first mammoth luxury hotel in New York was the Astor House, which opened in 1836 and filled the Broadway blockfront between Vesey and Barclay streets. The Astor House, built of Quincy granite, was five stories tall and formed a hollow square around a central courtyard. The main entrance occupied the center of the Broadway façade, and was a bustling scene throughout the day and night, with guests arriving and departing, piles of luggage waiting to be taken to the railroad station or docks, and young men standing around the lobby and entrance watching the commotion. Few people thought that the unadorned Greek Revival Astor House was a beautiful building. Instead, it was either an impressive-looking or an unforgettable edifice. Shortly before its completion the *Evening Post* wrote that its "appearance far surpasses expectation; for size and solidity no building in the United States will compare with it." Frederick Marryat thought that the hotel, "although simple of architecture, is, perhaps, the grandest mass" in the city.

The Astor House was the first modern hotel in New York. Fifteen years after its opening, the *Home Journal* declared that it had been "such a bold stride in advance of the time to build so vast and complete a hotel that the time has scarcely yet caught up with it." The hotel had 309 rooms and regularly accommodated 500 guests, although as many as 800 people were sometimes known to stay there. It was the first hotel in New York to offer bathing and toilet facilities on every floor, a real novelty at a time when the finest mansions in the 1830s usually lacked such comforts. It also offered its guests gas light, fueled by its own plant. This convenience was not totally perfected, as guests learned at the hotel's opening celebration. "The house was lighted by this gas everybody is discussing," reported the *Constellation*, "but the quantity consumed being greater than common, it gave out suddenly in the midst of a cotillion. Gas is a handsome light, but liable at all times to give the company the slip; and it is illy calculated for the ordinary use of a family."

All these conveniences, together with a much-praised management and the Broadway location, made the Astor House the city's most fashionable hotel. Newer and more luxurious rivals opened farther north on Broadway in the following ten and fifteen years, but as late as 1853 the Astor House was "still the best hotel in the country . . . in the opinion of large numbers of competent judges," according to the *Home Journal.* Its glory faded in the early 1850s, as several "monster hotels" or "palace hotels" opened on Broadway. "During the last eighteen months nearly half a dozen new hotels, of differing sizes, have been opened in various parts of the city," wrote the *Herald* in August 1852, and "now nearly half a dozen more are ready to be opened in a very few weeks." In five years, 1850 to 1854, nineteen hotels, all of them luxurious, opened on Broadway alone.

The finest hotels dating from this building boom were the American Hotel at Broadway and Grand Street; the Union Place at 860 Broadway, at Fourteenth Street; the Carlton at 350 Broadway; the Union at 496 Broadway; the Collamore at Broadway and Spring Street; the Aeolian at 834 Broadway; the Metropolitan at Broadway and Spring Street; the City at 492 Broadway; the St. Nicholas at Broadway and Spring Street; the Prescott House at Broadway and Spring Street; the Albion at 769 Broadway; the St. Denis at Broadway and Eleventh Street; the Howard at 434 Broadway; the Carroll at 722 Broadway; the Astor Place at 733 Broadway; and the La-farge House, on Broadway opposite the start of Bond Street, which burned just before its completion in 1854 and finally opened two years later.

The expected crush of visitors to New York's Crystal Palace exhibition of 1853 spurred the building boom. These hotels also provided living quarters for the rising numbers of visitors coming to New York for business or pleasure from across America or from Europe. New York, according to the *Herald*, was becoming for America "what Paris is to France, and London to Great Britain . . . in trade and commerce, science, literature, and the arts."

During this period, the *Herald* asserted that each hotel owner "vied with the other to rear the most gorgeous structure." But it was the St. Nicholas, which opened on January 6, 1853, that excelled all its rivals. Its extravagance, services, and public acclaim have been occasionally equaled but never surpassed by New York hotels built in later years. "Comfort, convenience, magnitude, and luxury seem to have attained their climax . . . in the vast and magnificent St. Nicholas," the *Home Journal* glowingly reported. "It is now, beyond all controversy, the largest hotel in existence," and its Italianate building is "one of the principal ornaments of our city and a credit to American architecture." The public parlors and dining rooms were so grand that *Putnam's Monthly* thought "luxury could no farther go, that there was no beyond, in the progress of refinement." Indeed, the "resources of the upholsterer have been exhausted in furnishing its apartments, and all that carving and gilding can do to give gorgeousness to its appointments has been done." The St. Nicholas offered every service then imaginable to its guests. The hotel, according to the *Home Journal,* "embraces every requisite of personal comfort and luxurious ease, which the most exigent of Sybarites could desire."

The very numbers that described the hotel's size and services made it one of the most talked-about buildings in New York. The St. Nicholas originally ran 100 feet along Broadway and 200 feet through to Mercer Street but was hopelessly overwhelmed by thousands of guests and sightseers after opening day. So in September 1853 the proprietors opened a south wing running 75 feet down Broadway to the southwest corner of Spring Street. A north wing, which ran 100 feet along Broadway in the other direction, was completed in March 1854. Now the hotel extended 275 feet along Broadway, and the six-story façade contained close to 18,000 square feet of white Westchester marble. The hotel contained nearly 600 rooms, 150 of them family suites. Sometimes a thousand guests stayed at the St. Nicholas; they were served by a staff of from 250 to 400 men and women, depending on the season. There were two miles of halls, all lavishly decorated and carpeted, and thirty miles of piping for heat and plumbing. The hotel, including the land, building, and appointments, had cost $2 million.

The porticoed main entrance on Broadway opened into a broad marble-floored hallway lined with settees that were covered in wild animal skins. The walls were wainscoted in black walnut, and pilasters with gilt capitals reached to the arched frescoed ceiling. The first room on the left was the 17-by-50-foot gentlemen's parlor, also decorated with black walnut wainscoting and a frescoed ceiling. Behind the pair of sliding doors at the end of the room was a reading room with a richly ornamented dome. The main hall ended at the reception desk and bookkeeper's office; the entrance to the washroom and hotel bar were off to one side. Opposite the hotel office stood the grand staircase, built of white oak, which led to what the *Herald* called the "brilliant surprise" of the second floor.

As guests reached the second floor, they came upon a hall, nearly 200 feet long, that ran from the front of the hotel on Broadway to the rear along Mercer Street. At night a seemingly endless line of mirrors along the walls reflected the crowds of modishly dressed guests passing up and down the hall beneath the glare of gas-light chandeliers and wall sconces. The second floor, which was the grandest in the hotel, contained several public parlors, the main dining room, and some guest rooms.

The ladies' parlor, facing Broadway, was "gorgeous in the extreme," according to the enthusiastic Isabella Lucy Bird. The 24-by-50-foot room included an Axminster carpet in a medallion pattern and "gold-colored brocade satin damask window curtains, interwoven with bouquets of flowers"; Miss Bird estimated the cost at $25 a yard, or $700 a window. This same fabric covered the Louis XV furniture, which *Gleason's Pictorial Drawing-Room Companion* thought "leaves little for luxury to desire." The $1500 grand piano had been made for the 1853 Crystal Palace exhibition.

St. Nicholas Hotel: dining room

The second floor also included the bridal suite, which *Putnam's Monthly* called "one of the newly invented institutions of hotel life." The massive rosewood bed was covered with white lace and satin, surrounded by white satin cushions, and topped by a canopy, also of white satin. The walls, too, were covered in white satin, and the same niveous fabric was used for the curtains. Elaborately carved woodwork, an excess of gilt, imported French furniture, and four crystal chandeliers contributed to the room's accoutrements. In all, the suite was so "scandalously splendid," according to the magazine, that "timid brides are said to shrink aghast at its marvels . . ."

Perhaps the grandest room at the St. Nicholas was the main dining room, on the second floor, overlooking Mercer Street. This 50-by-100-foot room was "an exquisitely beautiful example of a banqueting room," said *Putnam's Monthly*, "and shows to what a high condition the fine art of dining well has already been carried in this city." Highly polished black walnut tables and rosewood "spring chairs," covered in crimson velvet, filled the room. The walls were decorated with gilt pier mirrors, and a line of twenty-four pilasters

reached a daring twenty feet to the frescoed ceiling. All this "ornamental work and frescoing is rich but not tawdry or glaring," the *Herald* assured New Yorkers. The room was well lit by day from windows on Mercer Street, and, with sunset, three enormous chandeliers were "prepared to bid defiance to the night."

Dinner was one of the great moments of the day at the St. Nicholas and other Broadway hotels. At five o'clock the dinner bell sounded, and liveried servants smartly opened the double doors leading into the dining room. The headwaiters escorted the guests to their assigned places, whether at one of the long rectangular tables or at one of the small circular tables, where each found a folded linen napkin and the menu for the day. The menu at the St. Nicholas and all other Broadway hotels, except for the Astor House, listed all the dishes in French. Naturally these menus confused many of the American guests. "It is amusing to see the wry faces made by one of the uninitiated when a dish with an unintelligible name is presented to him," commented the *Knickerbocker* in 1846. "A simple-hearted man, who has grown gray under the solid material of beef and mutton, looks at the dish with distrust; yet to avoid being ignorant or rude, asks quietly of his neighbor what it is that he is called upon to eat; his neighbor is probably quite as ignorant as himself."

The waiters at the St. Nicholas and some of the other hotels served the dinner in a militarylike drill. "A whole regiment of waiters stood along the tables, waiting for the signal to begin serving the meal," wrote the *British American Guide Book* for 1859. When all the guests were seated, the headwaiter rang a silver bell, and each waiter "reaches over his arm and takes hold of the handle of the dish. That is the first motion. There they all hold for a second or two, when, at another signal, they all at the same moment lift the cover, all as if flying off at one whoop, and with as great exactness as soldiers expected to 'shoulder arms.' " These hotel waiters appeared to be French, wrote Lady Emmeline Stuart-Wortley, who visited New York in 1849–1850, but their accents "betrayed" them as Irish. Wearing a stylish beard and mustache, "Paddy seems quite transmogrified into a 'whiskered Pandoor or a fierce Hussar,' which seemed unnecessary for the peaceful occupation of laying knives — not without forks — and handling cream-ices.''

Large staffs of low-paid blacks and Irish immigrants filled the dining room and kitchens, but such ''new and wonderful patent contrivances'' as dumbwaiters, steam tables, and steam-driven roasting spits eased, if only a little, the burden of serving five meals a day. ''The gastronomic program of the day is perpetual,'' observed the *Herald* in 1855. The usual meal schedule was breakfast from five to noon, lunch from one-thirty to three-thirty, a dinner in one sitting at five, a tea from six o'clock to eight, and a late supper from nine to midnight. In addition, the kitchen prepared meals at any hour for guests who chose to eat in their rooms and often served a banquet or large private party in the ballroom or one of the dining rooms.

Technology's impact spread far beyond the hotel kitchen and, in fact, made it possible for the Broadway hotels to offer so many luxuries and so many services to so many people at so reasonable a rate. ''The great glory of the Americans,'' wrote Anthony Trollope in 1861, ''is in their wondrous contrivances — in their patent remedies for the usually troublesome operations of life.'' Trollope particularly liked the annunciator, which summoned a bellhop or brought one of a number of services to a guest's room. In the early nineteenth century, guests in country inns and small hotels rang a hand bell to summon a servant. The din and chaos of several hundred bells was obviously out of the question in the city hotels with hundreds of guests. The annunciator, invented in the 1830s, enabled a guest to push a button in his room, thus activating a device down at the first floor office. The instrument would emit a buzz, alerting the deskman, and cause a metal disk with a room number to drop to the bottom of the case, indicating which room wanted service. By the time the St. Nicholas was built, annunciator dials were marked with various labels, like Ice Water, Bellhop, or Room Service. The guest turned the dial to the item he wanted and pushed the button.

The St. Nicholas offered the central heating and luxurious bathrooms in almost every room that travelers had come to expect in fine hotels by the 1850s. One service that still amazed most travelers, however, was the "rapid laundry." Isabella Lucy Bird was "surprised to see gentlemen traveling without even carpetbags." Once she "understood the mysteries of these hotels," she realized that a man with one shirt could pass as the owner of half a dozen. While he took his bath, the laundry would clean the shirt and return it "in its pristine glories of whiteness and starch." She reported that the laundry used a "churn-like" machine, powered by steam, and that the clothes were "wrung by a novel application of the principle of centrifical [sic] force." Then the clothing was "dried by being passed through currents of hot air" from the furnace. A traveler in America "need not to encumber himself with great loads of underclothing in his excursions," reported William Chambers. "Anywhere, in an hour or two, he can get everything washed and dressed, as if he had just started from home."

Young Miss Bird also learned that "even razors and hair brushes were superfluous" for guests in New York hotels. A barber usually rented a shop on the ground floor of a Broadway hotel and served New Yorkers as well as hotel guests. The city's most fashionable barber, Phalon, rented the store just to the right of the main entrance of the St. Nicholas. *Gleason's Pictorial Drawing-Room Companion* warned that "the American who visits New York, and does not go to Phalon's Hair-Cutting Saloon [is] in infinite danger, during the next fifty years, of departing this life without having had the slightest idea of what it is to be shaved."

Phalon's served only gentlemen, so the St. Nicholas hired a hairdresser to attend to lady guests at any hour, a particularly thoughtful service for women who had been traveling all day. Indeed, the St. Nicholas tried to provide every convenience for its guests. The lobby alone included a post office that sold stamps and stationery; a bookstall with newspapers, books and magazines; a travel agent who had tickets for any means of conveyance to almost anywhere in the world; a telegraph that provided quick communication to much of America. The hotel also offered separate rooms for the guests' servants. Parents traveling with their children were delighted to learn that within the hotel was a nursery with attendants and even a separate dining room, where,

158

according to the *Herald,* "every provision has been made for the comfort and convenience of the little folks."

The Broadway hotels were so large and included so many necessities — as well as the luxuries — of life that European visitors described them as cities within a city. They were "a little world from which all the disagreeables are quietly excluded," thought the *Home Journal.* To create this happy illusion, the proprietors spent "three times as much as mere comfort requires" on their furniture, according to the magazine, and "their tables are spread at three times the expense which health and good digestion crave." Furthermore, "they are situated where ground and rent is highest." Yet hotels like the St. Nicholas were good investments, both for the rich businessmen who most often built them and for the professional managers who leased the buildings for fixed rents. In one good year, 1854, the profit for the manager of the St. Nicholas was $53,600; of the Astor House, $49,000; of the Metropolitan, $45,000; and of the New York, the smallest hotel on this list, an incredible $100,000.

Broadway (Spring to Prince streets), ca. 1855 (OVERLEAF)

The chance for profits such as these lured hotels, shops, and theaters to Broadway even if the move meant buying and renting some of the most expensive property in the city. By 1850 there were only two or three vacant lots on Broadway below Union Square. So the hotel builder or shopowner purchased a row house or mansion recently vacated by a rich family that had moved uptown. When Dr. John C. Cheesman, the fashionable physician, moved uptown in 1852, he sold his wide granite mansion at 473 Broadway, between Grand and Broome streets, for $100,000. Dr. Cheesman's house and lot, which ran 200 feet through the block to Mercer Street, were large even by Broadway standards and commanded a premium because of the location, just a block from the new Metropolitan and St. Nicholas hotels. That same year a house at the southeast corner of Broadway and Broome Street, standing on a 24-by-99-foot lot, sold for $30,500. In the mid-1830s that lot, which is all the purchaser of 1852 really wanted, would have sold for $5000 to $6000.

In the 1850s each of New York's newspapers published several articles a year on the rebuilding of Broadway and the northward drift of trade toward Union Square. "They are

159

tearing away the entrance of dwelling after dwelling in Broadway, to rebuild them all in fanciful modern style and convert the premises into shops, bewildering with costly fabrics, gilt mirrors, plate glass windows, and pretty buyers," wrote the *Daily Tribune* in 1850. Just two weeks before that, the newspaper had reported the "unfronting" of a dwelling opposite the Metropolitan Hotel, "for the purpose of converting it into a store." If present trends continued, wrote the *Daily Tribune*, Broadway would, in just a few years, "present three miles of unbroken shop front" from the Battery to Union Square.

Although hotels and small shops had begun to displace the dwellings along Broadway between Houston Street and Union Square in 1851 and 1852, the most intense commercial development, the greatest hotels and best-known shops, were still appearing on Broadway between Canal and Houston streets. But real estate speculators were so certain that Broadway north of Houston Street was ripe for great hotels and shops that they began to buy property, still best suited for private homes or fashionable boardinghouses, at prices that were more in keeping with the busy activity half a mile downtown. In 1852 a house at the corner of Broadway and Ninth Street sold for $23,000, and a year later 865 Broadway, near Thirteenth Street, sold for $21,000. These prices made the speculators very accurate prophets about the future of commerce in the area. In 1854 Charles A. Dana, writing in the *Scenery of the United States Illustrated,* observed that "below Prince Street, there is now scarcely a single private residence [and] above Prince Street, the dwelling houses are not entirely rooted out . . . but the waves are rising in that quarter also, and stately shops have begun to appear quite thickly."

In the summer of 1853 the *Daily Tribune* counted thirty-seven demolition or construction sites along Broadway between the Battery and Union Square, and three years later building activity was still so widespread that the newspaper believed "there is not the least hope to be entertained that building operations on this street will ever cease." Real estate speculation on Broadway was, if anything, more frantic in the late 1850s than in the early years of the decade. Prices for buildings like Dr. Cheesman's mansion, which had seemed so fabulous in 1852, were commonplace on the eve of the Civil War. Property on Broadway sold for $4000 a front foot by 1859, according to *Life Illustrated,* so it cost $100,000 for "a decently fronted lot," $250,000 for a "moderate show," and about $1 million for a "splurge."

New Yorkers were delighted to read newspaper articles that reported these inflated real estate values, and wondered if Broadway would ever be finished. Broadway's grandeur and the ever-northward movement of shops and hotels were sure signs of New York's rising population, wealth, and influence across America. Recollections of what Broadway had been in the 1820s and 1830s proved to New Yorkers how great their city had become in the previous twenty or thirty years. "It was a street of three-story red brick houses," reported George William Curtis in *Harper's Magazine* in 1862. "Now it is a highway of stone and iron, and marble buildings. The few older ones that remain are individually remembered as among the best of their kind and time and are now not even quaint but simply old-fashioned and unhandsome."

But most New Yorkers, and perhaps even Curtis, did not realize that the great hotels and shops of the 1850s might share the fate of the dwelling houses they displaced, and someday be called ugly and old-fashioned. Even as New York applauded the St. Nicholas Hotel in the early 1850s, farsighted businessmen knew that Broadway north of Canal Street would someday fall before the northward advance of the wholesale trade, then located a mile downtown, south of Chambers Street. In 1855 one real estate speculator completed several fine wholesale warehouses on Broadway opposite the St. Nicholas Hotel. The buildings had white marble façades with elaborate ornamentation and "will not probably be occupied by other than retail merchants for some years to come," wrote the *Daily Tribune.* They were, nonetheless, ready for the eventual and profitable fall of the area to wholesale trade.

10

As the city pushed up Broadway and past Fourteenth Street, around 1845, New Yorkers predicted that the homes and streets rising uptown would dwarf all earlier triumphs in their "city of sensations." "How this city marches northward!" boasted George Templeton Strong in 1850. "The progress of 1835 and 1836 was nothing to the luxuriant rank growth of this year." The splendor of the houses and churches uptown likewise seemed "out of all reason and measure" to Strong. The streets, agreed the *Builder*, a British magazine, were "springing up, lined, not with houses but with palaces," and soon Fifth Avenue would surely rival the greatest streets of London and Paris, "with all their accumulations of the wealth of a thousand years."

Awestruck New Yorkers recalled the story of Aladdin, "rising from his bed in the morning and looking out the windows" to see the "stately and gorgeous palace which the genii had erected for him during the night, glittering in the sunlight . . . on a spot where the day before there had been a barren plain." The story, observed *Putnam's Monthly*, grew "tamer and tamer" each day, for "we also are Aladdins, and for us the genii of the lamp truly work."

Despite the praise for the rapid growth of the city above Fourteenth Street and the magnificence of the homes there, something else had to be happening to excite the imagination of the city and fill people with talk of magic and Aladdin's lamp. Mansions and neighborhoods, no matter how impressive, were fragile things in nineteenth-century New York, where change was the one unchanging aspect of life. New Yorkers knew that most of the extravagant mansions of the 1840s would be surpassed by those of the 1850s and that they, in turn, would be surpassed by those of the following years.

What did make New Yorkers so proud of their city was the sudden improvement in their daily lives, thanks to the technological wonders of indoor plumbing and central heating and the city's first steps toward becoming the modern metropolis of the future. This move into the future first appeared during the mid-1840s in the homes of the well-to-do in the growing uptown district. Here, declared *Putnam's Monthly*, "the new city has risen up like enchantment telling

A Bird's-Eye View of New York, 1849

of new times, a new people, new tastes, and new habits."

The gateway to this uptown area was Union Square, a three-and-one-half acre park, bounded by Broadway, Fourteenth Street, Fourth Avenue, and Seventeenth Street. The land was once part of Elias Brevoort's farm, but in 1762 he sold twenty acres lying west of the Bowery Road, or Third Avenue, to John Smith, whose heirs subsequently sold it to Henry Spingler for $4750. In 1807 Broadway was regulated from Astor Place to the vicinity of Twenty-third Street, and in 1815 the city designated part of the land that became Union Square as a public park. The city, however, did not take title to Union Square or lay out the land as a park until 1831. A report by the Board of Assistant Aldermen declared: "It is worthy of remark, that almost every stranger who visits us, whether from our sister states or from Europe, speaks of the paucity of our public squares; and that in proportion to its size, New York contains a smaller number, and those few of comparatively less extent than perhaps any other town of importance." The report had recommended the immediate acquisition of the property for Union Square because, "now that the ground is unoccupied, the purchase can be effected, which, in the lapse of a few years, when valuable buildings are erected, will be impracticable, on account of the great expense." Then "future generations" of New Yorkers would lose the advantages of having a park, the most important one being that parks serve as "ventilators to a densely populated city."

With its enviable location at what was then the northernmost limit of Broadway and just half a mile north of stylish Bond Street, Union Square was assured of a fashionable destiny, predicted the *Herald* as early as 1836. Just three years later the *Mirror* reported: "Around Union Place new blocks of houses, capacious and stately, are springing up with surprising celerity . . . Fourteenth Street will doubtless be considered the heart rather than the extremity of the town in the course of a few years." These fine row houses stood virtually alone in fields, half a mile beyond the edge of the built-up city, surrounded by shanties of the poor and run-down former country houses. A 150-year-old Dutch farmhouse still stood on Fourteenth Street down by Second Avenue.

The outer edge of the city reached Fourteenth Street about five years later. In 1845 the *Herald* reported that "the growth of the city in the upper wards is astonishing. Whole streets of magnificent dwelling houses have been erected in the vicinity of Union Square within the last year." "Improvement" had become the "watchword" of the neighborhood, according to the *Herald* in 1848, and "the sound of the hammer is constantly to be heard from one end . . . to the other" of Fourteenth Street. The growth of the Union Square area was so "astonishing" that the *Herald* believed Fourteenth Street was "now nearly the center of the fashionable *faubourgs*, whilst a year or two since it was quite the boundary line of the city in that direction."

Palatial row houses and mansions began to rise, facing Union Square itself, after the Bank of Manhattan sold the lots it owned around the perimeter of the park in 1845. James F. Penniman built a five-story, 46-by-85-foot mansion on the south side of Union Square, between Broadway and University Place; it was one of the first in the city to have a brownstone façade and to display the Italianate style. The architects were Trench and Snook, who designed A. T. Stewart's store and many of the uptown houses. The Penniman mansion, which the *Daily Tribune* hailed as "almost equal in size and architectural elegance to Venetian palaces," had cost nearly $100,000 and included several parlors, an Elizabethan-style dining room, and a greenhouse complete with small trees and a fountain.

Another extravagant home on Union Square was the Henry Parish residence, at 26 East Seventeenth Street. This house included seven toilets and eleven tubs and wash basins, at a time when most New Yorkers were just getting their first indoor bathroom. The *Herald* described Parish's house as "magnificent" and "faultless," and Isabella Lucy Bird thought it "about the largest private residence in the city, and one which is considered to combine the greatest splendor with the greatest taste." She continued:

We entered a spacious marble hall, leading to a circular stone staircase of great width, the balustrades being figures elaborately cast in bronze. Above this staircase was a lofty dome, decorated with paintings in fresco of eastern scenes. There

Union Square, ca. 1855

were niches in the walls, some containing Italian statuary, and others small jets of water pouring over artificial moss.

There were six or eight magnificent reception rooms, furnished in various styles — the Medieval, the Elizabethan, the Italian, the Persian, the modern English, etc. There were fountains of fairy workmanship, pictures from old masters, statues from Italy . . . porcelain from China and Sèvres; damasks, cloth of gold, and *bijoux* from the East; Gobelin tapestry, tables of malachite and agate, and "knick-knacks" of every description . . . I saw one table the value of which might be about 2,000 guineas.

Like most European visitors of the 1850s, Miss Bird was surprised by the city's mansions. Although she professed that they "were rather at variance with my ideas of republican simplicity . . . and surpassed anything I had hitherto witnessed in royal or ducal palaces at home," she conceded that in the Parish residence "there was nothing gaudy, profuse, or prominent in the decorations or furniture; everything had evidently been selected by a person of very refined taste." George Templeton Strong thought otherwise. For him, the Parish mansion was "hideous but spacious."

The streets around Union Square delighted William Chambers, particularly the frankly ostentatious display of "richly decorated" façades, sparkling plate-glass windows, "silvered . . . door handles, plates, and bell pulls," and the "furnishings and interior ornaments of a superb kind." For *Putnam's Monthly*, the "richly furnished [and] well-built" uptown homes had become "the distinguishing characteristic of the metropolis."

The reasons for the rapid growth of the Union Square area went beyond the city's rising population and the swelling ranks of the rich. The serene, tree-shaded streets north of Fourteenth Street were a pleasant contrast to the increasingly noisy and traffic-filled streets just a mile downtown. "Not a store is to be seen" in most residential streets uptown, wrote the *Herald* in 1852; "nothing but the dwellings of the aristocracy, who moved up here out of the noisy and dusty part of the city." The spread of trade, more than anything else, drove status-conscious New Yorkers from their homes downtown. "Aristocracy," observed *Putnam's Monthly*, is always "startled and disgusted with the near approach of plebian trade which already threatened to lay its insolent hands upon her mantel, and to come tramping into her silken parlors with its heavy boots and rough attire . . . Alas for the poor lady, every day drives her higher and higher."

The decline of St. John's Park, which began in the mid-1840s, came as no surprise. The red brick Federal row houses were now twenty years old and too small and architecturally restrained for the taste of the mid-nineteenth-century city. The square, however, had the patina of beauty that comes only with time and the surrounding streets a serenity uncommon even in the streets uptown. In 1846 James F. Watson, a newspaperman, wrote that "the large growth of trees and the abundance of grateful shade, make it, in connection with the superiority of the uniform houses which surround it, a place of imposing grandeur." St. John's Park, he concluded, had "a peculiar aspect of European style and magnificence." A year later the *Evening Post* praised St. John's Park as "a spot of Eden loveliness and exclusiveness."

But the park's location, south of Canal Street and just a few blocks from the Hudson River, eventually ruined its serenity. No desirable neighborhood had ever been located that close to the Hudson, except for the first few blocks of Greenwich Street at the Battery. By the mid-1840s workmen, traffic, and warehouses from the busy waterfront had taken over the stretch of Greenwich Street just a block from St. John's Park. Rowdy young men and outright criminals, who would never have dared enter the area in earlier years, now began to invade the streets around the edge of the park. In 1846 the *Herald* reported the arrest of two pickpockets who had been working the crowds entering and leaving the First Baptist Church at Laight and Varick streets. Two years later the Mayor ordered the streets around St. John's Park lit with gas street lamps, because the neighborhood "is in the night time infested with base and unprincipled persons, who take advantage of the darkness in which it is shrouded, in consequence of the dense foliage of the trees, and the dimness of ordinary oil lamps, to perpetrate acts of violence upon . . . unprotected persons . . ."

Another blow to St. John's Park came in 1851, when the Hudson River Railroad ran tracks along Hudson Street, the west side of the square, to its downtown terminal at Chambers Street and College Place (later renamed West Broadway). The trains, which came down the Hudson, were broken up at the railroad's main terminal between West Thirty-first and West Thirty-fourth streets and then hauled downtown by horses on Tenth Avenue, then West Street, and, once past Canal Street, along Hudson Street to the Chambers Street terminal. Although the calm of the park had been shattered forever, Trinity Church still thought enough of the area's future to remodel the interior of St. John's Chapel during the summer of 1856. The houses facing the park at least retained their respectability, if not their glory, into the 1860s.

Nathaniel Parker Willis had observed, in the early 1840s, that fashionable New Yorkers must live "above Bleecker," and the erosion of St. John's Park bore out his statement. But Willis' dictum was outdated when trade on Broadway decisively crossed Bleecker Street in 1851 and 1852. Rich families left their homes along Broadway as far north as Union Square and, in the rising panic over the fate of all neighborhoods south of Fourteenth Street, began to flee the still-impeccable Bond Street area. By 1853 the *Builder* declared that "Bond and Bleecker Streets, that were then the *ultima thule* of aristocracy, are now but plebian streets." Bond Street became known for the offices of dentists patronized by the city's nabobs; in 1857, *Leslie's Illustrated* said that "the number of teeth that are pulled out or 'filled' in Bond Street in one day would afford a curious statistic."

A number of houses on Bond Street and neighboring blocks had already become boardinghouses filled with immigrants. "The nobbish door plates have been removed from the houses," lamented the *Daily Tribune*, "and the walls are ornamented with portentous German signs, indicating that beer and boarding, tobacco and private lodgings are furnished to immigrants on the most favorable terms." Even the homes of families who were not panicked into abandoning the handsome neighborhood began to "assume an appearance of *having been* in the aristocratic precincts," wrote Charles Astor Bristed, who lived in genteelly decaying Lafayette Place. Gentleman, sometime writer, and cousin of William B. Astor, he was qualified to judge.

Any doubts old-fashioned New Yorkers may have had about the flight of rich families uptown vanished in 1851, when the *Herald* published its list of the city's 200 wealthiest men, along with dollar estimates of their fortunes. Half of these men lived north of Fourteenth Street that year, and their number increased each succeeding year thereafter. Five years earlier just twenty of them had lived north of Fourteenth Street. The uptown street that appeared on this list as an address more often than any other was Fifth Avenue.

New Yorkers were surprised at Fifth Avenue's sudden emergence as the city's most fashionable address. As recently as 1840 it had been a muddy rutted road leading northward into an area noted for its "singular air of desertion." Even the country houses and farm buildings here "seemed but little cared for," and James Fenimore Cooper could "not remember ever to have seen the immediate environs of so large a town in such a state of general abandonment." As late as 1836 and 1837, boom years for real estate, lots on newly laid-out Union Square sold "with difficulty" for $1000, and lots on Fifth Avenue near Twenty-third Street sold for $400 to $500 each. Ten years later this same property readily fetched $10,000 to $12,000 a lot, and the Fifth Avenue lots near Twenty-third Street commanded almost as much.

With wonder and pride New York watched Fifth Avenue's rise as a "street of palaces," but did not understand why this street, above all others, was becoming "the holy of holies . . . " Several blocks to the east, the Stuyvesant family had attracted a number of rich New Yorkers to Second Avenue and the pretty park aptly named Stuyvesant Square. In 1846 the *Evening Post* named Second Avenue, along with Fifth, as "the two great avenues for elegant residence." The sidestreets east of Second Avenue, however, never were truly fashionable, and shortly before the Civil War were filling with the immigrant poor. Second Avenue itself, between Third and Eighteenth streets, one block north of Stuyvesant Square, remained impressive-looking for a few more decades. Many of the fine homes, however, had become boardinghouses.

Second Avenue was not the only uptown street unable to fulfill the predictions of fashion. Around 1850 there was even talk, incredible, as it soon proved, that Seventh Avenue, as it ran through the Chelsea neighborhood north of Fourteenth Street, would become the most sought-after address in the city. Instead, it became a street of shops with apartments for the middle class on the several upper floors.

Charles Astor Bristed offered the best explanation for the rise of Fifth Avenue. "The general course of fashion has been necessarily northward (as the city, built on a narrow island, cannot expand laterally) with a slight inclination westward." Fifth Avenue did occupy just the right location. It started on the north side of Washington Square amid the red brick houses of the Row and, at Fourteenth Street, was just a few

Brevoort residence, Fifth Avenue and Eighth Street

hundred feet west of Union Square, which was attracting the families fleeing trade along Broadway.

"But many accidents help to make a particular quarter fashionable," observed Bristed. The first people to live on Fifth Avenue were rich and socially prominent. Perhaps the first house there was the Henry Brevoort residence, 24 Fifth Avenue, at the northwest corner of Ninth Street. Brevoort was one of New York's few millionaires in the 1840s. His father had owned a farm roughly bounded by Eighth Street, Fourth Avenue, Thirteenth Street, and Sixth Avenue. Henry first enjoyed the wealth from this property, which became more valuable every year, and then increased his fortune by shrewd investments in the stock market. He and his wife had moved into their Greek Revival house on an otherwise empty Fifth Avenue in 1834. When they gave their first party late in 1838, Philip Hone declared: "It was a grand affair. There is not a house in the city so well calculated to entertain such an assemblage. Five large rooms open on one floor, and a spacious hall besides, with a noble staircase." The Brevoort house was almost the only house of any consequence on Fifth Avenue until the middle of the next decade.

Then the mansions that began to rise on Fifth made the Brevoort house look modest indeed and reflected the rising wealth of the city and the ways in which rich men chose to spend it. William Lenox built a $100,000 Gothic Revival brownstone mansion at the northeast corner of Fifth Avenue and Twelfth Street, where he collected a library that eventually became a part of the New York Public Library. Across the street, at the northwest corner of Twelfth Street, stood the home of August Belmont, American agent for the House of Rothschild. Moses Grinnell, the merchant, owned what the *Herald* called "one of the most majestic piles in that *distingué* neighborhood" at the northeast corner of Fifth Avenue and Fourteenth Street, and Richard K. Haight, another merchant, selected the southeast corner of Fifteenth Street for his mansion, one that the ubiquitous Isabella Lucy Bird described as "unquestionably . . . the most elegantly fitted up" in all New York.

Haight had a passion for extraordinary homes, and lived at the most fashionable addresses and within some of the finest

Grinnell mansion

products of architectural skill that New York offered during his lifetime. If one followed Haight's shifts of residence, one could trace the northward march of fashion and the changing tastes in architecture, which culminated in the late 1840s with the Italianate Fifth Avenue mansion. After leaving his family's Federal house on Whitehall Street near the Battery in 1820, Haight lived in a red brick row house on Dey Street, just off Broadway. In 1828 Haight left Dey Street for Le Roy Place, the granite terrace on Bleecker Street that was New York's first attempt to imitate the glories of the terraces rising around Regent's Park in London. From here Haight moved to Lafayette Place in 1834 and into the white marble Colonnade Row. When Lafayette Place began to fade in the late 1840s, Haight sold his home to William B. Astor, who lived across the street, and settled in his brownstone mansion, which helped assure that a budding Fifth Avenue would become "the location sacred to fashion."

According to Bristed, men such as Haight, Lenox, Belmont, Grinnell "were influential enough to draw other friends around them, and give a name and reputation to the avenue." By the early 1850s impressive groups of row houses and occasional mansions sitting behind iron fences lined Fifth Avenue to Twenty-third Street, and the towers of vaguely Gothic or Italianate churches rose high above the lines of the flat-roofed dwellings every block or two. On the eve of the Civil War, Fifth Avenue had become "an almost continuous line of brownstone palaces" stretching from Washington Square to the crest of Murray Hill at Thirty-seventh Street.

Fifth Avenue, as *Putnam's Monthly* commented in 1853, was already "perhaps the finest street in the New World, but not, by any means, more desirable than many others as a residence." Fourteenth Street was also an address favored by the rich. "In it there are no stores — nothing but the dwelling houses, which are substantial, highly finished, and first class ones," declared the *Herald* in 1852. Like other crosstown streets uptown, Fourteenth Street had the 800-foot-long blocks, which made for impressive sweeping vistas of residential houses. Moreover, it was the first of the periodic 120-foot-wide crosstown streets, like Twenty-third or Thirty-fourth streets, which were grander and of better scale for the highly ornamented brownstone-front houses than the usual 60-foot-wide streets. Although Fourteenth Street was at its most desirable in the blocks nearest Union Square and Fifth Avenue, it had, in the words of the *Herald*, fulfilled its destiny as "a noble thoroughfare . . . from river to river."

Once mansions and row houses began to blossom around Union Square in the mid-1840s, the park was planted with lawns, flower beds, trees, and shrubbery. Gas street lights were installed by 1849. Union Square was just the place to see some of the city's richest men strolling down the gravel paths, nursemaids pushing baby carriages, and young men and women courting. Even the birdhouses in the park reflected the nearby residents' concern for money, according to *Wood's Illustrated Handbook*. The "ingeniously contrived miniature buildings for these little birds, placed among the branches of the trees . . . represent different business departments as 'The Post Office,' 'The Custom House,' 'The Exchange,' etc., etc., etc., and it is very amusing to see the little creatures enter these different edifices, their busy, hurried air irresistibly giving the idea that they really know where they are going and have a purpose in it." As charming as these birdhouses may have seemed to some, old-moneyed New Yorkers, many of them still living below Fourteenth Street, remarked that the residents of Union Square and nearby Fifth Avenue were so immersed in daily business that even the neighborhood birds had to be busy at work all day long.

Broadway resumed its northward course at East Seventeenth Street, the upper edge of Union Square, but never enjoyed the vogue that it did south of Fourteenth Street. Comfortable red brick buildings, some private dwellings and others middle-class flats with shops on the ground floor, lined this stretch of Broadway, which now began its westward course and intersected Fifth Avenue at Twenty-third Street. The grandest building here was Peter Goelet's mansion, at the northeast corner of Nineteenth Street, which had peacocks strutting in its yard.

The other street leading north from Union Square was Fourth Avenue. New Yorkers had expected that Fourth

Fifth Avenue: view north from Twenty-eighth Street, ca. 1865

Gramercy Park

Avenue would become a fine residential street like nearby Second Avenue and Fifth Avenue. In the mid-1840s, Peter Cooper, the millionaire founder of Cooper Union, lived at Fourth Avenue and Twenty-eighth Street, and Josiah Cary, the dry goods merchant, lived on Twenty-fourth Street, just off Fourth Avenue. Churches with wealthy congregations also thought Fourth Avenue a good location. Calvary Episcopal Church opened in 1847 at the northeast corner of Twenty-first Street, where it still stands. In 1855 the Church of All Souls built an enormous Romanesque building across the street, between East Twentieth and East Twenty-first streets; its 106-foot dome loomed over the entire neighborhood. The walls of this $105,000 church were made of alternating horizontal bands of white and black stone, and All Souls soon became known as the "Church of the Holy Zebra." The other church in this stretch of Fourth Avenue was St. Paul's Methodist, a white marble Romanesque edifice at the northeast corner of Twenty-second Street, which opened in 1858.

Fourth Avenue, however, was "devoted to trade in the beginning," as *Putnam's Monthly* noted in 1854, though some private homes for the middle class were built on it, including an attractive row on the west blockfront between East Eighteenth and East Nineteenth streets, set back from the street on fifty-foot-deep front yards. Most of Fourth Avenue was built up in three- and four-story red brick flats with stores on the ground floors. Residential hotels, all of them respectable but few really first-class, stood on many of the corners. The avenue was "wide, stately, and quiet," according to *Life Illustrated* in 1858, and formed a "sort of connecting link between the aristocratic purlieus of Fifth, Madison, and Lexington Avenues, and the busy, unpretentious bustle of Third, Sixth, and Eighth."

Just a block east of Fourth Avenue was Gramercy Park, already one of New York's most beautiful and serene spots. It was the only private park in the city besides St. John's Park, two miles downtown. Samuel B. Ruggles had deeded the one-and-one-half acre park to the owners of the sixty surrounding lots, and they alone had the keys to open the gate of the iron fence around Gramercy Park. Because of the private park, the lots around Gramercy Park were built upon several years before the outward-moving edge of the city reached this point. As early as 1845, George Templeton Strong thought that Gramercy Park "looks like a comfortable place." Three years later Strong married Samuel B. Ruggles' daughter, Ellen, and built a house at 74 East Twenty-first Street, just off Gramercy Park. His father, George Washington Strong, and his aunt, Olivia Templeton, built their houses a few doors down the block.

Strong's thirty-five-foot-wide house was quite a financial undertaking for a twenty-eight-year-old man, even one with an independent income. The house cost $25,000, and Strong admitted in his diary that "going into so large a house and starting on so grand a scale is not in accordance with my 'private judgment.'" But both his father and father-in-law had told him that he was "safe," and he hoped "it will prove so." For all his trepidation, Strong's house was merely typical of those on the sidestreets north of Union Square. The façade was brownstone, plainly ornamented around doorway and windows, with a handsome bow window from basement to roofline. The interior was simple for the period, "quite free, I think from the epidemic of humbug and sham finery and gin-palace decoration," wrote the tasteful householder in 1850.

Like nearly all the houses built north of Fourteenth Street after 1845, the Strong residence included such modern conveniences as running water, fully equipped bathrooms, gas light, and central heating. *Putnam's Monthly* declared in 1854 that "it seems hardly possible that anything more compact, cozy, comfortable, and elegant in the shape of a dwelling house will ever be invented than the first-class houses now built in the upper part of the city." In terms of these amenities, the row houses of the 1840s more closely resembled the dwellings of the early twentieth century than those of the 1830s, just a decade earlier. The incorporation of such comforts into the city's houses signaled the start of New York's progress from an overgrown town, which was nearly medieval in many respects, to a modern metropolis.

Before the completion of the Croton water system in 1842, New Yorkers drank hard, often brackish water drawn from pumps at street corners. Aside from its unpleasant taste and the annoying shortages during summer droughts, the water sometimes spread sickness, particularly yellow fever, which ravaged the city every few years. Household garbage and raw sewage, which New Yorkers threw into the middle of the streets or carted to the Hudson and East rivers, polluted the water drawn from the pumps, as did the demolition of buildings and the digging of cellars, which disturbed the subsoil. Not surprisingly, some New Yorkers drank barreled spring water brought into the city from rural upper Manhattan, or the rainwater that drained from the roofs of their houses into the brick cisterns buried in the back yards.

New Yorkers had tried to improve their water supply even before the Revolution. In 1774 a group of citizens built a reservoir east of Broadway in the vicinity of Prince Street. Water was pumped into this reservoir from the wells that dotted the area and then was distributed throughout the city in wooden pipes. This enterprise collapsed in the chaos that accompanied the outbreak of the war and the British occupation of New York, but street excavations for the next century occasionally unearthed rotted wooden pipes buried there years earlier.

In 1799 another group of New Yorkers, Aaron Burr among them, received a charter of incorporation from the State Legislature to supply the city with fresh water. This group, the Manhattan Company, built a reservoir on Chambers Street, between Broadway and Centre Street, and even laid some of its own wooden pipes. But the Manhattan Company never completed the laying of the wooden pipes or the network of iron pipes designed to bring water from Rye Pond in Westchester County to the city. The company's real aim, it turned out, was the establishment of a bank. The bill of incorporation included an innocuous-looking clause that permitted the company to invest surplus capital in any activity not inconsistent with state law. Before then, the Bank of New York, which was controlled by Alexander Hamilton and his fellow Federalists, was the only state-chartered bank in the city. The Federalist-dominated State Legislature refused to charter any rival institutions. Now, thanks to the clause that Burr's group had inserted in its bill of incorporation, the

Republicans had their own bank. The Bank of Manhattan disposed of the Chambers Street reservoir in the mid-1850s but maintained a water tank nearby on Centre Street into the early twentieth century, should it ever have been asked to fulfill the terms of its charter. The Chase Manhattan Bank is the Bank of Manhattan's successor.

The early nineteenth century saw other schemes to supply New York with water, among them the drilling of artesian wells in the city, and the cutting of a canal from the Housatonic River in New Jersey to bring water into New York by pipes beneath the Hudson River. The lack of a reliable supply of pure water was a threat to New York's continued growth and its standards of public health, which were already abysmal. Seepage from churchyards, which were still receiving the dead by the thousands in the early nineteenth century, posed another threat to the purity of the city's water. Many graveyards and burial vaults had just been covered over by streets and buildings. In the dry goods and shipping district along the East River, there had been graveyards on the site of the Middle Dutch Meeting House on Nassau Street, between Cedar and Liberty streets; on John Street, next to the John Street Methodist Church; on Maiden Lane; on Frankfort Street; and near Burling Slip. City Hall and the A. T. Stewart store occupied the site of an old Negro burial ground, where hundreds of blacks were buried in 1770 during a smallpox epidemic. Even Washington Square had been a potter's field until the city transformed it into a public park.

Beginning in the nineteenth century, the city periodically passed laws prohibiting the burial of the dead in vaults beneath the streets or in churchyards in built-up areas. These laws were not stringently enforced in the 1820s and 1830s, because New Yorkers weren't all that worried about public health. Despite repeated warnings by doctors and scientists that the city must get a steady supply of pure water, New Yorkers did nothing until recurring fires in the dry goods district threatened their livelihoods. Then in 1835 New Yorkers voted $12 million to dam the Croton River in upper Westchester County and build a forty-five-mile-long masonry conduit to a fifteen-million-gallon receiving reservoir at Eighty-sixth Street, later part of Central Park.

Croton Reservoir

The Croton water system was a massive undertaking. Charles King, President of Columbia College, called it "the crowning glory and surpassing achievement of the latter part of the half century." By damming the Croton River, the city's engineers created a reservoir forty feet deep, on average, and five miles long, which contained 9,500,000,000 gallons of water. The masonry conduit built to carry the water from there to the Eighty-sixth Street reservoir was roughly eight feet in diameter. In its forty-five-mile route, the conduit crossed twenty-five streams below grade, had sixteen tunnels from 160 to 1263 feet in length, and carried sixty million gallons of water a day.

When water was officially introduced from the Eighty-sixth Street receiving reservoir into the distributing reservoir at Fifth Avenue and Forty-second Street (now the site of the New York Public Library and Bryant Park) on July 4, 1842, the entire city enjoyed the fanfare and parades, which went on for days. Even months later, Philip Hone wrote: "Nothing is talked of or thought of in New York but Croton water . . . Fountains, aqueducts, hydrants, and hose attract our attention and impede our progress through the streets . . . Water! water! is the universal note which is sounded through every part of the city, and infuses joy and exultation into the masses."

185

The city levied a one-time tax for the introduction of Croton water to a two-story house and twelve dollars for a three-story house. Plumbers, who advertised their services in the newspapers, installed pipes and bathrooms in existing, as well as new, private houses. In 1842 the *Evening Post* carried this plumber's advertisement:

A. Brower, at 244 Water Street, gives notice that he will supply all persons, who are in want of pipes for the conveyance of the water of the Croton Aqueduct to their houses, that he has the necessary fixtures prepared, with a supply of patent lead pipes, and compression faucets peculiarly adapted to the purpose, being able to withstand a heavy pressure.

Philip Hone installed running water and bathrooms in his mansion at Broadway and Great Jones Street soon after the completion of the Croton system, and George Templeton Strong considered the new bathroom in his father's Greenwich Street home "a great luxury — worth the cost of the whole building." Strong spent so much time "paddling around the tub" that he wondered if he might not be "part amphibian."

Despite all the celebration that greeted the completion of the Croton Reservoir, New Yorkers were slow to use the water. By the end of 1844, just 6175 residential houses in a city of some four hundred thousand people had Croton water. For one thing, the pipes, valves, and fixtures were expensive because they were not yet mass-produced. And many New Yorkers were not certain that the water was safe to drink, though European visitors, like Sarah M. Maury, thought that "the water is of the finest kind . . . No city in the world is now more plentifully supplied with pure and wholesome water than the city of New York." But Strong had been told that the water "flows through an aqueduct which I hear was used as a necessary by all the Hibernian vagabonds who worked upon it." The young man who had so happily taken to bathing wondered if it were true, as rumor had it, that Croton water "is full of tadpoles and animalculae." He swore, "I shall drink no Croton for some time to come." His friend Jehiel Post had drunk some, he reported, and was "in dreadful apprehensions of breeding bullfrogs inwardly."

With stories like these sweeping the city, plumbers advertised that they would also install filters at each faucet, to remove any sediment or impurities from the water. Some New Yorkers, as late as the 1850s, used the few remaining corner pumps, rather than the Croton hydrants, to get their water. But the scare over the purity of the Croton water disappeared almost as quickly as it began, and when the price of plumbing and bathroom fixtures dropped in the mid-1840s, most new housing included running water and bathrooms. Ten years after the completion of the aqueducts, 1852, New Yorkers were using thirty million gallons of water every weekday and forty million on Saturday. "Think of it!" exclaimed the *Daily Tribune*. Philadelphia consumed just nine

High Bridge

ROCHFORD & WORLEY'S
PATENT PORTABLE BATH TUBS,

WITH HEATER ATTACHED.

This is the most economical, as well as the most convenient Bath and Heater in the world. The extra charge more than any common Bath Tub is only six dollars. The fuel for heating a bath does not cost more than three cents, and it requires not more than twenty minutes to heat the water sufficiently to bathe in.

This heater is so simple in its construction, that it can be attached to any bath tub in one hour's time; it measures but ten inches in diameter, and can be placed on any part of the tub as the situation may require.

N. B.—We have also Bath Tubs without Heaters.

"By this treatment the bad juices are brought to discharge themselves from the skin."

ROCHFORD & WORLEY,
No. 82 VESEY STREET, (opposite Washington Market.)

million gallons a day, and London, with a population of two million, used no more water than New York, with its half-million people.

The profligacy led to frequent shortages in the 1840s and 1850s. During a prolonged spell of hot weather in August 1846, the *Daily Tribune* reported that "the demand for water is so great in the present hot weather that it is found impossible to keep up the supply in the distributing basins as fast as it is taken out." If New Yorkers did not conserve water, continued the newspaper, the city government would be forced to forbid the watering of the streets or sidewalks during daylight hours, as it had done in a drought two years earlier. Even when the reservoirs were full, some houses, particularly those on hills, had low pressure on their upper floors. The Croton system was serving many more buildings than the engineers had ever dreamed possible when they laid out the plans ten to fifteen years earlier. Every year the city dug up miles of streets to install water mains. By 1852 there were 200 miles of pipe beneath the streets; by 1853, 236 miles; and by 1854, 256 miles.

Indeed, by the early 1850s, indoor plumbing was an accepted part of life for a large number of New Yorkers. The five-story uptown houses had two or three fully equipped bathrooms, one on each bedroom floor, and lovely marble sinks set in black walnut cabinets in the dressing rooms off the bedrooms. Nothing was too grand for these homes: bathroom floors were marble, the walls frescoed or paneled in fine woods, the fixtures brass, silver, sometimes even gold. The servants, however, still used chamber pots in their rooms and bathed in a tub in the kitchen. Only the most enlightened mistress added a servants' bathroom near the kitchen, and even that was a long walk from the top-floor servants' quarters.

As the price of piping and fixtures dropped because of mass production, houses for the middle class and tenements for the poor contained bathrooms. Middle-class New Yorkers wanted their bathrooms to be fine-looking as well as functional. "What was known a few years ago, even as a luxury, is now a necessity," remarked the architect Samuel Sloan in the 1860s. "Now the polished metal tub and tubular shower

A bathroom, ca. 1860

with silver, marble, and walnut setting are esteemed necessary for comfort, even in very moderate houses."

Not everyone could keep up with the increasing luxury
and complexity of the plumbing marvels now found in hotel
and home bathrooms. Observed the *Builder*:

These conveniences of plumbing have been overdone. Frequently a marble slab basin or an enameled bath is seen with
invisible inlet or outlet for water, and only a fancifully en-
riched plated knob, perhaps over the center of the affair. In
perplexity this is pulled at, but it will not draw out. A lucky
turn to the right sends a rush of hot water streaming into the
basin or bath. This is soon too hot, and you look in vain for
some friendly tap of a cooler element. Another turn of the

knob, and, with a gurgling swirl, the water as quickly disappears, and all is empty, whilst vexation and embarrassment disturb all ideas of comfort.

The introduction of Croton water had one unwanted and unexpected effect: the water table began to rise ominously above its former level because people were no longer taking ground water from the corner pumps. To keep the basements of thousands of buildings in the city from being flooded, New York hurriedly embarked on a sewer-construction program, which physicians and scientists had been urging for years for reasons of public health. The *Herald* thought that "the most important subject that can occupy the thoughts of our city government is sewerage . . . for it involves comfort, health, life, the fate of offspring." But until the rising water table threatened property values, sewers and their importance to public health were "a question to which no serious attention had been paid by our city fathers, and comparatively little by a community too busily engaged in the pursuits of wealth, pleasure, or ambition."

Box drains had been built in Manhattan as early as 1676 to carry off storm water from low-lying areas. The first sewer, in a modern sense, was installed under Canal Street early in the nineteenth century to carry off the water from the underground springs that had fed Collect Pond and the Lispenard Meadows. The Canal Street sewer, which carried some household wastes as well, proved a terrible nuisance rather than a civic blessing. The engineers did not install air traps, and a stench filled the neighborhood on warm or still days. Memories of this smell and the decline of property values along Canal Street, until the problem was fixed, hindered sewer proposals in the 1830s and 1840s.

Once New Yorkers decided that their city must have sewers in the mid-1840s, the construction work proceeded with the same speed and skill that had marked the introduction of Croton water to the city. By 1849, 45 miles of sewers were either completed or in progress. At the beginning of 1852 there were already 148 miles of sewers, completed at an average cost of $3.12 a foot. Annual cost for cleaning and repairing the sewers ran $116.00 a mile, and there was a one-time $10.00 tax to connect a house to the system.

191

Now property owners clamored for the city to speed up its sewer-installation work. New Yorkers had come to appreciate streets that did not have pools of stagnant household waste everywhere, and new houses were virtually unsalable unless the street had a sewer underneath. The sewers, which were dug thirteen feet below the ground, lowered the water table two or three feet below what it had been before the level began to rise, and cellars could now be dug several feet deeper than previously to a practical eight or nine feet. Late in 1854 the *Daily Tribune* could report that every street in New York from the Battery to Forty-fourth Street would have sewers "in a very short time."

Still, some New Yorkers complained that sewers weren't worth the cost or the inconvenience of their installation. In 1847 the *Herald* reported that dirt and debris from the construction of sewers beneath Maiden Lane, John Street, and Fulton Street was piled as high as the second- and third-floor windows of nearby buildings. "It is with the greatest difficulty that pedestrians can make their way through the piles of dirt, boards, gas pipes, and laborers that choke up the sidewalks, or store keepers reach their places of business," reported the newspaper. To emphasize what it called the "sufferings of the downtown people," the *Herald* printed a cartoon showing men and women painstakingly making their way up and down great mounds of earth. One boy in the foreground had taken advantage of the situation to slide down one of the mounds.

On a more serious note, the *Daily Tribune* complained that "in all the old streets, where sewers have been put down at such trouble and expense, we do not believe one house in ten is connected with the sewer, and consequently no one can see that the street has one whit benefited." The *Daily Tribune*, however, realized that it would take years before all existing buildings in the city, particularly those housing the poor, would have indoor plumbing connected to sewers that would "convey, unseen, all the slop water of all the kitchens and chambers of all the hundreds of miles of houses, away to the ocean, without offending the eye or nose of those who walk the pavements."

Central heating was another comfort that advancing technology brought to the everyday lives of many New Yorkers in the 1840s. Before that, houses relied on cozy-looking but inefficient wood-burning fireplaces for heat. Although some families preferred coal to the traditional wood because it gave a more constant heat with less tending, wood remained "the chief, and indeed, almost the only fuel consumed here," reported an Englishwoman, Mrs. Felton, in the mid-1830s. "It is certainly much healthier and cleaner than its sable substitute, but the matter of dollars and cents has its share of influence."

The price of coal, however, dropped dramatically around 1840 because of the opening in 1825 of the Erie Canal, which reached the coal fields around the Great Lakes; the building of the Delaware and Hudson Canal in 1825–1829 to bring coal from Pennsylvania; and the growth of the railroad system into New York in the 1830s. Philip Hone, who had invested in the Pennsylvania coal fields, reported in his diary in 1839 that production of the mines around Lehigh had risen from 365 tons in 1820 to a million tons that year. The Delaware and Hudson Canal, he also reported, shipped 122,000 tons of coal in 1839, quite a jump from the 7000 tons handled in 1832.

Around 1840 New Yorkers began to burn coal first in their fireplaces and then in the hot-air furnaces, which appeared in the houses of the middle class in 1844. Two years later the *Evening Post* declared that "the improvements in the mode of warming dwelling houses, which have been introduced in the city of New York within the last two years, have effected almost an entire revolution in this department of our domestic arrangements." The first type of furnace in wide use sat in the cellar in a brick vault roughly six by nine feet. Wide wooden troughs brought outside air into the vault, where it was heated by contact with the surfaces of the furnace and then forced through tin pipes to floor or wall registers in the rooms upstairs. The operation of the hot-air furnace was fairly simple compared to the use of wood-burning or coal-burning fireplaces. Every morning a servant or a member of the family raked out the furnace and threw away the ashes. During the day it was twice stoked with coal, and at night the cinders were banked and the damper partly closed, to ensure even heat.

Trade card for a furnace manufacturer

Inventors and engineers were quick to improve upon the early forced–hot-air systems and, as early as 1846, introduced steam heat in radiators. That year the *Evening Post* reported that E. L. Miller of Brooklyn, who was "the first to introduce among us the present admirable system of air furnaces [has] recently, however, introduced into his own house, 89 Clark Street, an arrangement for warming air by radiated [sic] from water-heated surfaces only." Miller's rudimentary steam or hot-water heating system was slow to catch on. In 1854 the *Daily Tribune* observed that "doubts have been cast on the possibility of using water or steam to this extent." People worried that the steam would condense in the pipes before it had traveled any distance from the furnace, and, when that fear was allayed, other homeowners complained that the pipes and radiators were unsightly. That was an objection "for which no suitable remedy presents itself, as heating pipes to be serviceable, must necessarily be exposed," observed the *Daily Tribune*. But in that same article the newspaper reported that the Pennsylvania Hospital for the Insane, near Philadelphia, had a successful steam-heat system. Later that year the *Herald* reported that steam heat had been installed at the Metropolitan Theatre on Broadway and in a new building at the New York Hospital. Steam heat also began to appear in private residences.

English visitors were quick to notice, and complain about, central heating in New York homes and hotels. The former British consul in Boston, Thomas Golley Grattan, noted:

The method of heating in many of the best houses is a terrible grievance to persons not accustomed to it, and a fatal misfortune to those who are. Casual visitors are nearly suffocated, and the constant occupiers killed. An enormous furnace sends up, day and night, streams of hot air through apertures and pipes, to every room in the house. No spot is free from it, from the dining-parlor to the dressing closet. It meets you the moment the street door is opened to let you in, and it rushes after you when you emerge again, half-stewed and parboiled, into the welcome air.

The complaints about excessive heat appear somewhat exaggerated, considering the state of heating technology at the time. In the 1840s and 1850s, the hot-air system usually heated only the basement and first floor; the upstairs bedrooms still relied on the coal grates in fireplaces. Most homes of those in fortunate financial circumstances had two furnaces just to heat the lower two floors, but they seem to have been rather less than effective in the coldest weather. On January 8, 1866, "the coldest day for sixty years," with a wind that "blows lancets and razors," George Templeton Strong wrote that the temperature in his home, with both furnaces going and fires in every fireplace, was just 38°.

Gas light became the popular way to illuminate new homes in the 1840s. Gas had been readily available in New York since the 1820s, but people were slow in bringing it into their houses for fear of explosions. Gas for street lamps was a vast improvement over earlier means of lighting the city at night. In 1679 the city ordered every seven homeowners to join together to pay the cost of hanging a lantern with a candle from the seventh house on moonless nights. The light from these lanterns, though, was so weak that few New Yorkers ventured far from home on dark nights without carrying their own lanterns. In 1762 the city introduced oil-burning street lamps; these remained in use until 1825.

That was the year the New York Gas Light Company, which had been formed in 1823, began to lay pipes for the new gas street lights. In 1828 the new lights had been installed on Broadway between the Battery and Grand Street. Within several years, all the streets were lit with gas, and as early as 1829 Anne Royall was surprised by "the brilliancy of the gas in the windows, the lamps" along Water Street, "the profusion of lights to which I had long been a stranger."

Within five years of its founding, the New York Gas Light Company had laid over fifteen miles of pipes, and their gas works, at Rhynder and Hester streets, near the foot of Canal Street at the East River, was "one of the largest edifices in the city," according to *Goodrich's Picture of New York*. "The gas is measured by a curious machine called a meter, and passes out into all the principal streets south of Grand Street, through pipes of cast iron of various sizes, from six inches to two inches bore; and by lateral pipes into private houses, where the company pipes end, and the whole interior fitting is done at the expense of the person using the gas."

The public's fear of using gas in private homes had largely dissipated after 1840; by 1851, J. H. Ross, an Englishman, wrote that "gas is now considered almost indispensable in the city. So much so, that scarcely a respectable dwelling house is now built without gas fixtures." The statistics of gas consumption show its increasing acceptance in the period: in 1842 the Manhattan Gas Works sold 17 million cubic feet of gas, and in eight years the figure had risen to 103 million. Gas cost homeowners $3.00 per 100 cubic feet. Not only had gas light become "preferable to any other artificial light," according to Ross, but, as the *Home Journal* reported in 1854, the Astor House kitchens were sometimes cooking with gas.

One unfortunate result of the growing gas consumption was the spread of gasworks, which blighted their immediate neighborhoods. In 1856 the New York Gas Light Company, serving the entire city south of Grand Street, including three thousand street lamps, had its works between East Twenty-first and East Twenty-second streets from First Avenue to the East River. The Manhattan Gaslight Company, which supplied the city north of Grand Street, including seventy-three hundred street lights, had its works at the foot of Seventh and Fourteenth streets along the East River. The *Times* visited the Fourteenth Street works just before their completion in 1853 and reported that "six large tanks or gas holders, each of a capacity equal to about 368,000 cubic feet, and 97 feet in diameter, are to be built, while a space of ground 400 by 200 feet on Avenue C, between 14th and 15th Streets, is to be covered with purifying buildings. An entire block between Avenues C and D is to be occupied by the engine house, office, machine shop, blacksmith's shop, scrubbers, condensers, and three retort houses 240 feet long, to cover the whole width of the block." The coal yard occupied the land from East Fourteenth to East Fifteenth streets from Avenue D to the East River, a distance varying from 200 to 300 feet. Just five years earlier all the land occupied by the Manhattan Gaslight Company had been seventeen to twenty feet beneath the East River.

Gas light may have been convenient, but there was no overlooking its dangers. One evening in January 1867, George Templeton Strong had finished dinner and was pre-

JOHNSON'S
GAS FITTINGS,
AND
General Brass Work Establishments,
No. 1 DOYER STREET,
Principal Factory No. 111 Eighteenth Street,
ADJOINING M. G. LENGHI & Co.'s MARBLE WORKS.
GAS PIPES AND FITTINGS,
PLAIN & FANCY BRASS TUBING,
PENDANTS, BRACKETS, CHANDELIERS, &c.
Brass Bedsteads and general fancy Brass Work to order. Gas Burners of
every description. Cocks in every variety, &c. &c.

paring to drink some coffee and read the newspaper in the front parlor "when there came a prolonged vehement ringing at the doorbell. Two or three people rushed into the house the moment the door was opened shouting: 'The house is on fire!' " Strong ran upstairs with one of the servants and "found that a gas burner had lit up the lace and muslin curtains of the east windows of the third-floor front room. They or their fallen debris were blazing fiercely. So was the window frame." He put out the fire with basins of water before it did any real damage. "This is a repetition of the casualty that befell us in the Spring of 1860," he noted. Like most New Yorkers, Strong would not have given up the technological comforts of the 1840s and 1850s for anything, but he did realize that, at this early state of their development, "gas and hot-air furnaces are convenient but perilous."

11

Living at Gramercy Park gave Strong an exciting place from which to watch the northward growth of New York. When he had first visited Gramercy Park, in 1845, the neighborhood was virtually empty and was six or seven blocks beyond the northernmost edge of row-house construction. But by the time he moved into his East Twenty-first Street home, three years later, building operations had engulfed the park and the surrounding streets. The city's growth did not stop, or even hesitate, in these prosperous years, and by the early 1850s row houses and mansions were rising along Twenty-third Street. Several years later the city's northern edge reached Thirty-fourth Street and the gentle slope of Murray Hill. Row-house construction had pushed as far north as Forty-second Street just before the Civil War, and "still," proclaimed the *Herald*, "the cry is higher, higher, higher!"

Real estate speculators were not at all surprised by the speed with which the countryside receded farther and farther up Manhattan Island. The city was pushing northward at a rate of three streets a year in the 1840s and 1850s. The expansion of trade downtown was forcing residential neighborhoods to the north from the lower end of the island, and New York's population was growing at an astounding rate: 312,710 in 1840, 515,547 in 1850, 813,660 in 1860, and 942,292 in 1870. The city had reached Union Square in the mid-1840s, yet over half the city's population lived north of Fourteenth Street in 1864. Strong knew how rapidly the city was covering Manhattan without reading such statistics. In the 1830s he had gone no farther than Fourteenth Street in his regular evening walks to the edge of the city. His walks to open land were becoming longer every year, and in 1871 he reported, "Now they are up to 79th and 80th Streets."

In his own Gramercy Park neighborhood, the homes of the well-off went no further east than Third Avenue. Beyond that, the sidestreets were respectable but decidedly middle-class. Even when these blocks were solidly lined with row houses rather than sprinkled with middle-class flats, they looked different from the wealthier streets west of Third Avenue. The houses had red brick fronts, not the more expensive brownstone, and fewer homeowners and landlords had gone to the expense or trouble of putting trees along the curb and planting the front yards with shrubs and flowers.

These streets east of Third Avenue near Gramercy Park were attractive and well kept in the 1850s, but the East Side below Fourteenth Street was already turning into a working-class and poor neighborhood. The handsome houses that rose on the north side of Tompkins Square in 1846 did not accurately indicate the character of that area. Just a year later the *Daily Tribune* reported that a long row of "new and desirable tenements" had been completed on East Seventh Street, on the south side of Tompkins Square. Each apartment consisted of a parlor, three bedrooms, closets, and a kitchen with "one of Merklee's improved ranges." Rents on the second floor were $126 a year; on the third floor, $114; and on the fourth floor, $108. The ground floor contained stores, which rented for $200 a year. Although the *Daily Tribune* declared that "none but families of respectability and of quiet habits will be admitted," the construction of these buildings emphasized the decline of one of the East Side's most attractive spots.

In the 1850s immigrant Germans began to replace the native-born Americans who lived in the Tompkins Square area in modest row houses dating from the 1830s and 1840s. These two- and three-story houses would have been well suited to two families or a single family that took in boarders. Few immigrants could afford to rent or buy one of these houses, which cost $3000 to $4000, and the landlords were all too eager to cut them up into roominghouses and erect back buildings in the rear yards. Other real estate investors ripped down the houses to build tenements.

By 1860 the *Herald* declared that Avenues A, B, C, and D and the nearby sidestreets "all present that indescribably dusty, dirty, seedy, and 'all used up' appearance peculiar to the East Side of town." When the *Herald* wrote about the city's slums in 1869, it singled out "Ragpickers' Row," Fourth Street between Avenues A and B, and "Mackerelville," Eleventh Street from First Avenue to Avenue B, as among the worst "plague spots" in New York. The *Herald* also could have mentioned the intersection of Second Avenue and Houston Street, where a dozen slaughterhouses filled the nearby blocks with an awful stench.

The downhill slide of the blocks east of Second Avenue caused rich New Yorkers to worry about the future of that handsome street. House prices on Second Avenue, south of Fourteenth Street, remained constant or even declined, in a time of rapidly rising values elsewhere in the city. New Yorkers now wondered about the future of the East Side north of Fourteenth Street. The slums, they remembered, had spread northward from the Five Points into the Delancey Street area and then into the Tompkins Square neighborhood. So it seemed logical that the poor would continue to move in the same direction, past Fourteenth Street. These expectations were realized in the 1860s and 1870s as middleclass New Yorkers shunned the streets east of Third Avenue and north of Fourteenth Street, and real estate investors lined the East Side avenues with tenements all the way to Harlem.

When George Templeton Strong took his evening walks, he more often headed west than east. There he found the Hudson River waterfront and views of New Jersey that he had enjoyed as a boy living on Greenwich Street. He also liked the neighborhood, which was already called Chelsea in the 1840s. Much of the area had been the estate of Captain Thomas Clarke, with boundaries formed by Fourteenth Street, the Hudson River, Twenty-seventh Street, and Seventh Avenue. Thomas Clarke had expected that this estate would be his home in old age and, being a British soldier, chose the name from the Chelsea Royal Hospital in London,

General Theological Seminary, Ninth Avenue and Twentieth Street

a home for old soldiers and sailors. Though he died soon after buying the property, his widow built a mansion there; it stood on what came to be Twenty-third Street, 200 feet west of Ninth Avenue, on a hill overlooking the Hudson.

Several generations later, Chelsea passed to Clarke's grandson, Clement Clarke Moore, a classical scholar of some reputation, who is now best remembered as the author of "Visit from St. Nicholas." In the 1830s Moore realized that the city's growth, then filling in the skewed blocks of the West Village, was moving inexorably northward, so he mapped out his lands into building lots. A devout Episcopalian, the son of a past rector of Trinity Church, Moore gave a full block

204

Sixth Avenue and Twentieth Street: Gothic row houses, 1854

to the General Theological Seminary. Behind his gift lay a secular motivation as well. The presence of the seminary, he reasoned, could only enhance the value of his holdings nearby. Because Moore guided the area's growth by means of covenants in the deeds he gave to builders, Chelsea developed into an exceptionally handsome neighborhood. In 1846 the *Commercial Advertiser* reported, "The arrangements made by the original proprietors of the land in that quarter are such that no buildings can be erected for any purpose which will make the neighborhood disagreeable, and it is becoming a favorite place of residence."

Chelsea did not fulfill Moore's wish that it become a neighborhood for the rich. It was too far away from Fifth Avenue to be attractive. Many rich New Yorkers were too unsure of their newly won wealth and status to venture beyond the streets of the most fashionable district, the one that had Fifth Avenue as its axis, Third Avenue as its eastern boundary, and Sixth Avenue as its western limit. "West of Sixth Avenue no true codfish likes to swim. Not genteel. Not *bon ton*," observed the *Herald*. The lure of this district was so

205

Breakfast room in Fifth Avenue mansion, ca. 1860

strong by the 1860s that the prices of building lots outside its boundaries were stationary or declining, and values within its narrow limits were rising steadily.

Just 340 row houses and mansions stood on Fifth Avenue in 1860, and their residents paid dearly for the privilege of having the best-known address in America. In 1860 even the smallest row house on Fifth Avenue, perhaps sixteen or eighteen feet wide, cost between $20,000 and $25,000. The standard Fifth Avenue residence, a row house twenty-seven or twenty-eight feet wide and seventy feet deep, ran around $50,000 — more, if it stood on a corner. A freestanding mansion cost $200,000 to $300,000, not counting the cost of the furniture, stable, and horses that went with such an establishment. The yearly upkeep for such a house ran $25,000 a year.

206

Between 1860 and the end of the Civil War, the prices for houses on Fifth Avenue doubled. Some men refused offers of three and four times what their houses and furnishings had cost them in the 1850s. Rents for the few houses not occupied by their owners ranged from $4000 per annum (never less) up to a gentle and genial rental of $12,000, according to *Leslie's Illustrated*.

George Templeton Strong took a dim view of Fifth Avenue's attraction for thousands of New York business-men. "They are fighting hard for the grand, ugly house in the Fifth Avenue; for the gold and damask sofas and curtains that are ever shrouded in dingy coverings, save on the one night of every third year when they are unveiled to adorn the social martyrdom of five hundred perspiring friends." Strong may have been more than a little envious of this wealth. His income was not keeping pace with the inflation of the 1850s and 1860s, and his diary is filled with complaints about the cost of maintaining his household.

But other New Yorkers also lampooned the rich, generally *nouveaux riches*, residents of Fifth Avenue as "the Ave-noodles" and "the Shoddy Aristocracy." European visitors were quick to point out the common and often questionable ways in which Fifth Avenue residents had piled up their fortunes. Anthony Trollope noted, in the early 1860s:

I know of no great man, no celebrated statesman, no phi-lanthropist of note who has lived in Fifth Avenue. That gen-tleman on the right made a million dollars by inventing a shirt-collar; this one on the left electrified the world by a lotion; as to the gentleman at the corner there — there are rumours about him and the Cuban slave trade, but my in-formant by no means knows that they are true. Such are the aristocracy of Fifth Avenue. I can only say that if I could make a million dollars by a lotion, I should certainly be right to live in such a house as one of these.

Fifth Avenue was such a well-known address that almost any crookedness or foible of one of its residents became news. When one of the periodic "swill milk" scandals broke in 1858, the newspapers were quick to report that Bradish Johnson, a Fifth Avenue resident, was the proprietor of the offending dairy, located at the foot of West Sixteenth Street. *Leslie's Illustrated* even published a print of his handsome mansion, at the corner of West Twenty-first Street, implying none too subtly, that his chicanery had gained for him a luxurious life.

The New York newspapers also reported the marital difficulties of Isaac Merrit Singer, the sewing machine king, who lived at 14 Fifth Avenue. His name was familiar to most Americans, and he and his wife had literally taken their troubles to the streets. One morning, during one of their violent quarrels, Mrs. Singer decided that she had been beaten enough for that day and ran out the front door, her husband still screaming and beating her as she ran shrieking down Fifth Avenue. That morning she found refuge at a friend's house nearby; the next day she had her husband arrested at his office.

The most notorious resident of Fifth Avenue was Madame Restell, whom we last met when she lived on Greenwich Street. She had left her home there in the late 1840s for a handsome house on nearby Chambers Street, but did not stay for long. Realizing that the city and her clientele were moving ever northward, she erected, in the mid-1850s, a handsome brownstone mansion at 657 Fifth Avenue, on the northeast corner of Fifty-second Street. Only Restell knew why she chose to live in a spot that then was ten or fifteen blocks beyond the northernmost reaches of the city. She was not afraid to practice her trade in a densely populated area of the city, and had lived on Greenwich Street when it was still a fashionable residence. Perhaps, as the *Times* once suggested, she selected Fifty-second Street to be annoyingly close to St. Patrick's Cathedral and the Roman Catholic hierarchy, which tried so long and so unsuccessfully to put her out of business.

When the city did reach Restell's vicinity after the Civil War, her presence became a genuine embarrassment to the neighborhood. Restell was one of the few New Yorkers who could not buy their way into polite society with a Fifth Avenue address, a mansion, and fine horses. "There she has seated herself, in all the splendor of wealth, her great palace frowning down upon the street," wrote *Leslie's Illustrated*,

Residence of Madame Restell, 657 Fifth Avenue

"while, inside, madame sits a pariah, amid velvets and buhl, satin and rosewood, mirrors and bronzes, and longs for the sympathy and respect that all her wealth cannot buy, even in this city, where we are told it can buy anything." Restell's mansion lowered real estate values nearby, and the lots for 100 feet on either side of her home could not be sold, even at steep discounts.

Wealthy residents tried to buy her house and thereby rid the area of its objectionable owner, but she was as proud as she was rich, and scornfully rejected all offers for her property. To make matters worse, Restell flaunted her unwanted presence by taking an afternoon carriage ride every day. Her stylish equipage and liveried coachmen were well known to all who frequented the Fifth Avenue promenade and Central Park carriage drives.

Madame Restell had no effect, however, on the status of the rest of Fifth Avenue. Despite the high prices for property, New Yorkers were so captivated by the avenue that its blockfronts were filling up five, even ten, blocks in advance of the built-up city to the south. Like Broadway twenty or thirty years earlier, Fifth Avenue was leading the march up Manhattan Island.

No sooner had mansions begun to rise around Union Square and Fourteenth Street in the mid-1840s than it seemed that growth reached Madison Square. This seven-acre park, at the intersection of Fifth Avenue, Broadway, and Twenty-third Street, had been a potter's field, like Washington Square. By 1847, when the Common Council ordered Madison Square opened, owners of nearby property knew that the surrounding streets would become some of the most desirable in the city, and were ready to block anything that might diminish this splendid future. A group of New Yorkers proposing to build a free college in Madison Square met "with strong opposition from the property owners and residents in that neighborhood," according to the *Evening Post*. The opposition group reportedly wanted Madison Square saved as the future site of City Hall or municipal offices. What they were really interested in was keeping earnest but poor students out of their neighborhood. The Free Academy, later known as the College of the City of New York, or

CCNY, was built instead at Lexington Avenue and Twenty-third Street.

Three years after local property owners triumphed over the Free Academy, they proudly read in the *Daily Tribune* that their neighborhood "evidently will be the most fashionable part of our rapidly increasing city . . . that very nearly all the lots in its vicinity have been purchased by people of wealth, for the erection of spacious and costly edifices." The most famous buildings to rise near Madison Square at this time were seventeen brownstone row houses, which filled the south side of Twenty-third Street, between Lexington and Fourth avenues. The project, built by Brown Brothers & Company, cost some $250,000, including the land. Because of the economies of scale involved in so large an undertaking, each of the houses was sold for no more than what it would cost a gentleman to build a house for himself.

Another landmark near Madison Square was the Union Club, completed in 1855, at the northeast corner of Fifth Avenue and Twenty-first Street. The Union was the first men's club organized in New York and the first in the city to build its own clubhouse. In the 1820s, there had been several so-called clubs, generally consisting of six or eight friends who met for dinner and an evening's conversation at each other's homes. In 1824 James Fenimore Cooper, who was living at 3 Beach Street, near St. John's Park, founded a loosely knit group, called the Bread and Cheese Club, with the poets Fitz-Greene Halleck and William Cullen Bryant; James Kent, Chief Judge of the New York Supreme Court; Gulian Verplanck, scion of one of New York's oldest families; and Dr. John Francis, professor of obstetrics at the College of Physicians and Surgeons. In 1836 Philip Hone and eleven friends formed an association called the Hone Club, the members of which ate dinner together once a month for over ten years. These groups, however, lacked the paraphernalia of later men's clubs, the clubhouse facilities, and dues.

The Union, organized in 1836, was the first successful club in New York; it followed the model of the London establishments. Hone had helped form the club, which, from the beginning, attracted men from such select families as the Livingstons, Griswolds, Van Cortlandts, Van Rensselaers,

Stuyvesants, and Suydams, in addition to the "new Napoleons of wealth by trade." In 1837 the Union Club moved to its first clubhouse, at 343 Broadway, described by Hone as "well fitted up, the furniture neat and handsome, good servants, and above all a most *recherché de cuisine*." Hone saw the Union Club as "a great resource for bachelors, and 'men about town,' " and was delighted that "subscribers will get a better dinner and at one half the cost than at any hotel in town." But he wondered "how we married men can be induced to leave our comfortable homes and families to dine *en garçon* at the club, even under the temptation of M. Julien's *bon diner à la Paris*."

Whatever doubts Hone may have had about club life, the Union prospered and added more well-born and well-off men every year, until a waiting list had to be established. In 1842 the club moved to 376 Broadway, a large house owned by member William B. Astor, and in 1850 shifted a mile uptown to 691 Broadway, opposite Great Jones Street. Hone, who lived across the street, declared that "the club has never before been so well and pleasantly accommodated" and noted that "it will be convenient for me, also; perhaps too much so — it may cause me to visit it too frequently."

The club members were already looking for a permanent home farther uptown, where most of them now lived. In 1853 the club purchased from a member several lots at Fifth Avenue and Twenty-first Street for the same $42,000 he had paid for the property several years earlier. Here the Union Club built a $210,000 clubhouse, which the *Herald* called "perhaps the most conspicuous . . . among the many magnificent buildings which make up what is called the Fifth Avenue." Architects Thomas Thomas & Sons fittingly selected the Italianate style, inspired by the Florentine clubhouses in London. The boldly ornamented brownstone building, considered by *Ballou's Pictorial Drawing-Room Companion* "one of the greatest architectural attempts in this country," ran 65 feet along Fifth Avenue and 120 feet along West Twenty-first Street. The Union Club was only a ground-level basement and three stories tall, but the rooms had such high ceilings that the building was 85 feet tall and loomed over the nearby mansions and row houses.

212

The interior appointments and services at the Union Club rivaled those of the Broadway hotels. The drawing room, overlooking Fifth Avenue, was 56 feet long and 35 feet wide. The 60-by-40-foot dining room, with its 22-foot ceilings, seated as many as 150 guests and, as the *Herald* proudly noted, was "a truly noble apartment . . . said to be finer than the dining rooms of any of the London clubhouses." All the woodwork and furniture in the dining room, including an enormous buffet along one wall, was of the finest black walnut.

Union Club, Fifth Avenue and Twenty-first Street

The kitchen, which occupied the basement, along with the wine cellar, store rooms, and manager's office, was the last word in the mechanical wonders of the age. The "patent smoke revolving pit" was the "very perfection of art," according to the *Herald*. "By a simple contrivance, the smoke, as it passes up the chimney, is made to turn a small wheel that communicates with the revolving cylinder on which the meat is placed, and which is capable of being regulated in its speed like the paddle of a steamboat." Another clever feature was the speedy transmission, an "almost telegraphic rapidity," of guests' meal orders from the dining room to the kitchen downstairs. The waiter slipped the order into a hole in the wall and dropped it into the mouth of a tube, which carried it downstairs by gravity.

Other gentlemen's clubs followed the Union soon after its organization. The New York Yacht Club was founded in 1844, the New York Club in 1845, and the Century in 1847. A sure sign of the success of these men's clubs was the criticism directed against them by old-fashioned New Yorkers and newspapers. Clubs were "a blow against marriage, a protest against domesticity," accused the *Herald*. Moreover, clubs were evidence, in the newly urban and industrial nation, that the "boundaries which separate different classes are daily growing wider and more distinctly marked." Henri Junius Browne saw clubs as "the late fruit of a high civilization — the outgrowth of leisure, luxury, and cultivated unrestraint." New York already had more than enough "idlers," reported the *Daily Tribune*. These were defined as "half-pay officers, annuitants, rich bachelors, and waiters on Providence." The club also attracted hard-working merchants and businessmen who wanted a place to meet their friends outside the home, who longed for the status that membership in a fashionable club would endow. A. T. Stewart, for instance, wanted quite badly to be a member of the Union Club. The year he opened his department store, 1846, Union Club members blackballed his name because they looked down on Irish immigrants in general and on a man so deeply involved in trade in particular. When Stewart was finally admitted, he rarely went to the clubhouse. The distinction of membership apparently fulfilled his heart's desire.

The Union was the only club to breach the residential precincts of Fifth Avenue before the Civil War. The other clubs were located on Broadway, just below Union Square. New Yorkers concerned with propriety were unhappy that such a glaring affront to home life as the Union Club had moved to Fifth Avenue, the most fashionable, the most proper street in the city. Worse yet, the members were known to sit in the tall drawing room windows admiring the young ladies promenading up and down the street. What Fifth Avenue needed, the reasoning went, was not club-houses but more churches.

Fifth Avenue was, indeed, the favorite location for churches. In 1855 the *Herald* counted twenty within half a mile of Madison Square, and, ten years later, there were fourteen churches on or just off Fifth Avenue itself. Trollope thought that the churches enhanced the appearance of Fifth Avenue, but James McCabe wrote that "in some localities, especially on the fashionable streets, they crowd each other too greatly." The *Herald* wondered "whether this centralization of churches is an argument more against the clergy or the community of this section." Perhaps the clergy, "led there by a spirit bending lower to Mammon than to God," knew that they would receive larger salaries from congregations with full purses than from those with turned-out pockets. Yet again, thought the *Herald*, still searching for the truth, maybe "it is the moral condition of this section of the city which requires so much religion."

The Church of the Ascension was the first to build on Fifth Avenue. Its brownstone Gothic Revival church, at the northwest corner of Tenth Street, was completed in 1840. The congregation had previously worshiped in a church — modeled, however unfittingly, after a Greek temple — on Canal Street, just a block east of Broadway. After that church had been completed, in 1828, one of the first gasworks in New York was established less than a block away. The white stucco front of the church had become very dirty in the intervening years, and the neighborhood, despite its proximity to Broadway, had turned into a mixture of small factories and badly run-down houses. The church burned in 1839, obligingly providing the congregation with an excuse to move uptown.

The Church of the Ascension was not for long the only church north of Washington Square. The University Place Presbyterian Church, also known as Dr. Potts' church, opened for services in 1845 at the southeast corner of University Place and Tenth Street. The next year ground was broken for the Church of the Ascension on West Fourteenth Street between Sixth and Seventh Avenues, and for the Church of the Puritans, sometimes called Dr. Cheever's church, at the southwest corner of Union Square and Fifteenth Street.

The grandest church, and the one with the most interesting history, to build uptown in the 1840s was the First Presbyterian Church, which occupied the west blockfront of Fifth Avenue between Eleventh and Twelfth streets. This congregation, it will be remembered, had worshiped in a church at 5 Wall Street, the oldest one in the city before its destruction by fire in 1834. First Presbyterian later built another church at this site, even though some, like Philip Hone, thought that the congregation should sell the land and move to a more residential location. By 1844 so many parishioners lived several miles uptown, and the Wall Street property had become so valuable, that First Presbyterian built its church on Fifth Avenue. The land that the Wall Street church and its cemetery occupied was divided into five lots and sold for a total of $110,000. The church itself was carefully dismantled and sold for $3000 to a Presbyterian congregation in Jersey City, which re-erected the building at the corner of Washington and Sussex streets, one of the highest points in that city. Its tower was the tallest object in the Jersey City skyline and could easily be seen from New York.

As First Presbyterian's new church was rising on Fifth Avenue, George Templeton Strong, who would become a vestryman of Trinity Church, pronounced the building "an abortion . . . a travesty of a Gothic church." Several months later he wrote that the church grew "uglier and uglier, and when its tower is finished it will resemble a corpulent Chinese gander with its neck rigid, stout and tall, and its square-built rump and broad expanse of back, sturdy, squat, and not easily to be shaken." Strong's dislike of Dr. Phillips, First

216

Presbyterian's rector, and of the Presbyterian church in general had clouded his usually sound aesthetic judgment. First Presbyterian never was among New York's most imposing churches, but certainly it has always been one of the prettiest. Its greatest distinction is not its architecture but the spacious tree-shaded grounds, surrounded by the same iron fence that had encircled the church grounds and cemetery on Wall Street. "We wish that other societies would follow the example of this church corporation, and give their buildings such admirable settings of turf and trees," wrote *Putnam's Monthly*. "It is refreshing to see these little bits of verdure and leafiness in the midst of our city."

The Gothic Revival churches were a charming sight among the rows of red brick and brownstone houses uptown, but their evocation of medieval England and village churchyards was out of character with the extravagant display that was a part of the Sunday services. Services were so elaborately staged and the congregations so handsomely dressed that the *Herald* thought some uptown churches lacked only box seats to make them the equal of the opera or theater. Many of these churches prided themselves on their music, and hired professional musicians and opera singers for services. "How precise and elegant is everything and everybody in the church!" exclaimed Henri Junius Brown. "The music is executed faultlessly and after the style of the Academy [of Music]. You forget the words and place in the skilful execution of the trills and bravuras. 'The members of the choir sing well,' you whisper to your neighbor. 'Why should they not?' he answers. 'They are paid very liberally for it.' "

A musical program every Sunday cost $3000 to $4000 a year in the 1850s and was frequently considered the highpoint of the services at churches like Grace Episcopal. "Many of the pews are vacated soon after the best of the morning music is concluded," reported the *Herald*.

The New York churches were so worldly that in 1859 *Life Illustrated* wondered "how on earth the Fifth Avenue people ever expect to get to heaven! Are they going to drive up to the gates in their emblazoned carriages, and send in their cards by liveried John? Or do they suppose a flight of stairs,

balustraded with rosewood and carpeted with velvet, is to be let down for their patrician feet, with a little angel at every turning to announce their coming?"

New Yorkers sometimes answered these criticisms by pointing out that the number of churches in the city had grown from 32 around 1800 to over 250 in 1850 and over 350 by 1868. What they failed to point out was a proportionate increase in the city's population and the embarrassing fact that most church services showed a "beggarly array of empty benches." In 1860 the Episcopal churches in New York had seats for 110,750, but the average Sunday attendance was just 28,613, "This seems to show," wrote *Putnam's Magazine*, "not that we want churches, but people to go into them."

The handful of stylish churches had no trouble filling their pews every Sunday or selling these pews at high prices. When Grace Church was completed in 1846, it received well over $100,000 for its 212 pews, with some members of the congregation paying as much as $1200 to $1400 for their. Besides making a contribution to the collection plate, each member paid an 8 percent levy on the cost of his pew. Hone was appalled that the "word of God, as it came down to us from fishermen and mechanics, will cost the quality who worship in this splendid temple about three dollars every Sunday." The high cost of worshiping at Grace Church "may have a good effect," he thought, "for many of them, though rich, know how to calculate, and if they do not regularly go to church they will not get the worth of their money."

It was the churches in deteriorating or poor neighborhoods whose poor attendance lowered the overall figure for the city's houses of worship. Even a fashionable church lost much of its congregation and income if its neighborhood started to decline. In 1851 the *Herald* noted that the price of pews in St. Bartholomew's Church at Lafayette Place and Great Jones Street had dropped that year. "The truth is, we believe, that St. Bartholomew's is not now a fashionable church," remarked the newspaper. "This we think is the secret of the matter . . . It is decidedly unfashionable to appear in a church that is not resorted to by the aristocracy." The *Herald's* statement about St. Bartholomew's diminishing status was a bit harsh. A good number of well-born New

Yorkers still attended the exquisite Greek Revival church, but worshiping at St. Bartholomew's was no longer the acme of fashion it once had been, and the area had run down so badly after the Civil War that in 1872 the church wisely moved to the southwest corner of Madison Avenue and Forty-fourth Street.

St. Bartholomew's might have moved uptown years earlier if the congregation could have sold the church and land at a profit to someone who wanted the site for a warehouse or office building. But Lafayette Place did not fall to trade in the 1850s and 1860s. It simply underwent slow decay, as the old row houses became boardinghouses, and tenements were built a block away on the other side of the Bowery. Property values around St. Bartholomew's declined or, at best, remained stationary in the mid-nineteenth century.

Many churches in the downtown business district sold their property for sums far in excess of what they had spent on the land and construction twenty or thirty years earlier. In 1825 there were 84 churches in New York, 45 of them south of Canal Street. By 1857 there were 290 churches, just 17 of these south of Canal Street. Some New Yorkers justified the disappearance of churches downtown by pointing to the loss of population as the residential streets were taken over by trade. But the population of the six wards south of Canal Street had actually risen from 80,731 to 107,598 between 1840 and 1850, a period when fifteen congregations deserted their churches there.

The Roman Catholic diocese bought several churches from Protestant congregations that were moving uptown. The population of the six downtown wards did decline somewhat in the 1850s, but the percentage of Catholics in that number rose sharply as Irish and German immigrants moved into much of the remaining housing south of Canal Street. The Catholics usually purchased churches in out-of-the-way downtown areas that remained residential. The churches on or near busy thoroughfares were too valuable to be converted into anything but what was suitable for commercial occupancy. The Middle Dutch Church, which stood on Nassau Street since 1729, became the main Post Office in 1844. During the Revolution, the British Army had used the building as a riding school for its troops and a prison for American soldiers and civilians. The First Congregational Church, erected on Chambers Street west of Broadway in 1821, was transformed into the Bank for Savings in 1843. Christ Episcopal, which had stood on Worth Street off Broadway since 1823, became the office for the Commissioners of Immigration when the congregation moved to a new church on West Eighteenth Street, just off Fifth Avenue.

New Yorkers understood that the congregations sought the highest possible price for their properties so that they might have more money for their new churches uptown. Christ Church, however, went too far. It posted the following notice on the front door of the old Worth Street building: "To Let, this Church, for religious meetings, lectures, hotel, stables, or any other purpose." Other congregations sold or rented their downtown buildings for uses so offensive that New Yorkers and the newspapers despaired over the desecration of buildings once hallowed and the "triumph of the World over Church." The German Reformed Church on Nassau Street, near Maiden Lane, was a restaurant for many years before its demolition in 1857 for warehouses. The South Baptist Church on Nassau Street, between Fulton and John streets, served as a patent medicine warehouse in the 1840s and 1850s. The Methodist Episcopal Wesleyan Chapel on Vestry Street was a stable for American Express for several years in the 1850s. And a small church on Franklin Street, just west of West Broadway, which had housed a number of congregations since its erection by the Presbyterians in 1823, became a market for meat, butter, and eggs in 1855.

Some churches even became tenements. The Abyssinian Baptist Church on Worth Street, between Church Street and West Broadway, had housed a black congregation since 1810; it became a tenement for blacks in 1855. A Baptist church on Mulberry Street, near Chatham Square, also was converted into a tenement in the mid-1850s. The *Daily Tribune*, after an inspection of the property in 1857, reported that it had "seldom seen a dirtier tenant house, or one containing more poverty and wretchedness."

221

The most grisly fate, however, was reserved not for the church buildings but for their surrounding cemeteries. When a congregation sold its church to another congregation or to a builder, many of the bodies buried in the churchyard were claimed by their descendants and were re-interred in one of the countrified cemeteries outside the city, like Greenwood in Brooklyn. But once the congregations were busy erecting new churches uptown, they often forgot about the graves lying unclaimed in their downtown churchyards. As an abandoned church was demolished, the work crew dug up the yard, and the "crumbling coffins and mouldering remains . . . thrown rudely into the glare of the day," wrote Hone, were carried to the city's potter's field or were hauled away with the rubbish of the old church building.

The Brick Presbyterian Church thoughtfully moved all unclaimed bodies from its downtown vaults to Cypress Hills Cemetery in Brooklyn when it moved uptown in 1857. Brick Presbyterian was one of the best-known congregations in the city. The church had stood since 1767 at the northeast corner of Beekman and Nassau streets, a block from City Hall Park. The first pastor, Dr. John Rodgers, was hailed as "the father of Presbyterianism" in New York. The second pastor, Dr. Gardiner Spring, took over in 1810 and served as pastor for sixty-two years. By 1849 so many members of the congregation lived uptown, "above Bleecker," that Brick Presbyterian began to hold its evening services in Hope Chapel at 720 Broadway.

The congregation, however, did not seem eager to move uptown. With the removal of the First Presbyterian Church from Wall Street in 1844, its church became the oldest Presbyterian Church in the city, a shrine to the memory of Dr. Rodgers. Furthermore, the churchyard, bounded by Park Row, Nassau Street, Spruce Street, and Beekman Street, could grow only more valuable with each passing year. By the early 1850s New Yorkers were beginning to say that the Brick Church property was the best place to build the new Post Office, to replace the hopelessly inadequate operations in the old Middle Dutch Church nearby. What finally convinced the congregation of the necessity of a move uptown was a combination of gain and loss. First, the property promised to fetch a high price. Then, the loss of a fifteen-foot-wide strip of the churchyard and some of its finest buttonwood trees during the widening of Beekman Street in 1854 made the church less attractive to the congregation.

As Brick Presbyterian began negotiations in 1854 for the sale of its property for the Post Office, the *Daily Tribune* declared that the church "has uniformly been conceded to occupy that most eligible locality in that neighborhood for this purpose." But what the newspaper called "the cupidity of the church proprietors" prolonged the negotiations. The chances for a sale to the United States Government vanished in 1856, and that year the church and its yard were sold at auction for $270,000. Less than two weeks later the congregation held its final service in the church, which was demolished in March 1857. The *Times* building, not a post office, rose on the site.

Whatever sorrow the congregation felt at leaving the old church was assuaged by the grandeur of its new home, at the northwest corner of Fifth Avenue and Thirty-seventh Street. The new Brick Presbyterian, described in the newspapers as "Corinthian," "Grecian," and "Italian," was an enlarged and embellished version of Sir Christopher Wren's London churches. The church, which sat on a $58,000 lot, had cost $230,000, displacing the Union Club from its pinnacle of costliness. The Thirty-seventh Street location was somewhat beyond the built-up portion of the city, church members complained, and as far from some of their homes as the downtown church had been. But Thirty-seventh Street marked the brow of Murray Hill, making it the most desirable street in that neighborhood, and all New York knew that this stretch of Fifth Avenue would equal, if not surpass, the splendors of Union Square or Madison Square to the south. That the most expensive building yet erected in New York should rise here was further evidence of Murray Hill's irresistibility.

For one thing, Murray Hill had the advantage of freshness in a New York that clamored for change and novelty. After ten years, Union Square and its mansions were so well

known as to be considered commonplace. New Yorkers welcomed a new neighborhood to talk about. Moreover, Murray Hill had a higher elevation than any other area built up in New York so far, and hills meant an abundance of sunlight, fresh air, and drainage, which, in turn, assured good health. Lastly, Murray Hill was free of the occasional frame house or tavern, remnants of a countrified past, that were so obtrusive in other fashionable neighborhoods. A paint store in a ramshackle frame building, for example, stood on Fifth Avenue next to the Church of the Ascension until John A. C. Gray built a mansard-roofed townhouse there in 1857.

Murray Hill took its name from Robert Murray, whose country house stood at the present-day intersection of Park Avenue and Thirty-seventh Street. During the Revolutionary War, tradition says, Murray's wife served tea to General Howe and his staff, thereby delaying their troops and allowing the Americans to escape to the north. Murray's home was long gone by the mid-nineteenth century. What most New Yorkers remembered about Murray Hill's past was the Coventry Waddell mansion, a yellow gray stucco Gothic Revival villa, built in 1844–1845 on the west side of Fifth Avenue between Thirty-seventh and Thirty-eighth streets. The mansion's marble-floored halls, picture gallery, ballroom, and winding staircase leading to a tower were well suited to the Waddells' frequent entertaining. Anne Sophia Winterbotham Stephens used a thinly disguised version of the Waddell mansion as the home of the main character in her popular novel, *Fashion and Famine.* "This dwelling so graceful in its architecture — so fairylike in its ground — had risen as if by magic among those old trees . . . Grand, imposing, and unsurpassed for magnificence by anything known in our city." Not everyone was as captivated by the house as Mrs. Stephens. When Waddell's brother first saw the house, he said he would call it Waddell's Caster rather than Waddell's Castle, because the towers, bay windows, and porches reminded him of a mustard pot, pepper bottle, and vinegar cruet on a table. These towers, however, gave the Waddells views of the Hudson and East rivers and the countryside to the north of their home.

The Waddells lost much of their fortune in a brief financial

225

panic in 1854–1855. They sold their home and the eight lots directly on Fifth Avenue for $100,000, not a bad price, considering the $9150 they had paid for the land in 1844. Isaac Delaplaine, the purchaser, did well, too. West Thirty-seventh Street, between Fifth and Sixth avenues, was "the empire street of Murray Hill," according the the *Herald* in 1855. After selling the corner property to the Brick Presbyterian Church, Delaplaine further guaranteed the block's desirability by adding to the building lots' deeds covenants stipulating that no stables or tenements be built there, only brownstone-front houses, with seven-foot-deep gardens set back from the street. Now the street's future looked so secure that New Yorkers paid high prices for its lots, even though it was at the edge of the city and no one had yet ventured to predict the quality of the houses that would be built on the other side of Murray Hill as it sloped down to Forty-second Street.

Looking around Murray Hill, rich New Yorkers could see the three brownstone mansions erected by Isaac Newton Phelps in 1851–1853, for himself and members of his family, on the east blockfront of Madison Avenue between Thirty-sixth and Thirty-seventh streets. These mansions, each thirty-three feet wide and seventy-three feet deep, stood on spacious grounds, and, according to the *Daily Tribune,* were "furnished in elegant and luxurious style." Then there was the Samuel P. Townsend mansion, built in 1853–1855, at the northwest corner of Fifth Avenue and Thirty-fourth Street. Townsend was something of an oddity, even for Fifth Avenue. He had made his millions by selling his sarsaparilla syrup, which he called the "wonder and blessing of the age." "Sarsaparilla Townsend," as he was called, spent between $200,000 and $250,000 to make his mansion "the finest and most costly decorated in the city," according to the *Daily Tribune.* To ensure the fame of his mansion, Townsend threw it open for one week, at its completion, to thousands of curious New Yorkers, who came to gaze and gape and whose twenty-five-cent admission fee went to the Five Point Mission.

The building's Italianate brownstone façade was not much different from others on Fifth Avenue and gave little hint of the surprises awaiting the visitors within. Once past the front doors, the crowds entered the great hall, where several tiers of gilt Corinthian columns supported galleries reaching up three floors to a stained-glass dome. A profusion of frescoes decorated the various rooms: scenes of Italy in the great hall and parlors, classical figures and fanciful scroll-work in the picture gallery and library, and nymphs and baby angels in the black walnut and marble bathrooms. The most expensive French furniture filled the various parlors, the largest of which was thirty by eighty feet.

Other Fifth Avenue mansions boasted boatloads of French furniture and fifty-foot entrance halls. With his "period rooms," Townsend forged ahead of his *nouveaux riches* rivals for the city's most improbable mansion. A Gothic chapel, sixteen-by-thirty-three feet, occupied part of the third and fourth floors. A single rose window filled the room with what the *Herald* called "the requisite amount of 'dim reli-

The Samuel P. "Sarsaparilla" Townsend residence, Fifth Avenue and Thirty-fourth Street, 1860

gious light,' properly colored." A door in his well-filled but little-used library opened into the Pompeii Room, "a unique apartment," which was supposedly a "facsimile in size and frescoes of a room in the exhumed city." His picture gallery, though not a period room, contained what everyone thought were the works of Italian old masters as well as the *Voyage of Life* paintings by Thomas Cole.

Another delight of the new Murray Hill district was Park Avenue, already one of the city's most beautiful streets. The New York & Harlem Railroad trains had been pulled down this street by horses on their way to the downtown terminal at Centre Street. In the early 1850s, the railroad dug a tunnel beneath this stretch of Park Avenue to eliminate the nuisance of trains' passing through the fashionable area and to avoid the trouble of pulling the trains up and then down Murray Hill. Once this work had commenced, the Common Council ordered forty-foot-wide malls added to the center of the street between Thirty-fourth and Thirty-eighth streets. And the work progressed, in the late 1850s, the *Herald* noted that "when the plots thus enclosed are enhanced with shrubs and flowers . . . they cannot fail to vastly enhance the general appearance of the locality." Real estate investors knew that rich New Yorkers would be enchanted by Park Avenue's gracious width and grassy malls, and posters advertising the sale of the property showed, prophetically, the malls as completed and handsomely planted. In fact, several years elapsed before this wish fathered the fact.

All the beauty of Park Avenue, the construction of several magnificent mansions, and even the completion of the Brick Presbyterian Church in 1858 did not allay the doubts of some New Yorkers about the growth of their city beyond Murray Hill. They had no questions about the desirability of Murray Hill, but they did not know what to expect as the city pressed onward beyond Forty-second Street. Some speculators, excited by the Crystal Palace Exhibition, on the site of present-day Bryant Park, and by the talk about Central Park, had built row houses as far up as the Forties and Fifties. But these were isolated rows of houses among fields, and none could be called grand. Upper- and middle-class New Yorkers were afraid to move beyond Murray Hill because of the shanty-

*Park Avenue: view north
from Thirty-fifth Street*

Property map: Park Avenue

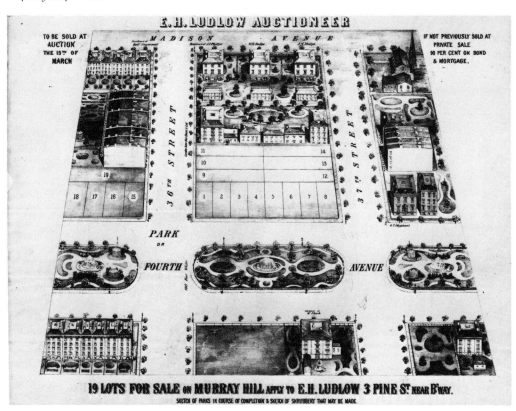

towns, slaughterhouses, and charitable institutions north of Forty-second Street. Besides, New Yorkers received the double blow of the Panic of 1857, which slowed all business operations, including row-house construction, for a year, and the probability of a civil war, which they believed would threaten the city's prosperity and growth.

12

The Panic of 1857 was a severe shock to
New York. With the exception of the brief recession in
1854–1855 that had hurt the Waddells and a few others, the
city had prospered and grown every year since the end of the
Panic of 1837. In 1850 the *Evening Post* declared that "the
rapid growth of New York has long since ceased to be a
matter of astonishment." Late in that decade the *Herald* estimated that seventy-five hundred houses and tenements had
to be built each year to accommodate the swelling population, quite an increase over the two thousand buildings
completed in most years of the 1840s. The *Home Journal* estimated that there were two hundred thousand buildings in
New York, three million windows and doors, one hundred
fifty thousand chimneys, and twenty-five thousand awnings
or lampposts.

Few New Yorkers in 1857 believed their prosperity imper-
iled. Houses were in such demand that rents throughout the
city rose 15 to 30 percent; in the most prestigious locations
the increase was up to 40 percent. Rents in business areas
had gone up just as much, and the behavior of landlords
toward their tenants changed noticeably in 1857. In earlier
years landlords had been "suave, obliging, and conciliatory
to their good tenants — they 'hope the apartment suits,'
and that the 'rent is not too high,' and the like," reported the
Herald. Now "the landlords are 'masters of the position,' and
are careful to let their tenants know as much." The builders
were particularly busy at this time, because investors de-

cided to erect business buildings, tenements, and row houses, all of them profitable enterprises. "The builders . . . have more work than they can possibly attend to," reported the *Herald,* and, accordingly, the price of vacant lots, building materials, and construction workers' wages rose to heights undreamed of.

The frenzied speculation that characterized real estate transactions now informed most business activities. "Business is pushed to its furthest limits," warned the *Herald.* "The mania for sudden success pervades every class." The *Daily Tribune* blamed "hazardous and sterile speculation" on members of the younger generation; they "despise the plodding ways and patient gains of their laborious, frugal sires, and rush to the cities or mines, to cards or corner lots, in quest of sudden and enormous wealth."

The boom ended when the New York–based Ohio Life and Mutual Trust Company went bankrupt on August 24, 1857, and dragged down several Wall Street brokers to ruin. Other banks and businesses failed in the following weeks, and the Panic began to spread across the nation. On October 13, all banks in New York, except Chemical, suspended specie payments, and the railroads, which had seemed the most secure of investments, went bankrupt one after the other. The spreading calamity threatened even New York's richest men. "Were I offered Aspinwall's paper tonight with thirty days to run, or Grinnell's, or Moses Taylor's at fifty cents, I would not take it," wrote George Templeton Strong. "All confidence is lost, for the present, in the solvency of our merchant princes — and with good reason. It is probable that every one of them has been operating and gambling in stocks and railroad bonds."

Construction activity in New York virtually stopped, and even wealthy men slowed or entirely halted work on their Fifth Avenue mansions, so uncertain were they about the future and so anxious to hold on to their money. By the end of the year thirty thousand to forty thousand laborers had lost their jobs in New York alone, and mobs gathered regularly in the streets or in Tompkins Square calling for food and work. The United States Government stationed troops at the Customs House and Assay Office to guard the buildings from mob violence.

New York escaped serious violence in the months after the onset of the Panic, and by early 1858 the crisis was easing. Banks resumed specie payments on December 12, 1857, and the rash of business failures ended soon after. By March 1858, *Harper's Weekly* was justified in reporting that good times were slowly returning to the nation. Real estate values and rents in New York began to return to their former levels, though almost no buildings were finished in 1858 because so few had been started the previous fall, at the height of the Panic.

As building operations resumed in 1858, rich New Yorkers still faced the earlier problem of whether to build on Fifth Avenue past Forty-second Street. "Perhaps Fifth Avenue

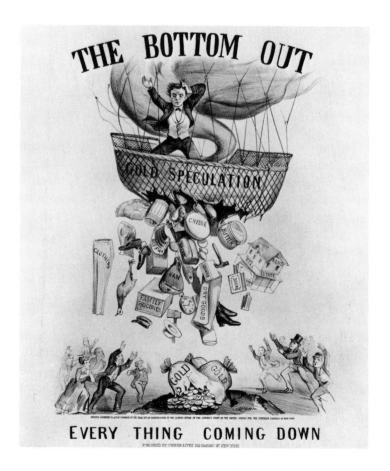

"The Bottom Out"

above Forty-second Street will command lower prices, and cease to be the special line of costly improvement," wrote Strong in 1858. The looming Croton Reservoir, which occupied the west side of Fifth Avenue between Fortieth and Forty-second streets, made a suitable boundary to the line of brownstone houses that stretched all the way from Washington Square, thought Strong. "By the time buildings have reached that latitude, I think the frontage on the Central Park will be more coveted by millionaires."

The *Herald* agreed that "things do look . . . dubious for those respectable people" thinking about living on Fifth Avenue between Forty-second Street and Central Park. "After passing 42nd Street, the first thing they did would be to run their heads against an Asylum [the Colored Home for the Aged and Indigent] on 43rd and 44th Streets; and if they ventured further on, they would plunge over head and ears into the great swash lying all along up to 47th Street; and then, with a slight lurch to the right, they would bring up against another public Institution [St. Luke's Hospital] on 51st and 52nd Streets. These things all looked bad, and some of them smelt bad."

What was true in the 1850s was unchanged in the 1860s. Manhattan north of Forty-second Street was not pleasant countryside; it was garbage dumps, shantytowns, and decrepit taverns, all punctuated by outcroppings of rock. Today's Central Park was some of the ugliest land on Manhattan, and only with thousands of men and millions of dollars did Frederick Law Olmsted and Calvert Vaux make it a thing of beauty.

One census counted over ten thousand squatters living north of Forty-second Street. The shantytowns were morasses of "poverty, misery, beggary, starvation, crimes, filth, and licentiousness," according to the *Daily Tribune*. Worst of all, except to those who lived in them, these shantytowns destroyed the value of all adjoining property. For the titillation of its genteel readers, the *Daily Tribune* described the shantytown known as "Dutch Hill," at the foot of East Forty-second Street, overlooking the East River. With 200 to 300 shacks and well over a thousand full-time residents, this shantytown merited both a name and a branch post office.

The rutted, garbage-strewn streets were crowded with the poor of "all ages . . . together with untold numbers of children, chickens, cats, dogs, and pigs." The "dwellings are not generally fashioned after those in the Fifth Avenue," observed the newspaper at its most arch, but "are quite as *outré* in their architectural designs." Each shanty had one room five or six feet tall and was "built of slabs, old boards, timber from torn-down houses, old tin roofing rolled up and spread out again," reported the *Daily Tribune*. "If the owner possesses a horse, a cow or a pig, the animal has a room as good as his owner directly alongside the dwelling." The city broke up these miserable settlements as soon as row-house development began to approach their borders.

"Dutch Hill" shantytown, Forty-second Street, near the East River, ca. 1860

Another nuisance, more stubborn than the squatters, was the livestock pens and slaughterhouses that also cursed some downtown neighborhoods. A "sickening overpowering odor" filled the streets for blocks around the yards where cattle were fattened for slaughter. When the city health wardens closed one sprawling yard at Lexington Avenue and Fifty-seventh Street, they found that the pigs ate "refuse, animal matter, such as sheeps' heads, bones, dead horses, etc." and then were sold as "country pork." The yard's owner saw nothing wrong with the diet and directed the health wardens to a yard at Broadway and Fifth-eighth Street. Here the "country pork" was eating dead rats, cats, and dogs gathered from the streets.

By the mid-1860s, fifteen thousand head of live cattle, hogs, and sheep came into Manhattan every week, all destined for the abattoirs. Families living nearby had to "endure the perpetual lowing and bleating of starving stock waiting their turn . . . at sacrifice," according to the *Daily Tribune*. The killing usually commenced around 1:00 P.M. or 2:00 P.M. in outdoor pens; between 11:00 P.M. and 5:00 A.M. the tanner arrived to carry away the hides in his cart, the bone boiler's man came for the horns, hoofs, and large bones, and the butcher removed the remains of the carcass to his shop or market stall. Nearby residents were spared these sights because of the hours, but during the afternoon slaughtering women going out for a few hours or children on their way home from school sometimes saw the killing in the open pens.

Most of the slaughterhouses were a block or two from the Hudson River so that the cattle, from New Jersey, could be quickly transported from the railroad yards and ferry stops. But the slaughterhouses on Houston Street, First Avenue, Rivington Street, and Stanton Street were some distance from the West Side depots, and the only means for getting the livestock to the East Side was the cattle drive, down the city streets. No location, not even Fifth Avenue, was spared this indignity. Not only were the hundreds of bellowing cattle and the hollering cowboys an assault to the eyes and ears, but they threatened the safety of nearby pedestrians and snarled the traffic.

Cattle drive: a cartoon

In 1850 the city forbade cattle drives south of Thirty-fourth Street in the daytime, and in the following years gradually eliminated the problem. The *Daily Tribune* was not satisfied with just stopping the cattle drives, however; it also wanted to prohibit the carrying of live animals in carts through the city streets. "Such exhibitions as we have seen of calves and sheep, with legs tied and heads hanging over end boards, rattled away through Broadway, are enough to provoke the indignation of any person who has a spark of sensibility left," wrote the newspaper in 1850. "Nay, we have seen a wagon seat tossed upon the bodies of these animals and two great boys sitting upon the board as coolly as if lolling upon a sofa, while their weight was fairly crushing the poor creatures beneath."

Another distressing sight connected with the slaughterhouses was the bone-boiling works. A few bones, such as the thighs, became toothbrush or hairbrush handles. The rest of the bones, horns, and hoofs were turned into bone-meal fertilizer, Prussian blue, and glue. In 1851 and 1852 the city closed all bone-boiling works in Manhattan, producing an unexpected consequence. The man who had the city contract to remove dead animals from the streets, William Reynolds, now had no place to dispose of these carcasses or to salvage the valuable byproducts. Obviously the removal of the animals from the streets was crucial to the health and appearance of New York. In August 1853, Reynolds cleared from the streets a "veritable farm yard": 577 horses, 69 cows, 883 dogs, 111 cats, 14 hogs, and 6 sheep. In the same month he collected 1303 tons of "butcher's offal," 277 tons of "other nuisances," and 62 tons of "refuse bones, etc." from the slaughterhouses. He also bought baskets of bones, which the poor had gathered from the streets and garbage dumps. So the city wisely leased Reynolds an island in Sheepshead Bay, miles from the city, where he could continue his essential work without offending anyone.

The city, however, did nothing to save New Yorkers living on the outskirts of town from the chaos surrounding the construction sites. From early spring to late fall, when windows were open, "sections of the city are beclouded with brick and mortar dust," reported the *Herald*, and "the music of laborious enterprise is everywhere heard, mingling the ring of the trowel with the more sullen hammer beat." The sidewalks and streets in front of construction sites were filled with dirt left over from cellar digging, piles of building materials, and construction debris. This mess knew no social boundaries. In the 1850s and 1860s, Fifth Avenue, from Thirty-fourth Street to Central Park, was filled with "mammoth piles of bricks, huge masses of stones, long lines of lumber, monster appliances for mixing mortar, paving stones, dirt carts, barrels, boxes, wheelbarrows, doors, and window frames." New Yorkers almost despaired of taking carriage rides up Fifth Avenue and into Central Park because of the swirling clouds of dust, the miserable rutted condition of the roadway, and the rubbish piles, which "almost positively blocked" the street in many spots.

The rock outcroppings, which marred much of the uptown landscape, had to be removed before streets were opened or row houses constructed. Explosions rocked the upper periphery of the city from dawn to dusk during the building season. On September 2, 1852, some rock blasting near Union Square sent a 400-pound boulder into the air and through the roof of Dr. William B. Moffatt's mansion on East Seventeenth Street. The boulder crashed its way through

floor after floor in a cloud of plaster dust until it came to a house-shaking halt between two beams in the parlor ceiling. Additional fragments from the same explosion had nearly hit two children playing nearby, and the contractor admitted that the day before "he had put a stone through Colonel Webb's door and another into a stable."

Dr. Moffatt's experience was not uncommon. Just a week earlier, Henry Haslem "discharged a blast" on West Fortieth Street that showered destruction for a block around. One piece of rock badly damaged a nearby house and struck a young women resident on the forehead, nearly killing her. "Another piece, weighing about 500 pounds, fell upon the roof of a house occupied by Mr. McDowell, tearing away everything before it, until it reached the ground floor," reported the *Herald*. "Another piece, about 700 pounds in weight, flew into the air, and coming in contact with the chimney of a small dwelling, tore it away. The devastation here ended."

Aside from all these nuisances, the gentility faced social uncertainties by living at the northern edge of the city. The *Herald* declared that some gentlemen who had built good houses beyond the established limits of Murray Hill "have since wished that they had paid more for lots and built lower downtown." This "new country [is] thinly settled and contains few of the old Knickerbocker families, few of the wealthy nabobs, distinguished merchant princes, and others of that class." More important, any street at the edge of town had many empty lots, and "you don't know how these vacant lots may be improved." The deeds for most lots near Fifth Avenue had restrictions limiting the use of the land to only "first-class improvements." No stables, tenements, shops, or small factories could be built on these lots. Some owners, reported the *Herald*, "don't mind taking the bits of restrictions in their teeth, and bidding defiance to law drivers."

Several families purchased brownstone houses uptown only to find one of the buildings forbidden by the deed restrictions being erected on the vacant lot next door, "right under the very nose of your dignity." West Thirty-fifth Street, between Fifth and Sixth avenues, for example, appeared to

A mansion next to a shack: cartoon, ca. 1868

have a splendid future in the mid-1850s. Fine brownstones and mansions, including Sarsaparilla Townsend's residence, were rising nearby on Fifth Avenue and on Thirty-fourth Street. The block's proximity to fashion proved its ruin. The residents of the mansions on the north side of West Thirty-fourth Street often owned double lots, which ran the full 200 feet through the block to the south side of West Thirty-fifth Street. Here they built their servants' quarters and stables, out of sight and smell to them but not to the residents of West Thirty-fifth Street.

Blocks other than West Thirty-fifth Street had been given over to stables of nearby mansions, both earlier and later in Manhattan's growth. East Ninth Street, from Second to Third avenues, still contains some of the carriage houses that served the homes on St. Mark's Place and Second Avenue. West Thirteenth Street, between Fifth and Sixth avenues was the location of the carriage houses belonging to the mansions along West Fourteenth Street. The residents of Fifth Avenue who did not have stables just around the corner from their homes often kept their horses and carriages just west of Sixth Avenue, the limit of the fashionable district. Several of these

243

former stables still stand between West Fourteenth and West Thirtieth streets west of Sixth Avenue.

Rich New Yorkers could avoid the cares of living at the edge of the city by paying more money for a house in a finished neighborhood; middle-class families often had no choice but to live in a partly built-up area. House prices and rents were rising faster than the wages of the heads of the households, and tenements were overwhelming former middle-class areas like Tompkins Square. The newspapers began to complain that New York was becoming a city only of the rich and the poor. Walt Whitman said that "nothing" was being built in New York "between a palatial mansion and a dilapidated hovel." In 1865 the *Times* wrote that "New York furnishes the worst place of residence of any city in America." The rents that countinghouse clerks, shop owners, teachers, and young doctors and lawyers "are compelled to pay have become so intolerably high as to trench on their daily necessities, to crowd them into smaller and smaller spaces, and drive thousands of them from the city." Housing was cheaper in suburban Brooklyn and New Jersey than in Manhattan, and an 1853 advertisement for a real estate development in the East New York area of Brooklyn typically proclaimed, "Now every family can own a home." But some middle-class families wanted to stay in Manhattan, even if it meant they had to live far beyond the established residential part of the city.

Horse-drawn "street railroads" enabled New Yorkers to live on the outskirts of town and still hold jobs four or five miles downtown around Wall Street and City Hall. The New York & Harlem Railroad, chartered in 1831, opened its first line along Fourth Avenue from Prince Street to Harlem in 1832. The first cars, which were similar to stagecoaches, were balanced on leather springs and had three compartments, each with a side door. The driver sat on top and braked the cars with a foot pedal.

Other street railroad lines began operations in the 1850s: the Sixth Avenue line in 1851, the Third Avenue line in 1853, the Eighth Avenue line in 1855, the Ninth Avenue line in 1859. Lines along First, Second, and Seventh avenues opened in the 1860s. Routes on such east-to-west streets as

Eighth, Fourteenth, and Twenty-third streets linked both sides of town and carried people getting off the Brooklyn or New Jersey ferries to the lines running along the north-to-south avenues.

The opening of the New York & Harlem Railroad spurred the growth of the East Side. Country houses and estates, which had dotted the grassy banks of the East River north of Fourteenth Street since the eighteenth century, were sold for building lots once the city growth neared them. In 1847 the *Evening Post* reported that the East Twenties around Third Avenue were "rapidly filling up with private dwellings. In many places, entire blocks are going up, and in a few years this will be one of the most thickly settled parts of the city." A few years later the Phelps family sold its estate in the low Thirties east of Second Avenue. During one sale in 1854, the Phelpses sold 150 lots on East Twenty-ninth, Thirtieth, Thirty-first, and Thirty-second streets, some for as much as $5900 on the corners of Second Avenue and others for as little as $960 on the sidestreets close to the East River.

A crowded "street railroad," 1867

By this time the stretch of Third Avenue north of Four-teenth Street was not much different from the Bowery, a mile downtown. The tenements and erstwhile private houses had grocery stores, bars, secondhand furniture stores, and cloth-ing shops on the street level and apartments on the floors above. Between Murray Hill and Harlem, Third Avenue was unbuilt in the early 1850s and was still "the exercise and trial ground of all fast trotters and pacers in the city," according to Charles Astor Bristed. "In these five miles of road there are just as many hills, not steep, but gradual, and pretty equally distributed, so that every third or quarter of a mile presents a different level." At the top and bottom of each hill the horse-men came upon a tavern and livery stable, so man and beast could be refreshed before setting out on the next portion of the ride.

Third Avenue had been a favorite with horsemen since the 1820s. The roadway was in such "excellent order," according to the *Evening Post* in 1836, that "scarce a hollow is to be found on the whole length of the road [and] carriages pass over it so swiftly, noiselessly, and easily that it seems as if the horses drew them without an effort." When the city paved Third Avenue around 1850, only the middle strip was macadamized. "The sides," reported Bristed, "are left soft earth for the benefit of the trotters, whose feet would be broken to pieces by hard pavement at their rate of going."

Third Avenue's days as a racing ground were already num-bered by the 1850s. Brick row houses for the middle class were being built on the crosstown streets from Third Avenue to the East River. Four- and five-story tenements lined First, Second, and Third avenues and, beginning in the 1860s, began to fill in the empty lots on the sidestreets. By 1860 the city had pushed as far north as Fifty-ninth Street on the East Side. In 1861 *Harper's Monthly* viewed Manhattan from a boat in the East River and noted that around Fifty-seventh Street the shoreline is "exchanging the metropolitan aspect of the city . . . for something like its ancient rocky and wooded look. The streets are fast finding their inexorable way, however, to the river in this neighborhood, as they had done below."

One particularly handsome spot on the East Side was Beekman Place, the two-block-long street that runs along the bluff of the East River between East Forty-ninth and East Fifty-first streets. In 1860 the *Herald* described it as "desirable . . . for residences." George Templeton Strong, after one of his walks through the city, in 1871, found Beekman Place "unlike any other part of the city . . . The outlook over the East River is nice and includes a clear view of the penitentiary, the smallpox hospital, and the other palaces of Blackwell's Island." (Blackwell's was later renamed Welfare Island, and, after we became self-conscious, was changed to Roosevelt Island.) Strong thought Beekman Place's "brownstone houses look very reputable," but he noted that they were "separated from civilization by a vast tract of tenement rookeries and whiskey mills, and streets that absolutely crawl with poor little slatternly pretty children." The vast tract was the area between Beekman Place and the respectability of Madison and Fifth avenues.

Although the Beekman family had sold its estate years earlier, its former country home, built in 1763, still stood on East Fifty-first Street, east of First Avenue. It was the strangest sight in the neighborhood. Not only was it a country house with no surrounding countryside, but it stood alone on a rocky mount twenty feet above the street, which had been cut through the outcropping twenty years before. The house was torn down in 1874.

The least attractive street in the East Forties and Fifties was Park Avenue, strange though that may seem to us now. Open railroad tracks and switching yards ran down the middle of Park Avenue north of Forty-second Street, and factories, garbage dumps, and stockyards lined its desolate-looking sidewalks. The F. & M. Schaefer brewery stood on Park Avenue between Fiftieth and Fifty-first streets, a site now occupied by St. Bartholomew's Church. The block bounded by Park Avenue, East Forty-ninth Street, Lexington Avenue, and East Fiftieth Street was a potter's field, which was broken up during the Civil War for the construction of the Women's Hospital. The Waldorf-Astoria Hotel now occupies the site.

The West Side grew as rapidly as the East Side. Chelsea

248

was not even half built up by 1850, but builders were already erecting rows of frame and brick dwellings beyond Forty-second Street. In 1847 a builder completed a row of modest frame houses on West Fortieth Street between Sixth Avenue and Broadway. The rent was $130 a year. In 1850 Sanford, Porter & Stryker built a similar row of eight houses on West Fifty-second Street, between Tenth and Eleventh avenues. Their advertisement in the *Sun* read:

To Let — Eight entirely new, two story cottages, piazzas, and verandah fronts, courtyards thirty-five feet deep, filled with elegant forest trees . . . Each house contains four bedrooms, two parlors, and kitchen, and hard-finished walls with cornice and center piece . . . Possession given immediately; terms very moderate.

Stryker's Cottages, West Fifty-second Street

Working-class New Yorkers gladly moved into Stryker's cottages, even though the street railroads were not yet running on Sixth or Eighth avenues. The Hudson River Railroad and stagecoach lines were the only public transportation downtown.

In 1851 William B. Astor began construction of 200 brownstone row houses, three to five stories tall, on West Forty-fourth, Forty-fifth, Forty-sixth, and Forty-seventh streets, between Broadway and Ninth Avenue. Contractors were clearing away the rocky outcroppings on the line of Sixth Avenue so that the street could be opened north of West Forty-fourth Street. As they opened and graded each block of Sixth Avenue, builders began to erect tenements and row houses there and around the corners on the sidestreets. Even Tenth and Eleventh avenues were thought to be respectable residential addresses, and were built up past Forty-second Street by the mid-1850s.

Another attraction of the West Side, besides its moderately priced housing, was the character of the worthies who lived there. In 1860 the *Herald* described the West Side as having "a superior class of residents than those on the East Side of town." *Leslie's Illustrated* wrote that the West Side had "a good English or rather American population." The city's acquisition of land for Central Park in 1856 for $5.5 million also encouraged New Yorkers to move into the West Forties and Fifties.

The enthusiasm over Central Park, in fact, led some New Yorkers to believe that the West Fifties around Seventh and Eighth avenues might replace Fifth Avenue as the address with the most cachet. This area was well west of the Sixth Avenue boundary of residential fashion and still "very high uptown," admitted the *Herald*, "but the aristocracy . . . must ultimately come to the conclusion that westward the empire runs." The land was elevated, which was considered healthful, and was served by street railroad lines running downtown, which was convenient. By 1860 Seventh Avenue was "very wide and well paved" and the site of "a number of fine edifices . . . in course of erection, under the pressure of the Central Park excitement." Building lots there commanded "prices which would have seemed fabulous a few years ago," noted the *Herald*.

To some New Yorkers, Central Park was nothing more than the city's attempt to guide real estate development in their city. Work on the park, begun in 1857 partly to give work to the unemployed, quickly attracted speculators into the West Forties and Fifties. What was more important, Central Park saved Manhattan Island from becoming one unbroken mass of buildings. The pleasures of a walk along the East and Hudson rivers, which New Yorkers had enjoyed in the early nineteenth century, vanished as shipping, warehouses, and factories took over almost the whole waterfront. With the exception of a few small parks, like Washington Square or Madison Square, buildings packed Manhattan from river to river. North of Madison Square, there were no comparable small squares of greenery to relieve the density of building.

Although the poor and the working class had no alternative to living packed in tenements, "even the wealthy crowd their mansions together within the limits of the bustling city that they may share in the life and breathless whirl of business and pleasure that center in its narrow area," reported the *Herald*. A mansion standing on handsomely planted grounds, or a row house with one or two adjacent lots kept empty for a garden, was "a phenomenon in an American city," wrote Bristed. "A man will sip Cordon Bleu or Latour every day, or buy two hundred dollar handkerchiefs for his wife, or pay a fancy price for a fast trotter; but to lose the interest on a town lot by making a garden of it, is an extravagance not to be thought of."

Instead, New Yorkers spent their money making their homes impressive. The Italianate row houses had lofty black walnut or mahogany front doors, plate-glass windows, elaborately carved ornamentation around the windows and doors, and a boldly protruding cornice supported on brackets. These houses were a full five stories tall, even though the top floor was "as empty as a ballroom, save once a week, when a clothes line may perchance be run through it," noted the *Herald*. The ceilings, which were sometimes sixteen or eighteen feet high in the parlors, made these row houses taller still. "Every man who builds a new house," observed the *Daily Tribune*, "seems ambitious to have the roof a foot or

252

two higher, the marble steps a few inches broader, or the cornice and entablature a little richer than his neighbors'."

The higher the houses, the more they crowded the narrow crosstown streets and blocked the sun from the pavement. "Nothing can be further removed from genuine aristocracy than the people who buy and occupy these houses," declared the *Herald.* "Bah! Is such a street, can such a street, be aristocratic? No, never! It is just fit for what, like Bleecker and other once fashionable streets, it ultimately will be — boarding and other houses, fashionable tenement houses, on an extravagant scale." A truly stylish and handsome street, thought the *Herald,* should have yards with trees and flowers around the houses. "Let the houses stand well back from the noise and dust of the street, with plenty of space between the houses. Build up a street in this style, and you have doomed it to everlasting gentility. It is fit for nothing else. The houses are not big enough for boarding houses, hotels, etc. In short, there is so much of the value to the land, and so little comparatively in the house proper, that nobody but a man of wealth is able to own and occupy it."

The continuing desirability of St. John's Park, even though it was a mile south of Union Square, showed the wisdom of the *Herald*'s remarks. The few spots that developed in a *rus in urbs* manner in the 1850s and 1860s, such as Gramercy Park or Park Avenue in Murray Hill, were as attractive to New Yorkers then as they are today. But land in such sections of Manhattan was simply too expensive for anyone but the richest man to build on it a house surrounded by a beautifully planted yard. The building lot was nearly half the cost of a house on Fifth Avenue in Murray Hill.

New Yorkers did soften the canyonlike character of the streets by planting shrubs and flowers in the space between the sidewalk fence and the ground-floor windows. A family might grow wisteria up the front of its home on guide wires, which extended to the cornice; another would plant a tree near the curb. (The trees most popular for this purpose were the ailanthus and silver maple.) Other families moved into the so-called cottage rows, which sat twenty to thirty feet back from the street on handsomely planted front yards. The two cottage rows that are still remembered by many were

London Terrace, a severe Greek Revival row along the entire north side of West Twenty-third Street, from Ninth to Tenth avenues, demolished in the 1920s for the apartment buildings by that name, and the Rhinelander Gardens, the row of red brick houses with handsome Gothic Revival cast-iron porches rising to the roofline, at 102–116 West Eleventh Street. The Gardens were torn down in 1955 to make way for Public School 41.

These cottages were a startling sight in the brownstone-lined streets north of Fourteenth Street. The *Herald* thought no other city had such "wonderful uniformity"; almost all the houses were built by speculators, who adopted a standard architectural design and interior layout that made the buildings easy to sell at a quick profit.

The interior decoration of the uptown brownstones was as unvarying as the façades and showed how unimaginative some New Yorkers were in choosing their surroundings. The homes of the prosperous in the 1870s seemed to *Appleton's Magazine* "painfully lacking in individuality." Thirty years earlier Nathaniel Parker Willis had declared that

the twenty thousand drawing rooms of New York are all stereotyped copies, of one out of three or four styles — the style dependent only on the degree of expensiveness. The proprietor of almost any house in New York might wake up in thousands of other houses, and not recognize for a half hour, that he was not at home. He would sit on just such a sofa in just such a recess — see a piano just so placed — just as many chairs identically in the same position [and see] nothing . . . but perhaps a little difference in the figure on the carpet . . . or the want of a spot on the wall where his head leans in napping after dinner.

The uptown houses were "built on a plan to suit everyone and all, and no one in particular."

In 1860 New Yorkers began to worry that the prosperity that paid for all these luxuries might vanish if the South seceded from the Union, precipitating civil war. A war would give Southern merchants license to repudiate their debts to Northern businessmen, and trade would be ruined for years. What made the prospect of this financial calamity all the more upsetting was that New York had never been so

A parlor filled with typically elaborate furniture, 1854

prosperous as it was in 1860. That year more than one third of the nation's exports and more than two thirds of its imports, as computed by goods' values, passed through the city. It imported more goods in 1860 than had the entire country just ten years earlier. This pre-eminence in trade had long ago attracted the nation's leading banks and insurance companies to New York, and by 1860 the city was not only the financial center of the nation, but was home to the main offices of fast-growing corporations. New York was also becoming an important manufacturing center; its swelling immigrant population supplied cheap labor and its rail and water transport lines offered quick access both to raw materials and to markets for the finished goods. The value of those goods was $105 million in 1850 and $160 million in 1860.

The onset of the Civil War did bring disaster to New York's businessmen. As had been feared, the Southern merchants refused to pay $200 million in debts to New York firms, and the South's privateers, like the *Alabama,* attacked the city's merchant ships on the seas. Merchant houses in New York briefly held up payments, and many firms went bankrupt. New York's banks suspended specie payments for a short time at the end of 1861. "The fabric of New York's mercantile prosperity," declared the *Daily Tribune,* "lies in ruins beneath which ten thousand fortunes are buried . . . Last Fall, the merchant was a capitalist; today he is a bankrupt."

Although some traditional trade and banking activity had disappeared, New York's businessmen soon discovered that new, even more profitable opportunities existed in financing the war and outfitting the Union army. A. T. Stewart, realizing that the war was inevitable, had, just before the outbreak of hostilities, contracted to buy nearly all the blankets and uniform cloth to be manufactured in the country for the next few months. The United States Government had no choice but to approach Stewart for most of the goods necessary to clothe its army.

The financial distress of 1861 had disappeared by 1862 and soon the city was busier than ever. The Broadway stores were so jammed with customers, the fashionable restaurants so crowded, and the carriage drives in Central Park filled with so many stylish equipages that the *Times* repeatedly warned New Yorkers that their extravagance was diverting money from the Union cause. The enormous profits of the hotels was another surprise. Before the Civil War, New York hotel managers had assumed that much of their business depended on the travels of Southern planters. "There has probably been hardly a Southern planter seen in the North for the last two years," observed the *Times* in 1863, "yet we believe the hotels are at present fairly patronized. There are few of them which do not turn away every day nearly as many guests as they receive."

The building trades did not share in this boom. Whereas several thousand single-family houses were completed almost every year in the 1850s, that figure fell to 467 in 1861, 539 in 1862, 1247 in 1863, 773 in 1864, and 1190 in 1865. Building operations had collapsed in 1861 because of the financial panic in New York and the uncertainty over the outcome of the war. Houses were in brisk demand in 1863, but construction was held back by ongoing doubts in the currency market, the rise in the price of building materials, and the shortage of workmen, who were in the army or were working in war-related industries.

Rents for all kinds of housing had risen because the demand was far greater than the supply. Workingmen came to New York from across the country in hopes of good jobs along the bustling waterfront, in the dry goods trade, or at one of the factories. Businessmen came to New York from Southern or Western states to make more money or perhaps spend some of what they had made at home. Many West Indian, Mexican, and South American families, said the *Times*, were living temporarily in New York, "attracted by the advantage of doubling a gold income by converting it into currency, thereby enabling them to enjoy the luxuries of the metropolis at the cheap rate." Handsome brownstones on Fifth and Madison avenues, which had rented for $2000 to $3000 before the Civil War, fetched double that figure by 1865. Working-class families faced the same steep rise in rents. Houses that had rented for $500 to $700 in 1860 now went for $700 to $1000, and the tenants, reported the *Times*, "have to go a-begging to get them for that."

In spite of the need for housing, building activity during early 1865 stayed at the depressed war-time levels. But then wages and the price of materials began to decline, and the number of houses completed each year soon increased to prewar levels. Some 1190 houses were completed in 1865, 1670 in 1866, and 2000 in 1867.

New Yorkers no longer worried where the rich would live, once Fifth Avenue in Murray Hill was built up. After the Civil War, the grandest mansions and row houses were built on Fifth Avenue north of Forty-second Street. Building lots on Fifth Avenue around Forty-eighth and Forty-ninth streets, which had sold for approximately $4000 in the mid-1850s, now cost $20,000. The houses rising on this land cost $75,000 to $125,000, and were sold as quickly as the builders could finish them. The orphanages, hog pens, and shanties, which had dismayed New Yorkers ten years earlier, were now disappearing one by one. Force of habit, the insatiable

Fifth Avenue: view north from Forty-second Street, ca. 1882

demand for fine homes at fashionable addresses, and the continuing work on Central Park assured Fifth Avenue's desirability past Forty-second Street.

New Yorkers could also point to Mrs. Mary Mason Jones' white marble mansion, complete with Parisian-style mansard roof, at the northeast corner of Fifth Avenue and Fifty-seventh Street. Although some New Yorkers thought Mrs. Jones a bit eccentric, they could not deny her wealth and near-legendary social position. In 1869 she left her Waverly Place home of several decades for the Fifty-seventh Street house, where her neighbors included the unfinished St. Patrick's Cathedral, Madame Restell, and shantytowns.

Mrs. Jones also startled New York by locating her bedroom on the ground floor and the formal reception rooms upstairs. Edith Wharton, her niece, explained the reasons for this unusual arrangement in *House of Mirth*, in which Mrs. Jones is the model for Mrs. Manson Mingott.

The immense accretion of flesh which had descended on her in middle life like a flood of lava on a doomed city had changed her from a plump active little woman with a neatly-turned foot and ankle into something as vast and august as a natural phenomenon. She had accepted this submergence as philosophically as all her other trials [but] the burden of Mrs. Manson Mingott's flesh had long since made it impossible for her to go up and down stairs, and with characteristic independence she had made her reception rooms upstairs and established herself (in flagrant violation of all the New York proprieties) on the ground floor of her house; so that, as you sat in her sitting-room window with her, you caught (through a door that was always open, and a looped-back yellow damask portierre) the unexpected vista of a bedroom with a huge low bed upholstered like a sofa, and a toilet-table with frivolous lace flounces and a gilt-trimmed mirror.

Mary Mason Jones had an unshakable faith in New York's northward growth.

It was her habit to sit in a window of her sitting room on the ground floor, as if watching calmly for life and fashion to flow northward to her solitary doors. She seemed in no hurry to have them come, for her patience was equalled by her confidence. She was sure that presently the hoardings,

*Madison Avenue: view
north from Fifty-fifth
Street, ca. 1870*

the quarries, the one-time saloons, the wooden greenhouses in ragged gardens, and the rocks from which goats surveyed the scene, would vanish before the advance of residences as stately as her own — perhaps (for she was an impartial woman) even statelier; and that the cobblestones over which the old clattering omnibuses bumped would be replaced by smooth asphalt, such as people reported having seen in Paris.

Perhaps the far-sighted Mrs. Jones was surprised by the even more daring plans other New Yorkers had for their booming city. In 1865 Hiram Cranston, proprietor of the smart New York Hotel, purchased the block bounded by Fifth Avenue, East Fifty-ninth Street, Madison Avenue, and East Sixtieth Street so that he could build an enormous hotel at the entrance to Central Park. A year later the *Daily Tribune* declared: "Gentlemen of the Legislature! Give us both the Underground and the Aerial Railway!" The newspaper recognized that these would enable working- and middle-class New Yorkers to live in reasonably priced homes on the east and west sides of Central Park. All the city's papers were predicting that it would not be long before trade would overwhelm Union Square and Murray Hill and that the finest mansions, unlike any New York had ever seen, would soon rise on Fifth Avenue as it ran along the edge of Central Park, north of Fifty-ninth Street.

13

Hiram Cranston never built his projected
hotel on Fifth Avenue opposite Grand Army Plaza, and the
construction of the elevated railroads and the growth of Manhattan on both sides of Central Park were still years in the
future. But in the booming post–Civil War years New
Yorkers did take steps that would, in time, transform their
city into a modern metropolis. These developments did not
occur in the unpaved, largely empty streets of upper Manhattan but rather in the oldest part of the city, downtown on
Wall Street and around Trinity Church.

In 1872 work began on the ten-story Western Union building, at the northwest corner of Broadway and Dey Street, and
the eleven-story *Tribune* building, at the northeast corner of
Nassau and Spruce streets. George Templeton Strong
thought that the Western Union building was a "hideous,
top-heavy . . . huge brick and granite nightmare." True, it
was richly ornamented and heavily massed but, architecturally, was no worse than many other buildings of the
early 1870s. What troubled Strong, although he did not say
so specifically, was its height. It was several stories taller
than any other building in New York at the time. Twenty
years later architectual critics pointed out that the construction of the Western Union and *Tribune* buildings was the
beginning of "the development of the high modern office
building."

These buildings were the skyscrapers of their day and,
among a people who often defined their city through its

buildings, reflected New York's ever-increasing financial might. In 1870 its imports and exports were valued at $569,337,000. New York produced more manufactured goods than any other city in America. It had fifty-six national banks with $73 million capital and thirty-six savings banks with $106 million in deposits. The assessed value of real estate in Manhattan was $762,134,350, and the value of personal property was estimated at $305,292,699.

This wealth provided the capital to erect huge buildings, and the growing need for offices filled them with rent-paying tenants. But the buildings could not have risen to such daring heights had not technology considerately produced the

Western Union Building

elevator. As early as the 1830s New York merchants had used simple steam-powered hoists to haul merchandise from one floor to another. The first building with passenger elevators was the Fifth Avenue Hotel, which opened at Fifth Avenue and Twenty-third Street in 1859. The city's first office building with elevators was the Equitable Life Assurance Company Building, completed in 1870 at 120 Broadway. The elevators, however, did not appreciably affect the building's design; it was just five stories tall. The Western Union and *Tribune* buildings, begun a few years later, were the first to take advantage of the possibilities of height offered by the new device.

A choice location for offices was Nassau Street, described by Henri Junius Browne as "crooked, contracted, unclean, with high houses and low houses, marble palaces and dingy frames." Offices were in such demand here that the buildings had become a jumble of "back offices and upper stories and creaking stairways and cobwebby corners and dingy crannies and undreamed-of lofts and out-of-the-way places generally."

Wall Street, however, was the busiest and best-known downtown street. Since the early years of the nineteenth century Wall Street, it will be remembered, had been the site of New York banks and insurance companies, as well as of the Merchants Exchange and Customs House. But it was the New York Stock Exchange and the fortunes made there that spread "the Street's" reputation as America's financial center across America.

Although the New York Stock Exchange was a market for corporate securities, it was better known by the 1860s for the "greatest gambling in the Republic," according to Henri Junius Browne. "No one asks nor expects favors. All stratagems are deemed fair in Wall Street. The only crime there is to be 'short' or 'crippled.'" Speculation had been part of the operations of the stock exchange long before the post–Civil War years. In 1835 and again in 1844 Philip Hone complained about "gambling" on the stock exchange. Occasionally stocks doubled and quadrupled in value only to fall back to their original levels a week later, after the speculators had taken their profit. By the 1860s questionable maneuvers such

*Nassau Street: view north
from Wall Street*

as this were no longer an isolated outrage but an accepted risk in playing the market.

Perhaps the favorite ploy of operators like Leonard Jerome, Daniel Drew, and Cornelius Vanderbilt was setting up a "corner" in the market. One speculator or a group would decide to push up the value of one stock. People willing to deliver thousands of shares in thirty days, usually at a slight advance over the current price, would be lined up, at which point the speculators would buy up, secretly, most of the selected stock. The men who had agreed to deliver the stock in thirty days did not usually own the shares, and as the delivery date neared they went into the market to purchase the stock so that they could fulfill their agreement. Finding the stock in short supply, they quickly tried to purchase some, and the law of supply and demand sent the price up, sometimes as

Wall Street, 1864

much as 30 or 40 percent. Now the speculators who set up the corner sold their shares. By gambling $5 million, much of it on margin, shrewd operators could make $1 million to $2 million from a successful corner.

The volume in the stock market was rising so rapidly that the Stock Exchange building, at 10–12 Broad Street, which had been completed only in 1865, was enlarged in 1870 and again in 1881. The board room now was 63 feet wide and 138 feet long, but still was not big enough, and the building was enlarged again in 1887. It was demolished in 1901, and the present New York Stock Exchange building opened in 1903 on the same site.

As the ranks of downtown office workers increased in the mid-nineteenth century so did the number of restaurants catering almost exclusively to businessmen. In the early years of the nineteenth century, most men returned home for their midday meal. By the 1850s and 1860s, the city was so large and time so precious that men began to eat lunch in a restaurant near their office. Nearly three quarters of the restaurants south of Canal Street, calculated Henri Junius Browne, survived on the lunch trade and closed once the business day was over.

Although a few downtown restaurants, like Delmonico's, offered leisurely and elegant lunches and dinners, most meals were served and eaten "with the haste of Americans intensified," according to Browne. From noon to three, these restaurants were "one continuous roar. The clatter of plates and knives, the slamming of doors, the talking and giving of orders by the customers, the bellowing of waiters are mingled in wild chaos. The solid wonder is how anyone gets anything; how the waiters understand anything; how anything is paid for, or expected to be paid for." Despite the confusion, New Yorkers thought that the food was good and the prices reasonable. Some of the favorite restaurants were Bode's, on Water Street near Wall Street; Gosling's, on Nassau Street near Maiden Lane; Nash and Fuller's, on Park Row; and Rudolph's, on Broadway near Cortlandt Street.

Businessmen in a hurry ate in stand-up counter joints. "A long counter is crowded with men, either standing elbow to elbow, or perched on stools, using knives, and forks, and

269

spoons; talking with their mouths full; gesticulating with their heads, and arms, and bodies," wrote Browne. Some men ate their meals and left the counter in five minutes. "The hungry are constantly satisfied — constantly going; but others, as hungry, as feverish, as garrulous, as energetic as they, are always coming to supply their places, and continue the chaos of confusion as before." There were even "a number of neat and cleanly coffee saloons," open twenty-four hours a day, for the fifty thousand men who worked downtown at night.

Because all available space in good locations produced rent from offices, shops, or restaurants, downtown land prices were high. The land under each of the banks on Wall Street cost as much as the three- and four-story building itself. In 1858 the Bank of New York spent $150,000 on its new building, at the northwest corner of Wall and William streets. The 40-by-130-foot lot, however, was worth $200,000.

In the 1850s many banks along Wall Street and lower Broadway replaced their Greek temple–style buildings with Italianate brownstone or marble edifices, which they apparently thought more elegant. The new buildings were up-to-date and included such conveniences as central heating and running water, but, because they had no elevators, were not much taller than the ones they replaced. As six- and seven-story buildings with elevators became the norm rather than the exception in the 1870s, the price of land in the most desirable locations increased to a level commensurate with the revenue generated by the additional floors of offices. It now made economic sense to tear down handsome buildings of the 1850s and 1860s that were only four or five stories tall.

One of the first office buildings erected as such was the Trinity Building at 111 Broadway, immediately north of Trinity Church and its graveyard. The New England Hotel and an old sugar house, built in 1751 and used as a prison during the Revolutionary War, had occupied the site. When the Trinity Building was completed in 1853, the *Daily Tribune* called it "a noble monument indeed to the growth of our commerce, the energy of our American merchants, and the prosperity of our country." The Trinity Building was enormous for its time: five stories tall, 44 feet wide, and 262 feet

Trinity Building

271

deep. Nearly 23,000 cartloads of dirt were removed when the cellar was dug; the foundation had 16,000 cubic feet of concrete; the walls included 26,500 cubic feet of stone and 123,457 cubic feet of brick. The interior had 207,000 square feet of plastering (about five acres), 87,000 square feet of flooring, one and a half miles of gas pipe, and two miles of steam pipe for heating. For all its vastness, the Trinity Building, designed by Richard Upjohn, who had designed Trinity Church, was not considered an architectural success. Critics complained that the façade was too simple and that brownstone or red brick should have been used instead of yellow brick.

The few office buildings erected on or near Wall Street in the 1850s and 1860s did not come close to meeting the demand for space by lawyers, brokers, and corporations. So after the Civil War, the twenty- and thirty-year-old counting-house buildings on Broad and Pearl streets were one by one converted into offices. Ever since the wholesale dry goods trade moved to Park Place and its environs in the late 1850s, the tenants of the buildings in the area had been small struggling wholesale firms, which paid one-third to one-half the rents the landlords had received in the 1840s and early 1850s. The influx of lawyers and brokers into the old counting-houses halted the slow decline of Broad and Pearl streets and made these buildings some of the most valuable property in the city.

Many downtown landmarks were destroyed or substantially altered after the Civil War. In 1868 workmen demolished St. George's Chapel, built in 1749, at Beekman and Cliff streets. "At present the graves of Revolutionary heroes serve as a depository for ashes and rubbish," reported the *World*. "Vessels are emptied daily from the windows adjoining, on places where a hundred years ago, was carved the sacred words never to be effaced, 'Requiescat in pace.' " The property, which Colonel Beekman had bought for £500 back in 1748, was now worth half a million dollars.

A year later, the New York Hospital, on the west side of Broadway between Duane and Worth streets, was torn down. The original hospital building had been started in 1775 but was nearly destroyed by fire just before its completion. It was rebuilt the next year but was taken over by the British Army as a hospital and barracks during its occupation of New York. The hospital did not receive its first civilian patients until 1791. Its grounds occupied two blocks along Broadway, and when the buildings were demolished Thomas Street was extended through the former property and wholesale dry goods warehouses rose on the site. The New York Hospital moved to the grounds of the former Herman Thorn mansion, running from West Fifteenth to West Sixteenth streets, just west of Fifth Avenue.

Another relic of eighteenth-century New York, the Walton house, still stood at 326 Pearl Street. Once the old mansion, built in 1754, was turned into a boardinghouse in the 1830s, it rapidly became nothing "but a ruin," according to John Austin Stevens in 1867.

One inscription — the Old Walton House — coarsely painted in dingy white on its muddy red walls, arrests the eye of the passing stranger . . . Its pitched tilings have given place to flat roof; its balustrades are seen no more; its portico and columns, its carvings and hatchments, even its doorways, are gone. The broad halls and spacious chambers where the courtly aristocracy of the Province was wont to meet in gay and joyous throng, have been broken into small rooms which now serve as petty shops for tailors and cobblers, or the humble abode of seamen.

The Walton house was demolished in 1881.

That same year the federal government sold the Middle Dutch Church on Nassau Street, which had been used as the Post Office since 1844, to the Mutual Life Insurance Company for $650,000. Less than a month later Mutual Life demolished the old church, built in 1727–1731, and erected an office building on the site. A year later New York lost yet another pre–Revolutionary War landmark, the Kennedy mansion at 1 Broadway. Cyrus W. Field purchased the old house, which was the Washington Hotel by then, along with the land stretching to Greenwich Street, and put up the Washington Building.

But eighteenth-century buildings were not the only landmarks to be torn down as lower Manhattan was rebuilt with office buildings in the 1880s and 1890s. In 1888 the *Times* building, which had occupied the site of the old Brick Presbyterian Church since 1857, was replaced by another, much taller building for the same newspaper.

In the midst of this swirling change, some things remained solidly in place in lower Manhattan. The Astor House still stood on Broadway, just a block north of St. Paul's Chapel. In 1853 *Putnam's Monthly* stated that the Astor House would be one of the city's best-known and most respectable hotels for the next fifty years. That prediction was on the mark; because of the Astor House's central location, the careful management, and the efforts to keep the hotel mechanically up-to-date, it survived. In 1868 it closed, but only temporarily. Elevators were installed, the rooms redecorated, and the old attic was replaced with a full fifth floor. In the 1870s James McCabe wrote that though the Astor House was too far downtown to be fashionable, "it is admirably located for merchants and others who have business in the lower part of the city, and to whom time is of value. A few old-time folks, who knew the house in its palmy days, still stop there."

The section of Broadway opposite the Astor House was still jammed with traffic in the post–Civil War decades. Here the omnibus and street railroad lines from the Brooklyn and New Jersey ferry slips joined the lines running north and south. Broadway merchants worried that the peril involved in crossing the street discouraged people from visiting their shops. So in 1866, at the urging of Genin, the hatter, a cast-iron footbridge was built across Broadway at Fulton Street, just below St. Paul's Chapel, at the cost of $14,000. A footbridge had been suggested for this intersection since 1852. No one, however, seemed to like the bridge once it was completed, particularly the long of flight of stairs at each end. Another hatter, Knox, and several merchants on his side of Broadway complained that it blocked the sun from their shops. The bridge was torn down in 1868.

The old A. T. Stewart department store still stood at Broadway and Chambers Street. The fashionable shopping district had moved up Broadway so quickly in the 1850s that Stewart had opened a new department store in 1859 at Broadway and Ninth Street. The Chambers Street store became his whole-

*Broadway Bridge at
111 Broadway, 1864*

sale offices, which were more profitable than his retail store. After Stewart's death in 1876, the marble store on Chambers Street became an office building and later the New York *Sun* building. The structure stands today, largely forgotten in the bustling City Hall district, its original architectural dignity assaulted but not ruined by the several stories added in the late nineteenth century.

Trinity Church was one of the few buildings downtown to remain unchanged over the years. Just by surviving, Trinity Church became a reference point by which to measure the changes that had taken place in lower Manhattan since its completion in 1846. At that time, Trinity Church visually dominated the four- and five-story buildings around the Broadway and Wall Street intersection and its spire was taller than any other object nearby.

By the 1860s the medieval-looking brownstone church, with its old graveyard, was already an anachronism on Broadway and Wall Street, crowded with hurrying countinghouse clerks and stock speculators. Trinity Church and the "thick rows of gravestones, all crumbling and stained with age . . . stare solemnly down into Wall Street," observed James McCabe, "and offer a bitter commentary upon the struggles and anxieties of the money kings."

The ten-story Western Union building and the eleven-story *Tribune* building were the first visual challenge to Trinity Church and its spire. But they stood virtually alone in the 1870s, despite the financial advantages accruing to the tall buildings that possessed floor space. Another depression swept America in 1873, and construction work in New York slowed down, as it had in earlier panics. Only 6916 buildings, worth $89,099,913, were begun between 1873 and 1877. The figures for the 1868–1872 period were 11,223 buildings, valued at $180,008,999, and, for the years 1878 to 1882, 11,248 buildings at a cost of $155,086,823.

Real estate values likewise declined for the duration of the Panic. First-class brownstones in good locations, which had cost at least $85,000 in 1873, could be purchased three years later for $60,000. Property values decreased because of a 30 percent drop in wages, the high price of building materials, and the soaring cost of lots.

Clustered skyscrapers, 1881

Once fortunes began to rise, in 1878 and 1879, downtown office buildings also began to rise, but none was taller than ten or eleven stories because exterior and interior stone or brick walls were all that supported the structures. The cost of this traditional form of construction and the valuable rental space lost to load-bearing walls precluded the erection of anything higher. The introduction of steel skeletons to hold up the walls of a structure permitted builders to break through the ten- or eleven-story limit and send up true skyscrapers.

The first building in New York with a steel skeleton was the eleven-story Tower Building, completed in 1889 at 50 Broadway. New Yorkers doubted that a building so tall yet so narrow was structurally sound. To demonstrate his confidence and allay all fears, Bradford L. Gilbert, the architect, rented the top-floor offices himself.

After the completion of the Tower Building, architects

277

began to use the steel skeletons to push buildings to new and startling heights. In 1890 the New York *World* moved into its sixteen-story, 309-foot building on Park Row at Frankfort Street, opposite City Hall. Soon after the building's opening, one visitor reportedly got off the elevator on the top floor and, in a loud voice, asked "Is God in?"

New York had entered the "age of skyscrapers," according to *Harper's Weekly*. In 1894 it published photographs of downtown Manhattan taken from Brooklyn Heights and the Hudson River. "We are getting to be more accustomed to lofty structures, and so conventional ideas, born of what we are accustomed to look at, are being gradually modified." Two years later the New York *Journal* published a panoramic drawing of the lower part of the island. The drawing, by Charles Graham, was entitled *The Skyline of New York*, and the word *skyline* caught on immediately. A year later, Montgomery Schuyler, the architectural critic, wrote in *Harper's Weekly* that few of the skyscrapers were architecturally distinguished in themselves but "it is in the aggregation that the immense impressiveness lies. It is not an architectural vision, but it does, most tremendously, 'look like business.'"

The steel skeleton, which enabled office buildings to become skyscrapers, was just one of the technological advances of the 1880s that dramatically changed the appearance of lower Manhattan. The 1880s were, in fact, much like the 1840s, when improving technology made life for most New Yorkers easier and more pleasant than it had been before. Alexander Graham Bell demonstrated his "speaking telephone" in New York for the first time in 1877, and the Bell Company opened its first exchange at 82 Nassau Street in 1879. Subscribers were billed $60 a year for service, and the first telephone directory was a card with 252 names.

Initially, businessmen and shops were the most numerous subscribers. By the early 1890s there were already nine thousand telephone users in New York. About 120,000 calls were made each day, nearly 99 percent of them from 8:00 A.M. to 6:00 P.M. Many subscribers averaged 60 to 70 calls a day; some made as many as 130.

Another dramatic change occurred in 1882, when Thomas

Edison produced electricity at his generating plant at 257 Pearl Street. Originally, Edison served the area bounded by Nassau, Pearl, Spruce, and Wall streets, but electricity was soon available to the rest of Manhattan.

The telephone, telegraph, and electric wires, unfortunately, ruined the appearance of lower Manhattan. By 1880 the utility poles on Broadway near Trinity Church had fifteen horizontal arms, each carrying over a dozen wires. Some telephone poles carried no less than fifty cross arms. The wires, aside from being unsightly, were dangerous. They often broke in storms, disrupting service, and the ones carrying electricity threatened life and snarled traffic. In 1884 the city passed a law requiring all telephone, telegraph, and electric wires to be buried underground, and the first conduits were dug beneath the streets in 1886. The terrible damage and service disruption caused by the Blizzard of 1888 speeded up the burial of utility wires, and a few years later New York streets were generally free of this short-lived visual horror.

Public transportation improved substantially in the decades following the Civil War. The traffic in lower Manhattan was getting worse every year because more and more omnibuses, wagons, and carriages poured into the narrow streets as the volume of business downtown increased. In the 1860s George Templeton Strong's ride from his Gramercy Park home to his office on lower Broadway often took an hour or more. The horse-drawn street cars, which had been introduced in the 1850s, did no better than the old-fashioned omnibuses, because wagons and carriages often blocked the tracks on which they ran.

Beginning in the mid-nineteenth century, politicians and businessmen regularly suggested that the major north-to-south streets be widened to accommodate more traffic. But any modest gain in roadway space was at the expense of the already narrow and pedestrian-filled sidewalks. Other people thought that the opening of another north-to-south artery along the central spine of Manhattan would relieve traffic on Broadway. One New Yorker proposed that traffic on Broadway run only downtown in the morning and uptown in the late afternoon and early evening.

The Blizzard of 1888

The surest way to speed up travel, however, was to remove mass transit from the streets entirely. Subways were proposed as early as the 1850s, and in 1869 the Beach Pneumatic Transit Company opened a 295-foot-long tunnel under Broadway from Warren to Murray streets. Alfred Ely Beach, the builder of the tunnel, was an owner of the New York *Sun* as well as a gifted inventor. At the American Institute Fair of 1867, held at the Fourteenth Street Armory, Beach displayed a wooden tube, six feet in diameter and one block long. Using a huge fan, Beach blew a car carrying ten people from the Fourteenth Street to the Fifteenth Street end of the armory and back again.

Beach thought that using this principle, he could operate a subway under Broadway, but he knew that Boss Tweed would stop any subway plans that would compete with the several surface transit lines he controlled. So Beach requested a charter from the State Legislature to dig a pneumatic mail tube under Broadway. Boss Tweed did not recognize the true purpose of the bill, and as soon as Beach received the charter, his crews began digging the tunnel beneath Broadway. Once it was finished, Beach announced its real purpose, and thousands of New Yorkers flocked to see the 295-foot-long tunnel, which had its entrance in the basement of the Devlin & Company clothing store, at the southwest corner of Broadway and Warren Street. The 120-foot-long waiting room was "elegantly furnished," with frescoed walls, a fountain, and oil paintings. Although New Yorkers were thrilled with Beach's daring plan for a subway, Governor John T. Hoffman vetoed his subsequent request, in 1871, to extend the subway under the entire length of Broadway. Beach's subway charter finally passed the legislature and was signed into law by a new governor two years later, but the Panic of 1873 struck the city, and Beach could not raise the needed money. The state withdrew the charter at the end of 1873, and New Yorkers did not get a subway until the turn of the century.

Another answer to the city's slow-moving omnibuses and horse-drawn cars, the elevated railroad, did become a reality in the 1870s. Boss Tweed thought Charles T. Harvey's request for a charter to build an elevated railroad was so ridiculous that he did not kill it in the State Legislature. Harvey built a half-mile track on Greenwich Street from the Battery to Dey Street, and on July 1, 1868, thousands of New Yorkers watched him drive a small locomotive at speeds up to ten miles an hour. Harvey's engine was not self-propelled, as it appeared to be, but was moved by the pulling of a fixed cable. The legislature subsequently authorized construction of an elevated railroad from the Battery to Spuyten Duyvil, and *Harper's Weekly* hoped that the "problem of rapid and safe locomotion through the crowded streets of the city has been solved."

By 1870 Harvey had extended his tracks along Greenwich Street to the vicinity of Fourteenth Street and from there along Ninth Avenue to West Thirtieth Street. But the stationary power source that moved his train was plagued with troubles, and Harvey's backers withdrew financial support.

Trial trip of the elevated railroad, 1867

The railroad went bankrupt and was purchased by the New York Elevated Railroad Company, which did almost nothing with the elevated railroad until the state ordered it, in 1875, to begin operations within five years. That same year the state also authorized the company to build another el along the Bowery and Third Avenue, and gave the Gilbert Company, later the Metropolitan Elevated Railroad Company, the right to run elevated lines along Second and Sixth avenues. The Sixth Avenue el opened in 1877, the Third Avenue line in 1878 to East One hundred twenty-ninth Street, and the Second Avenue line in 1880 to East One hundred twenty-ninth Street. The Ninth Avenue line also in 1880.

The elevated trains opened up for development large tracts of uptown Manhattan by bringing hitherto inaccessible areas within a reasonable commuting distance of downtown jobs. Moreover, the els permitted an even greater concentration of office buildings downtown, because the people who worked in all the skyscrapers could now reach their jobs without jamming the already overcrowded streets and omnibuses.

Office buildings had almost entirely replaced dry goods wholesaling warehouses along lower Broadway by 1870. In the following years office buildings moved northward along Broadway, first past St. Paul's Chapel at Fulton Street and then beyond Chambers Street. But the prime wholesale district was pushing up Broadway, too. By 1860 it had displaced the shops and hotels on Broadway as far as Canal Street. Taylor's, the "restaurant of the age" when it opened in 1853, closed forever in 1866. Its six-story building at Broadway and Franklin Street, which also housed the International Hotel, became an American Express office. "In Broadway the cellar and wareroom are invading the boudoir," observed George William Curtis, editor of *Harper's Magazine*, in 1862. "If you go below Canal Street of an evening, there is something ghostly in the gloom of the closed warehouses."

Wholesale trade did not even pause at Canal Street; after the Civil War it absorbed that stretch of Broadway which had been the setting for the grandest and most fashionable shops, hotels, and theaters in the 1850s. Tiffany's left its shop at 550 Broadway and moved uptown in 1870. Ball, Black & Company, a few doors downtown, closed in 1872 and Lord &

Taylor left its store at the northwest corner of Broadway and Grand Street in the same year.

The hotels along Broadway north of Canal Street adapted to a changing neighborhood and clientele. By 1870 even the fabled St. Nicholas was no longer one of the best hotels in the city. "When it first opened," observed Henri Junius Browne in 1869, "it was all the rage; but new houses were built, and the city grew and expanded, and the tide rushed by it to 14th Street and Madison Square." The St. Nicholas remained profitable through the 1870s, but, as Browne noted snobbishly, "everyone goes there . . . In its spacious halls and dining rooms you can encounter the representatives of every state . . . Fast persons affect it a good deal; and you are likely to encounter more pinchbeck material there than at any other house on the great thoroughfare." The public rooms and furniture, which had excited such envy at the hotel's 1853 opening, were now considered "too much given to show and something nearly resembling tawdriness." The hotel closed in 1884, just thirty years old, and a tall loft building rose on the site. Its greatest rival, the Metropolitan, survived until 1895, when it, too, was demolished for a loft building.

Once the wholesale trade took over this stretch of Broadway, it moved into the narrow streets east and west of Broadway where red brick dwellings had stood, and put up its warehouses. New Yorkers were delighted to see trade eliminate the infamous "ladies' boarding houses" of Greene and Mercer streets just as it had pushed them out of Church Street twenty years earlier. Anyway, the Greene and Mercer Street whorehouses had become distinctly second-class as Madison Square began to attract the most desirable hotels and brothels. The warehouses, which rose west of Broadway from Canal to Houston streets in the late 1870s and 1880s, now make up the lofts of the SoHo (for "south of Houston") district.

But the northward movement of trade also had undesirable consequences. In October 1866, Commodore Cornelius Vanderbilt purchased St. John's Park for $1 million. A year later workmen had felled the 200 trees in the park and removed their stumps. Vanderbilt's freight depot for the Hudson River Railroad rose on the site of the park. Trinity Church, the owner of St. John's Chapel, received $400,000 and the owner of each house on the square got $13,000, for its share of the park. The houses, which had once faced the park, now lost all appeal to well-to-do families and rapidly became overcrowded roominghouses. St. John's Chapel, from which churchgoers had looked down Hubert Street to the Hudson River after leaving Sunday services, now faced the walls of Commodore Vanderbilt's warehouse.

14

That New Yorkers lamented the loss of St. John's Park but did not press Trinity, the major landowner, to prevent its destruction shows how little people cared for their city's beauty. Most of them did not see any practical benefits in preserving a historic spot of their city's early-nineteenth-century past. When it came to the deterioration of the once-handsome houses that had faced the park, they could point to hundreds of grander-looking row houses and mansions built uptown every year. Even the loss of park land in a crowded area of the city did not seem important because New Yorkers looked to Central Park and plans for other parks in the northern end of Manhattan.

These people failed to realize that the tradition of destroying one spot — there were, after all, other areas to develop farther uptown — would eventually degrade their city's appearance and its quality of life. By the 1890s the city had grown as far north as Ninety-sixth Street, and wealthy New Yorkers decided that they did not want to build their homes beyond this point, either on the East or West side. New Yorkers now had to face, not avoid, the very nearly uncontrolled growth that had long been altering the area of the city that was already built up. Change frequently brought improvement, but it also destroyed some irreplaceable good things in New York, such as St. John's Park.

Unwelcome change had swept into Bleecker Street, too, in the 1860s. Browne noted that the family residences had become boardinghouses, standing "conspicuously in the thoroughfare, with a semblance of departed greatness, and an acknowledgement of surrendered splendor. The high stoops before which private carriages stopped, and emptied loads of feminine fragrance, the broad halls and airy drawing-rooms that were trodden by dainty feet, and filled with soft voices and voluptuous music are profaned today by more common uses."

By the 1880s Bleecker Street and the streets south of Washington Square had become one of the most shabby and unsavory areas in the city. Sullivan, Thompson, and Macdougal streets were an overcrowded black slum known as "Coontown." St. Benedict the Moor, the first black Roman Catholic church in the northern states when it opened in 1883, stood at 210 Bleecker Street, at the corner of Downing Street. French immigrants filled the houses on Wooster, Greene, West Third, and West Fourth streets, an area called "Frenchtown." Bars and concert halls were scattered through the neighborhood. The Black and Tan Concert Hall, also known as the "Chemise and Drawers," on Bleecker Street featured meagerly clad black dancing girls, who were available as prostitutes. "Scotch Ann's" was a brothel where the whores were young men with painted faces, effeminate voices, and women's names.

Rich families had begun to leave the handsome red brick houses on Bleecker Street around 1850, so its decline after the Civil War was no surprise to New Yorkers. But what shocked and upset the gentility in the 1860s was the influx of shops into Union Square. They took over the basements and parlor floors of mansions and row houses, some of which were less than ten years old, and none of them more than twenty years old. So families left their homes on Union Square for Murray Hill, an enclave supposed to be forever safe from the intrusion of trade. By 1865 the *Times* reported that nearly all the houses on Union Square had become boardinghouses.

Union Square had never been an exclusively residential location, like Fifth Avenue or Gramercy Park. In 1851 the *Daily Tribune* described Union Square as the favored location in the city for sumptuous family hotels. The Union Place Hotel, completed in 1850, stood at 860 Broadway, at the southeast corner of Fourteenth Street. The Clarendon Hotel opened in 1851 at the southeast corner of Fourth Avenue and Eighteenth Street, a block from Union Square. That same year, the Eolian Hotel opened at 834 Broadway, the southeast corner of Thirteenth Street. The Everett House, completed in 1854, stood at 41 East Seventeenth Street, on the north side of the park. And the Academy of Music, built in the same year, stood just a few hundred feet from Union Square, at the northeast corner of Fourteenth Street and Irving Place.

But boardinghouses and shops were another thing to the families living on Union Square, and if they weren't reason enough to move uptown, the rising values of houses in the area offered another incentive. By 1866 and 1867, houses on Union Square were selling for $125,000 to $180,000, up from

Bleecker Street, a slum

the $15,000 that lots in the area had fetched ten or fifteen years earlier. An ordinary house rented for $10,000 to $12,000 a year, and in 1870 one corner property was leased for $50,000 a year.

So many shops had moved into Union Square by the late 1860s that the *Herald* declared that the area was "fast becoming a center of business." Tiffany's purchased the Church of the Puritans, at the southwest corner of Fifteenth Street and Union Square, for $115,000 and put up a cast-iron building in 1870. Although George Templeton Strong thought the new Tiffany's was "hideous," he considered it an "improvement" over Dr. Cheever's meetinghouse. "Real jewels will be sold there instead of bogus ones. Cheever's pew holders paid high prices for their bogus acquisitions. Tiffany's customers will pay still larger sums, but they will secure a genuine article."

Shops also moved on to Broadway, just north of Union Square. Lord & Taylor opened its new store at the southwest corner of Broadway and Twentieth Street in 1871. Other stores whose names are still familiar moved into the Union Square area in the following years: F. A. O. Schwarz at 42 East Fourteenth Street, Gorham & Company at the northwest corner of Broadway and Nineteenth Street, and W. & J. Sloane at the southeast corner of Broadway and Nineteenth Street. The old Peter Goelet mansion, where peacocks once strutted in the yard, stood at the northeast corner of Broadway and Nineteenth Street until its demolition in 1898.

Union Square remained a fashionable shopping area until the turn of the century. In 1892 Richard Harding Davis wrote that the shops on the west side of the park showed Union Square at "its richest and most picturesque. The great jewelry and silver shops begin here, and private carriages line the curb in quadruple lines, and the pavement is impressively studded with white-breeched grooms." Davis observed that "long-haired violinists and bespectacled young women in loose gowns, with rolls of music in their hands, become conspicuous just above this — the music-shops are responsible for them." Union Square had also become a popular location for theaters and concert halls after the Civil War. Wallack's Theater opened at Broadway and

Thirteenth Street in 1861 and was considered to have the best stock company in the city. Steinway Hall opened at 109 East Fourteenth Street in 1866 and for the following twenty-five years was "the cradle of classical music in this country," according to *King's Handbook of New York.*

The distress that greeted the invasion of Union Square by shops, great as it was, paled before the shock over Fifth Avenue's fall to trade at the same time. Although the *Herald* had predicted in 1857 that Fifth Avenue would "in some future day be resonant with the clangor of traffic and that its princely palaces will be converted into busy stores," upper- and middle-class New Yorkers were surprised when a tailor opened his shop at the southeast corner of Fifth Avenue and Seventeenth Street in 1860. Two years later Delmonico's opened another restaurant at the northeast corner of Fifth Avenue and Fourteenth Street. An art gallery took over the former Myndert Van Schaick residence at the southwest corner of Fourteenth Street, and Brewster's carriage showroom opened at the northwest corner of Fourteenth Street in another former residence. Fifth Avenue, north of Fourteenth Street, replaced Broadway as the fashionable afternoon promenade.

Some of the houses on Fifth Avenue that still looked like private residences were actually select boardinghouses. These establishments quickly took over many of the sidestreets near Fifth Avenue, particularly Fourteenth Street. During his 1868 visit to America, Charles Dickens remarked that there were "300 boarding houses in West 14th Street, exactly alike, with 300 young men, exactly alike, sleeping in 300 hall bedrooms, exactly alike, with 300 dress suits, exactly alike, lying on so many chairs, exactly alike, beside the bed."

Some of the mansions on Fifth Avenue became clubhouses. The Manhattan Club purchased the Benkard residence at Number 96 for $110,000 in 1865, the year it was founded. The Blossom Club leased Number 129 in 1870, and the Travelers Club occupied Number 124, just across the street, in 1872. The Lotus Club occupied 2 Irving Place after its founding in 1870 but soon moved to the former Bradish Johnson residence at Number 147, just across the street from the Union Club.

Another Fifth Avenue mansion, the Richard K. Haight residence, at the southeast corner of Fifteenth Street, was the home of the New York Club from 1861 to 1870. But the Haight house assumed a more important role in the growth of New York in 1871 when it became one of the city's first apartment buildings. Previously, bachelors and childless couples had the choice of renting an entire house, with more space than they needed, or living in a boardinghouse or hotel, with the accompanying loss of privacy. Although the poor had lived in tenements for decades, middle-class and rich New Yorkers had moral and social doubts about living under the same roof with other, unrelated people. Rutherford Stuyvesant erected the first apartment building in New York in 1869 on the south side of East Eighteenth Street, about 100 feet west of Third Avenue. Each of the first four floors had four apartments, renting for $100 to $150 a month apiece. The fifth floor was artists' studios, renting for $75 a month. Stuyvesant's building was immediately filled, and other real estate investors who followed his example earned returns as high as 30 percent from their property. The social stigma of living in these so-called French flats slowly disappeared, and more and more New Yorkers began to live in apartment buildings.

Discreet brothels had opened in the vicinity of Union Square and Fifth Avenue even before shops made their appearance. Julia Brown, who had been one of the first madams to settle on Church Street back in the late 1830s, was operating a stylish establishment at University Place and Twelfth Street by 1860. Her immediate neighbors then included James Lenox, the multimillionaire whose library helped found the New York Public Library, merchant William H. Aspinwall, the Union Theological Seminary, Mrs. Peter A. Schermerhorn, and the Society Library. The apparent ease with which prostitution could flourish in so select a location reflects the social strains of the time as well as patterns of urban development.

Julia Brown represented the advance guard of vice north of Washington Square. In 1870 the *Gentleman's Companion*, a pocket-sized brothel guide for New York, counted fifteen "temples of love" within a two-block radius of Fifth Avenue and Fourteenth Street. Miss Ida Thompson's place of business on East Twelfth Street was "an elegant parlor house . . . furnished in the most elaborate and magnificent style" in the judgment of the guide. Miss Thompson and her "lovely young ladies are a very pleasant set, full of fun, love, and fond of amusement. The carpets, mirrors, furniture, and paintings are of the latest and most costly designs. This is truly a splendid establishment of the first class."

Eighteenth Street apartments

The busiest red-light district during the 1870s and 1880s was Twenty-fourth to Thirtieth Street, just west of Sixth Avenue. The *Gentleman's Companion* counted fifty-seven brothels on those streets, between Sixth and Seventh avenues, including twenty-seven on West Twenty-seventh Street alone. One of the most select houses in this area was the three-story brownstone at 105 West Twenty-fifth Street, kept by Kate Woods. The house had been furnished in rosewood furniture, gilt mirrors, wall-to-wall carpeting, and imported statues at a cost of $70,000. The oil paintings had run an additional $10,000. Kate Woods kept only three young women, but each one offered "rare personal attractions," according to the thorough vade mecum, and the "house receives the patronage of distinguished gentlemen from foreign countries." Clearly, this lent a seal of approval.

Brothels were clustered in the West Twenties to be near the fine hotels that opened on or near Madison Square in the 1860s and 1870s. Greene and Mercer streets, it will be recalled, were the red-light district in the 1850s, because hotels such as the St. Nicholas and the Metropolitan were just a block away on Broadway. The first major hotel in the Madison Square area was the huge, white marble Fifth Avenue, which opened in 1859 on the west blockfront of Fifth Avenue between Twenty-third and Twenty-fourth streets. Skeptics wondered how a hotel so far uptown would attract a clientele, but the overwhelming success of the Fifth Avenue led to the opening of the Albemarle at Broadway and Twenty-fourth Street in 1860; the St. James at Broadway and Twenty-sixth Street in 1863; the Hoffman House on Broadway between Twenty-fourth and Twenty-fifth Streets in 1865; the Victoria at Fifth Avenue and Twenty-seventh Street in 1871; the Brunswick at 225 Fifth Avenue, at Twenty-sixth Street, in 1871; and the Gilsey at Broadway and Twenty-ninth Street in 1871.

Just ten years after the completion of the scoffed-at Fifth Avenue Hotel, Madison Square had become the center of much that was fashionable and exciting in New York. The stretch of Broadway between Madison Square and A. T. Stewart's department store at Tenth Street now was the location of so many fine shops that it was called "the ladies' mile." Restaurants and theaters followed the hotels to Madison Square, and in 1876 Delmonico's moved from Fifth Avenue and Fourteenth Street to a building on the south side of West Twenty-sixth Street between Fifth Avenue and Broadway. The main dining room overlooked Fifth Avenue and the greenery of Madison Square, and the gentlemen's café faced Broadway. The three floors upstairs included private dining rooms and the ballroom which was the scene of the city's leading social events.

The "Ladies' Mile," Broadway, 1875

*Bums at a fountain in
Madison Square, 1877*

At first the hotels, restaurants, and theaters stayed on the west side of Madison Square, along Fifth Avenue and Broadway, which intersect at Twenty-third Street. Private houses still lined the three other sides of the park in the 1860s. But the enormous rents offered for property meant that one by one they, too, would become boardinghouses, shops, and clubhouses. In 1871 one man refused an offer of $25,000-a-year rent for the house at the southwest corner of Fifth Avenue and Twenty-third Street; the owner of a house on East Twenty-sixth Street, facing Madison Square, asked and received the same amount.

The most splendid home facing Madison Square was Leonard Jerome's at 32 East Twenty-sixth Street. In 1859, just two years after he became a millionaire by selling short in the Panic of 1857, Jerome began his six-story mansion, whose red brick façade, trimmed in white marble, and mansard roof made the house a startling sight among the somber brownstones around Madison Square. The interior was as flamboyant as the façade and matched Jerome's lifestyle, characterized by fortunes made and lost several times, the finest horses and carriages, and well-publicized love affairs. The white and gold ballroom held 300 people; the breakfast room seated seventy. Many of Jerome's young women protégées performed in the mansion's private theater, which seated 600 people. The part of his home dearest to the owner was the stable, three stories tall, built for $80,000. It was just down the street and was complete with black walnut paneling and wall-to-wall carpeting. "Except for the Emperor's mews in Paris, it is doubtful if any stable in the world . . . surpassed Jerome's," declared the *Daily Tribune*. But this manner of living, extravagant even for Madison Square, ended in 1868 when Jerome rented his mansion to the Union League Club.

While Madison Square was in its heyday in the 1870s and 1880s, trade was moving inexorably northward from the Fourteenth Street and Twenty-third Street areas toward Central Park, forcing well-to-do New Yorkers from their homes. In 1879 Egbert L. Viele observed that Murray Hill "was for a considerable time regarded as the synonyme of fashion, but in time it will be more strictly synonymous with shabby gentility." Fifth Avenue "has now become thoroughly invaded, from Washington Square almost to the Central Park, with fancy shops, jewelers, hotels, and boarding-houses, and its exclusiveness has vanished forever."

Few New Yorkers had expected trade to march up Fifth Avenue this quickly, particularly A. T. Stewart. In 1864 he purchased the Townsend mansion at the northwest corner of Fifth Avenue and Thirty-fourth Street so that he could build his own home on the choice site. Until then, Stewart had lived quite simply for a man worth $40 million to $50 million. Although he had lived at 331 and 355 Fifth Avenue from 1861

Thirty-fourth Street and
Fifth Avenue

on, his homes were nothing extraordinary for such an exalted avenue. But Stewart broke with his lifelong prudence when he began his white marble, mansard-roofed mansion, which took $3 million and nearly ten years to build and furnish.

Stewart's house, with its broad halls lined with sculpture, its gold dinner service, the ballroom, the sweeping stairway, set a new standard of extravagance. The art gallery "far surpassed in importance and value any other in this country," in the opinion of the *Times*. Although some newspapers predictably praised the house as "chaste," "elegant," and "a temple rather than a mansion," others pronounced it "hideous," "over-loaded with ornament," and "a vast tomb." Stewart enjoyed living in the house only a few years; he died in 1876, and by then shops and clubhouses had reached Thirty-fourth Street.

By the 1880s the only truly residential stretch of Fifth Avenue below Central Park began around Fiftieth Street. Rows of $100,000 to $150,000 brownstones had risen here after the Civil War, and the city laid out Grand Army Plaza in 1870 after acquiring the land by condemnation. St. Thomas' Church moved to the northwest corner of Fifth Avenue and Fifty-third Street in 1870, after occupying a site at Broadway and Houston Street since 1826. Fifth Avenue Presbyterian, which had been located at the southeast corner of Fifth Avenue and Nineteenth Street since 1852, moved to the building it still occupies, at the northwest corner of Fifth Avenue and Fifty-fifth Street, in 1875. The most impressive-looking church on all of Fifth Avenue was St. Patrick's Cathedral, on the blockfront between East Fiftieth and East Fifty-first streets, which opened in 1879, twenty-one years after the laying of its cornerstone.

In the 1880s the Vanderbilt family built four mansions on this stretch of Fifth Avenue, each one of them grander than the Stewart residence a mile downtown. William Henry Vanderbilt, son of the commodore, built a pair of Renaissance-style houses on the west blockfront of Fifth Avenue between Fifty-first and Fifty-second streets in 1880–1884. He lived in one, and his daughters and their families occupied the other. His son William Kissam Vanderbilt built a lovely Gothic Revival mansion next door, at the northwest corner of Fifty-second Street, in 1879–1881. His other son, Cornelius Vanderbilt II, had just begun his mansion at the northwest corner of Fifth Avenue and Fifty-seventh Street. When he enlarged this house to take in the entire blockfront between West Fifty-seventh and West Fifty-eighth streets, facing Grand Army Plaza, he achieved probably the grandest-looking and best-situated house ever built in New York. Across the street, at the northeast corner of Fifty-seventh Street, stood the Mary Mason Jones mansion, a reminder of how fast the city had grown northward and how much larger and more elaborate the homes of the rich had become since the 1860s.

While the Vanderbilts were spending $15 million in building and furnishing their four mansions, Fifth Avenue down around Madison Square was losing its exciting mix of fine shops, restaurants, clubs, and theaters. The hotels were fading because the establishments most favored by the elite were now farther uptown: the Holland House, at the southwest corner of Fifth Avenue and Thirtieth Street; the Waldorf, at the northwest corner of Fifth Avenue and Thirty-third Street; the New Netherland, at the northeast corner of Fifth Avenue and Fifty-ninth Street; the Savoy, at the southeast corner of Fifth Avenue and Fifty-ninth Street; and the Plaza, on the same site as the present-day hotel, which dates from 1907. Grand Army Plaza had replaced Madison Square as the choicest location for hotels. "Its situation is peculiarly advantageous," observed *King's Handbook of New York,* "surrounded by the homes of distinguished families, the architectural splendors of the 'swellest' club houses, and the most fashionable churches." Hotel guests were just a few minutes' walk or carriage ride from Central Park, "the loveliest pleasure-ground in America, with its drives and rambles; its lawns and forests; its statuary and fountains."

Madison Square, by contrast, was on the way to the office-building center that it became at the turn of the century. In 1893 Metropolitan Life moved its headquarters from Park Place to a $3 million, nine-story building at the northeast corner of Madison Avenue and Twenty-third Street. Office buildings, especially those occupied by publishers, such as the Methodist Book Concern, *Judge,* and Scribner's, soon

Fifth Avenue and Fifty-first Street

rose along Fifth Avenue from Fourteenth Street to Madison Square. The Twenties along Sixth Avenue, and West Twenty-third Street itself, had become a busy shopping area filled with huge department stores patronized primarily by the middle class. These stores and their customers apparently discouraged most of the brothels from remaining in the West Twenties. Adventuresome madams, however, were already moving into the West Thirties and Forties, following the drift of population and fine hotels northward.

By the 1890s the few blocks of Fifth Avenue between Washington Square and Twelfth Street had reversed a slow decline, which had begun after the Civil War. New Yorkers had predicted that the wholesale dry goods trade, then moving up Broadway, would overwhelm lower Fifth Avenue in the 1870s and 1880s as it moved north from the area south of Houston Street. Warehouses did rise on the streets east of Washington Square and along University Place, but enough people clung to their old family homes on Washington Square North, lower Fifth Avenue, and the adjacent side-streets that neither trade nor tenements could gain a foothold in the area.

Mariana Griswold Van Rensselaer was an art critic and poet, and, as her later history of seventeenth-century New York would show, cared much about her native city. In the early 1890s she wrote in *Harper's Magazine* that " 'good people' " not only lived on or near lower Fifth Avenue but that "the number is now increasing again year by year, desecrated dwellings being restored within and without, and a belief steadily gaining ground that, whatever may happen a little farther up the avenue, this quarter-mile stretch will remain a 'good residence neighborhood.' " Mrs. Schuyler Van Rensselaer, as she was, lived at 9 West Tenth Street and found it inconvenient to visit friends living several miles uptown, but she stood by the area's

exceptional convenience in almost every other respect. We are proud of the aroma of fifty years' antiquity which we breathe, and we delight to maintain that this is the only part of New York, outside of the tenement districts, where a "neighborhood feeling" exists. Sometimes, down here, we even call upon a newly established neighbor whom we know only by name. Perhaps, up near the Park, you do not do this, because people with such nice names are not apt to settle near you.

But Mariana Griswold Van Rensselaer had old-fashioned ideas, as well as three old New York names. By the 1890s most well-to-do families considered the height of fashion to be the Upper East Side, particularly Fifth and Madison avenues and the adjacent sidestreets as far north as, roughly, Ninetieth Street.

When the city swept past Fifty-ninth Street around 1870, the Upper East Side bore little resemblance to the thickly built district it would become twenty years later. The streets near Fifth Avenue were almost entirely open, except for shanties, occasional garbage dumps, quarries, and stockyards. A modest frame house sometimes stood on an unpaved road that would eventually become a paved city street. Despite the unkempt appearance of the area, rich families and real estate speculators already owned the vacant land along Fifth Avenue facing the eastern edge of Central Park. As soon as Olmsted and Vaux began work on Central Park, the newspapers had predicted that this property would someday be among the most desirable in the city. In 1862 Anthony Trollope thought that "the present fashion of Fifth Avenue about Twentieth Street will in course of time move itself up to the Fifth Avenue as it looks, or will look, over the Park at Seventieth, Eightieth, and Ninetieth Streets."

Despite rosy predictions for Fifth Avenue, the rest of the Upper East Side, specifically anything east of Madison Avenue, developed into a working-class and middle-class neighborhood. Growth in this part of the Upper East Side began as soon as the New York & Harlem Railroad reached Eighty-sixth Street in 1834 and Harlem in 1837. By 1858, a horse-drawn trolley ran up Second Avenue as far north as One hundred twenty-second Street, and the Third Avenue line reached Eighty-sixth Street. Detached frame houses and occasional groups of row houses were built on the Upper East Side for New Yorkers willing to spend long hours commuting in return for suburban living and low housing costs.

Rows of modest cottage residences were built in Harlem around One hundred twenty-fifth Street in the 1850s and 1860s, even though it was three miles above the northern edge of the city proper. In 1852 the *Evening Post* thought that Harlem "to a much greater extent . . . than . . . any other place on this island" was the best location for "the working and laboring classes wishing to settle themselves in New York at moderate rents." Surprisingly, the *Evening Post* believed that "this beautiful portion of our city" was the "most suitable location for all sorts of manufacturing purposes. The large front on the [East] River, the depth of the water, and the

Old frame house, 3 East Eighty-third Street

*Marsh drugstore, One
hundred twenty-fifth
Street, 1865*

easy slope of the shore render this section of the island decidedly the most suitable place unappropriated about the
densely populated parts of the metropolis for the construction
of shipyards, coal and lumber yards, and depots for the
various articles of trade required by this great market."

Harlem did not become the manufacturing center newspapers and local land owners had predicted it would; it developed much like the East Seventies or Yorkville to the south.
After the Civil War the tenements that lined First, Second,
and Third avenues south of Forty-second Street rapidly
pushed northward into the Upper East Side and eventually
into Harlem. Builders erected red brick and brownstone row
houses for middle-class families on the sidestreets of the Six-
ties, Seventies, and Eighties.

The Upper East Side began to lose the landmarks of its
countrified past. The small estates along the East River were
sold off in building lots and the country houses demolished
or turned into taverns or boardinghouses for a while. The

307

*Park Avenue vicinity, south
from Ninety-third Street*

Astor family's mansion, at the foot of East Eighty-eighth Street, was torn down in 1869. The Hopper house, which had stood at Second Avenue and Eighty-third Street since 1630, also disappeared. In 1879 workmen who were digging a cellar for an apartment building at the northwest corner of Lexington Avenue and One hundred fourth Street discovered a graveyard for British soldiers, dating from their occupation of New York during the Revolution. A few years later, tenement builders razed the nearby McGowan house, on the south side of East One hundred sixth Street between Lexington and Third avenues. The old homestead had been a military hospital during the Revolution and, more recently, the Red House Tavern, serving the horsemen who raced up and down Third Avenue.

The Upper East Side lost not only its landmarks but two small parks, which had been laid out as part of the grid street

Houses in open fields, West One hundred thirty-third Street

plan. In 1865 the State Legislature ordered East Ninetieth, Ninety-first, Ninety-second, and Ninety-third streets opened from Fifth to Park avenues, thereby destroying Observatory Place. Three years later the legislature closed Hamilton Square, bounded by East Sixty-sixth Street, Fifth Avenue, East Sixty-ninth Street, and Third Avenue. The Upper East Side now needed more than just access to Central Park in the way of open space, and in 1876 the city condemned the property east of present-day East End Avenue from East Eighty-fourth to East Ninetieth streets for what is now Carl Schurz Park.

The city guided the growth of the Upper East Side by leasing or giving away land in the area to hospitals, schools, and museums. In 1866 the city leased twenty lots on East Eighty-first and East Eighty-second streets, between Madison and Park avenues, to the Roman Catholic diocese for an industrial school for the Sisters of Mercy, and eighteen lots on East Seventy-seventh Street, between Park and Lexington avenues, to the German Hospital for fifty years at $1-a-year rent. The closing of Hamilton Square in 1868 gave the city even more choice land for institutions. By the early 1870s, Mount Sinai Hospital, a foundling hospital for the Sisters of Mercy, the Hahnemann Hospital, an asylum for the Association for the Improved Condition of Deaf Mutes, the Normal College (later renamed Hunter College), and a home run by the Ladies' Baptist Home Society were housed on the gentle slope of what became known as Lenox Hill.

In 1868 the State Legislature ordered the commissioners of Central Park to set aside a site on Fifth Avenue from Eighty-first to Eighty-fourth Street for the New-York Historical Society. The New-York Historical Society already had a handsome library and museum at the southeast corner of Second Avenue and Eleventh Street, across from St. Mark's-in-the-Bouwerie, so several years later the Central Park commissioners offered the excellent site to the Metropolitan Museum of Art, which had been incorporated in 1870. The Metropolitan Museum accepted the city's gift in 1872, and ground was broken two years later. The museum first displayed its paintings in Cooper Union, then rented 681 Fifth Avenue from 1871 to 1872, and occupied the former

Bloomingdale Road, 1862

Douglas Cruger mansion at 128 West Fourteenth Street from 1872 to 1879. The museum moved to its new building on upper Fifth Avenue in 1880.

The Upper West Side grew far more slowly than the Upper East Side. While horse-drawn trolleys ran up and down Second and Third avenues and builders hastily erected rows of modest houses on the nearby sidestreets, the Upper West Side was still open land, dotted by shantytowns, old country houses, small farms, and taverns. Until the early 1880s, West Seventieth Street, from Central Part West to Columbus Avenue, was the "main street" for one shanty village, complete with several shops and saloons. One tavern occupied an old frame house on a rocky outcropping, with a flight of shabby wooden stairs leading down to the unpaved street. Some shanties in this village actually came close to looking like houses. One might be "the home of some important personage in the community — possibly a milkman," reported *Harper's Weekly*. "There would be more tin on the roof, the windows would look as though they might be mates, and an extra chimney or two would impart an air of wealth and comfort to the ambitious structure." Several blocks to the northwest of West Seventieth Street was another shantytown, called "Wallhigh," and "Shantyhill" stood near what is now Seventy-ninth Street and Broadway, then called the Bloomingdale Road.

Country homes from the eighteenth and early nineteenth centuries stood on the elevated land overlooking the Hudson, but most of them had become taverns or boardinghouses by the 1860s and 1870s. Among the handsomest country homes was the Charles Ward Apthorpe mansion, built in 1764, at the present-day intersection of Columbus Avenue and Ninety-first Street. The front door, beneath a portico, opened into the hall, which was large enough for dancing parties. Like the walls and ceilings of the main rooms, the hall was paneled in English oak, imported by Apthorpe at enormous cost. After the Revolution, William Jauncey, a rich landowner living on Wall Street, bought the 200-acre estate and named it Elmwood. It was inherited by his son-in-law, Herman Thorn, whose good friend Philip Hone often left his children there for several days in the

summer to play with Thorn's sons and daughters. A year after Thorn's death, in 1859, his heirs sold Elmwood for $600,000. The old house became a tavern and was torn down in 1892 for a row of tenements.

Development by-passed the Upper West Side for many years because public transportation to downtown Manhattan was almost nonexistent. Until 1870, the Eighth Avenue street railroad ran a single car between Fifty-ninth and Eighty-fourth streets; it turned around and then returned south on the same track. The only other public transportation was the stage, which ran down the Bloomingdale Road every hour.

Despite its countrified state, New Yorkers saw a splendid future for the Upper West Side. The land was elevated and breezy and lay between Central Park and the Hudson. In 1865 William Martin proposed that the city build Riverside Drive and a park along the river, and the State Legislature approved the plan two years later. The city had acquired all the property by 1872, and work on the park began in 1877. The plans for Morningside Park were approved in 1868. That year the city widened the Bloomingdale Road and renamed it the Boulevard. (It would be called Broadway in 1899.) Unfortunately, several landmarks were destroyed during this work: the Bloomingdale Reformed Dutch Church, built in 1816 at West Sixty-eighth Street, and the old Somerindyke house, on the west side of the Bloomingdale Road between the present Seventy-fifth and Seventy-sixth streets, where Louis Philippe taught school during his exile in America.

The Upper West Side remained suspended in its undeveloped condition until the opening of the Ninth Avenue el in 1880. As work on the el progressed, New Yorkers excitedly anticipated the growth of the area. Egbert L. Viele, writing in 1879, was certain that the Upper West Side was

the section of the city that has been held in reserve until the time when the progress of wealth and refinement shall have attained that period of development when our citizens can appreciate and are ready to take advantage of the situation . . . Moreover, this entire region combines in its general aspect all that is magnificent in the leading capitals of Europe. In our Central Park, we have the fine Prater of Vienna, in our grand Boulevard the rival of the finest avenues of the gay capital of France, in our Riverside Avenue the equivalent of the Chiara of Naples and the Corso of Rome, while the beautiful 'Unter den Linden' of Berlin and the finest portions of the West End of London are reproduced again and again.

But the opening of the el in 1880 did not bring the immediate building boom that New Yorkers had expected. Thirty-four streets between West Fifty-ninth to West One Hundred Twenty-fifth streets were not yet completely opened, and even the avenues were still unpaved dirt roads. Riverside Drive was opened in 1880 but still lacked the finishing touches that made a great boulevard. Water and gas lines were few and far between.

Then, too, speculative builders, who had plenty of work on the Upper East Side, hesitated to enter a nearly empty area whose social character was not yet determined. Everyone agreed that mansions would line Central Park West and Riverside Drive, so prices for lots on these empty thoroughfares rivaled those for land on Fifth and Madison avenues on the other side of Central Park. But what about the rest of the Upper West Side? Was Viele correct in predicting that the area would become the home of only the rich? Or would the Upper West Side become a working- and middle-class district, like the Upper East Side east of Madison Avenue? The last was very much a possibility. The Upper West Side could become a noisesome tenement district, like the settled blocks south of West Fifty-ninth Street. In 1881 one builder filed plans for a row of tenements on West Seventy-second Street, west of Ninth Avenue. The tenements were never built.

The Upper West Side, by and large, became a desirable neighborhood. The success of Edward Clark's improvements on West Seventy-second and West Seventy-third streets, the first major project on the Upper West Side, encouraged other investors to build similarly luxurious housing in the neighborhood. In 1877 Clark, the president of the Singer Sewing Machine Company and a well-known real estate investor,

Central Park West, ca. 1873: open fields

purchased from August Belmont, for $280,000, the blockfront of Central Park West from Seventy-second to Seventy-third streets and the land running several hundred feet down those sidestreets. Early in 1880, Clark completed a row of handsome houses, designed by Henry J. Hardenbergh, on West Seventy-third Street. Later that year, Hardenbergh filed plans for an opulent apartment building on Central Park West between Seventy-second and Seventy-third streets. New Yorkers thought that the shrewd Clark had finally made a glaring blunder. The joke about the seven-story gabled and turreted building was that it was so far from genteel homes and in so desolate a location that it might as well have been in the Dakotas. The building was a great success, but the improbable name "Dakota" has stuck to this day.

As house construction on the Upper West Side slowly got underway in the early 1880s, operations clustered around the Ninth Avenue el stations at West Seventy-second, Eighty-first, Ninety-third, and One hundred fourth streets. A few years later the Upper West Side was in the midst of a boom, and builders were erecting rows of houses in nearly every part of the area. The *Times* wrote, in 1886:

The west side of the city presents just now a scene of build-ing activity such as was never before witnessed in that sec-tion, and which gives promise of the speedy disappearance of all the shanties in the neighborhood and the rapid popu-lation of this long neglected part of New York. The huge masses of rock which formerly met the eye, usually crowned by a rickety shanty and a browsing goat, are being blasted out of existence. Streets are being graded, and thousands of carpenters and masons are engaged in rearing substantial buildings where a year ago nothing was to be seen but mar-ket gardens or barren rocky fields.

The social composition of the Upper West Side was fixed by 1890, though not exactly in the way New Yorkers had forecast ten years earlier. Mansions and extravagant row houses did line Riverside Drive, "universally acknowledged to be the most beautiful and picturesque [street] in the world," according to one New Yorker. Eleventh Avenue, which had been renamed West End Avenue in 1880, had become a street of handsome homes, not the predicted mix of

317

Shanty on Riverside Drive

small shops and apartment buildings. On the other hand, the Boulevard was lined with shops and fashionable apartment buildings and residential hotels rather than mansions, as had been expected. A few mansions and fine row houses stood on Central Park West, but after the success of the Dakota, it became a street of elegant apartment buildings and hotels. By 1890 the San Remo and Beresford stood on the sites now occupied by later buildings with the same names. Ninth and Tenth avenues, which had been renamed Columbus and Amsterdam avenues in 1880, were filled with tenements, just as everyone had thought they would be, those on Amsterdam being of a better class than those on el-shaded Columbus. Nothing had come of the proposal to set the buildings on Columbus Avenue well back from the street, away from the noise and flying cinders of the rumbling elevated trains.

Montgomery Schuyler believed that the Upper West Side "offered an opportunity for a quarter of small houses," because "so much land was at once thrown open to settlement by the completion of the elevated railroad that its price was low enough for the wants of people of moderate means." But outside of occasional tenements and modest apartment buildings, the only single-family homes for the middle class were built on the blocks between Columbus and Amsterdam avenues, generally north of Seventy-ninth Street. The row houses on other sidestreet blocks were fairly substantial, particularly those just off Central Park West and Riverside Drive.

The streets of the Upper West Side displayed the architectural fashions that had replaced the long-dominant Italianate brownstone. The long rows of almost identical brownstone-front row houses on Fifth Avenue were no longer considered impressive; they were monotonous and ugly. Reminiscing about her childhood in *A Backward Glance*, Edith Wharton recalled "this little low-studded rectangular New York, cursed with its universal chocolate-coloured coating of the most hideous stone ever quarried, this cramped horizontal gridiron of a town without towers, porticoes, fountains, or perspectives, hide-bound with deadly uniformity of mean ugliness."

Around 1880, architects began to design row houses that combined several styles and a number of different stones and bricks at once. Ideally, each house was different from its neighbor, and a Romanesque home in brownstone might stand next to a Renaissance town house in limestone or a gabled and turreted Queen Anne building in red brick. Builders and architects working in the Upper West Side were quick to adopt the vogue of architectural eclecticism and variety. Schuyler thought that "the houses that now characterize the West Side are without doubt the most interesting examples of domestic architecture that New York has to show."

New Yorkers were proud of the Upper West Side — not only for its rapid growth but for its architecture, parks, broad avenues, and sweeping vistas. The Upper West Side was the embodiment of a new ideal of what New York should be: the City Beautiful. The idea was not new to the 1890s. Twenty years earlier *Appleton's Journal* declared: "We hear a great deal about The House Beautiful, of how art should enter our domiciles and give them grace and charm . . . We earnestly wish this aesthetic passion would enlarge its sphere to give the world The City Beautiful. No people excel Americans in a love for well-equipped and well-furnished homes, but no civilized nation is so indifferent to the general seemliness of its cities."

*

New Yorkers needed the ideals of the City Beautiful to guide its growth and continual rebuilding. They were proud of their city's wealth, its talented people, and the celebration of glamour and beauty, yet they tolerated abysmal poverty, hoplessness, and squalor. But New York has been a city of contradictions since the early nineteenth century. The Croton Reservoir, built at enormous cost and calling on the talents of skilled engineers, supplied the city with fine water, but the streets were some of the filthiest and worst-paved in the nation. New York built the imaginative and delightful Central Park where once there had been shantytowns and garbage dumps, but the wharves and waterfront, which generated so much of its wealth, were badly run-down and inefficiently arranged. New York "is very much like a fine beauty who always appears in dishabille, or like one whose embroidered robes are smirched and torn," criticized *Appleton's Journal*.

The City Beautiful was only a dream in the 1870s and 1880s. New York was not yet the modern metropolis it became at the turn of the century. The great task in New York, in the 1870s and 1880s was building rapid mass transit, introducing telephone service and electric lighting to everyday life, expanding the Croton water system, and burying the unsightly and often dangerous utility wires beneath the streets.

King Garbage: cartoon, 1891

By the turn of the century, New York had finally become a well-functioning modern city, and its leading citizens knew that it might yet become more livable and lovely. In population, area, and wealth, New York had exceeded the most optimistic predictions of the early nineteenth century. The city's population was 1,441,216 in 1890, quite a jump from the 515,547 of 1850 and the 813,660 of 1860. When the five boroughs were united as one city in 1898, the population of Greater New York was over 3.4 million. Except for parts of Harlem and Washington Heights, Manhattan was solidly built up from river to river. The city's growth reached into nearby parts of Brooklyn, the Bronx, Queens, and New Jersey. Manhattan had become the focal point of a metropolitan region that was tied together by mass transit, the local economy, and social patterns, as well as by political jurisdictions.

The island of Manhattan had ninety thousand residential buildings and twenty-five thousand commercial structures in 1890, with a total market value estimated at over $4.4 billion. There were 575 miles of streets, 444 miles of sewers, 685 miles of water mains, and over twenty-eight thousand street lights, nearly all gas lamps. The city consumed 170 million gallons of water daily. New Yorkers got around on five elevated train lines with a total mileage of thirty-three miles, on forty-two horse-drawn street railroad lines, and on numerous horse-drawn omnibus lines. Although the Brooklyn Bridge spanned the East River and several bridges crossed the Harlem River into the Bronx, there were thirty-eight ferry lines between Manhattan and outlying areas, including thirteen to Brooklyn and thirteen to New Jersey. Twenty-three railroads served Manhattan, although only four lines actually entered the island, three of them stopping at Grand Central Station. The Long Island Railroad depot was in Long Island City, and the lines from the South and West, such as the Pennsylvania, the Baltimore & Ohio, and the New Jersey Central, still stopped in Jersey City, where passengers and freight were loaded onto ferries to cross the Hudson River to New York.

New York was the richest city in America and the center of national business activity. At least two New Yorkers had fortunes in excess of $100 million, according to one survey in the early 1890s, six men were worth more than $50 million, thirty were worth from $20 million to $40 million, and 325 from $2 million to $12 million. Mere millionaires, apparently, were too numerous to be counted.

The 113 national and state banks and trust companies in New York had $88 million in capital and $1,055,000,000 in total assets. The clearinghouse's annual transactions ran between $35 million and $50 million, more than the amounts of all other cities in America combined. New York's twenty-seven savings banks had deposits of $325 million for eight hundred thousand people.

Exports then leaving America from New York totaled $346,528,847, or 39.2 percent of the national total; imports entering the city totaled $537,786,007, or 63.6 percent of the nation's total. The city was a major manufacturing center. By 1890, 25,399 businesses with over 350,000 employees produced $765 million in goods every year.

By the time New Yorkers realized that their city could be beautiful and livable as well as rich, powerful, and exciting, nothing could be done about the grid street plan, which had mapped out Manhattan into a monotonous series of rectangular blocks. But parks could relieve the density of buildings and people in the city. So Morningside Park was finally finished in 1887, and, by the turn of the century, the city had acquired or completed St. Nicholas Park, Colonial Park, and Inwood Park in upper Manhattan. Plans for parks in the still largely rural Bronx were even grander than those for Manhattan. In 1884 a commission selected 3945 acres, which cost $9 million, for Pelham Bay, Van Cortlandt, Bronx, Crotona, St. Mary's and Claremont parks. At the same time, the Pelham, Crotona, and Mosholu parkways were built to connect them. Under the Small Parks Act of 1887, the city relieved the unbroken stretches of buildings in lower Manhattan by acquiring land for the DeWitt Clinton, Washington-Lafayette, and East River parks.

The most important buildings erected in New York now affirmed the City Beautiful ideals. They were large, richly ornamented, and costly, as were buildings of earlier eras, but they were also monumental — set back from the street in

parks or plazas, reached by long flights of stairs, designed on
a scale that dwarfed men and the surrounding cityscape.
New York had its monuments — though they were just several years old: the New York Public Library (1898–1911),
which occupied the site of the Croton Distributing Reservoir
on the west side of Fifth Avenue from Fortieth to Forty-
second streets; the Pulitzer Fountain at Grand Army Plaza;
the Statue of Liberty (1886); the Columbia University campus
on Morningside Heights, which was first occupied in 1897;
the nearby Cathedral of St. John the Divine, begun in 1892
and still not finished; Grant's Tomb, completed in 1897; the
Washington Arch, built in 1892, just inside Washington
Square at the foot of Fifth Avenue; and Grand Central Sta-

Pennsylvania Station   tion, completed in 1913.

While work proceeded on this terminal, the New York
Central Railroad covered its sprawling rail yards along Park
Avenue, then called Fourth Avenue, from Forty-second to
Fiftieth streets and laid out a mall down the middle of the
street. An impressive array of luxury apartment buildings
and hotels soon stood tall on what had been one of the city's
ugliest streets.

The greatest triumph of the City Beautiful movement in
New York was Pennsylvania Station, built in 1906–1910. By
most accounts, it was the most awesome building ever
erected in the city — a symbol of the Pennsylvania Railroad's
might and wealth, the façade and vaulted waiting room
modeled by McKim, Mead, and White on the ancient Baths
of Caracalla, and the steel and glass arches and domes of the
train concourse an elegant acknowledgment of modern technology. Pennsylvania Station provided travelers with a dignified entrance to New York, as befitted the city's importance,
not just by its architectural magnificence, but by eliminating
the nuisance of the stop in New Jersey and the ferry ride
across the Hudson to one of the grimy, ill-equipped stations
downtown.

That Pennsylvania Station was razed in 1963–1966 shows
what little weight the ideals of the City Beautiful now carry.
The potential profits and novelty of a new building are still
more important than its appearance or its contribution to the

quality of life in the city. "Until the first blow fell," declared

the *Times* on October 30, 1963, "no one was convinced that Penn Station really would be demolished or that New York would permit this monumental act of vandalism . . . Any city gets what it admires, will pay for, and ultimately deserves. Even when we had Penn Station, we couldn't afford to keep it clean."

New York has been destroying its landmarks and amenities since the early nineteenth century, and, despite the moderating influence of the City Beautiful, went right on doing the same thing in the name of growth and progress during the twentieth century. One of the more glaring acts of destruction took place during the construction of the Seventh Avenue IRT subway in 1914–1917. The city decided to link Varick Street, which ended at Carmine Street, with Seventh Avenue, which began at West Twelfth Street, so it cut Seventh Avenue South through the twisting, brownstone-lined streets of the West Village. Seventh Avenue South destroyed hundreds of old houses, left others with their sides sadly exposed, and formed little triangular pieces of land, which are now gas stations and parking lots. In the process, the city also widened Varick Street, needlessly destroying St. John's Chapel and the few early-nineteenth-century houses still standing on either side.

Private interests have been just as thoughtless as the city government. The losses in the 1960s alone were staggering. The General Motors Building and its little-used sunken plaza replaced the Savoy Plaza Hotel, which had helped define the formal urban space of the Grand Army Plaza. The Brokaw mansions, at the northeast corner of Fifth Avenue and Seventy-ninth Street, which were significant not for their architecture but as reminders of what Fifth Avenue had been before it was crowded with high-rent, high-rise apartment buildings, were torn down to make room for yet another apartment building. The twenty-five-story Times Tower, one of the best-known and most distinctive buildings in New York, was refaced with bland white marble and reopened as the Allied Chemical Building. The nearby Astor Hotel, a good hotel and an anchor to the past on an increasingly raucous Times Square, was replaced by an office building. The Singer Building, at 149 Broadway, the tallest building in the world for a time and a delightful example of the Beaux Arts manner, gave way for the U.S. Steel Building. Another office building replaced the Metropolitan Opera at the northwest corner of Broadway and Thirty-ninth Street. The Metropolitan Opera Association sold the building on the condition that it be demolished so that no competitive opera company could occupy its old house.

The 1960s saw the conclusion of the building-by-building destruction of midtown Park Avenue, the only other post–World War II act of urban vandalism to rank alongside the demolition of Penn Station. Although the original thirty-foot-wide mall had been reduced to its present width in 1927 to add two more lanes of traffic, the great vistas of handsome, vaguely neoclassical apartment buildings and hotels remained unbroken until the construction of Lever House, on the west blockfront between Fifty-third and Fifty-fourth streets, in 1950–1952. Because of the fame of the Park Avenue address, companies in search of impressive headquarters or real estate speculators looking for a sure thing tore down the very buildings that had given the location its good name.

Although some of the buildings on Park Avenue, such as Lever House or the Seagram Building, are landmarks of our time and society, New York has forever lost this grand European-style boulevard and bastion of midtown living. Except for the mall running down the middle of the street and the size of the buildings, a once-unmistakable Park Avenue now looks no different from other midtown avenues or office-building streets anywhere in the nation.

Some people argue that whether New York is handsome or retains its distinctive places and historic landmarks has no effect on the problems facing the city today: bankruptcy, racial polarization, crime, a decaying housing stock and widespread building abandonment, and the loss of tax-paying middle-class families and their replacement by poor people on welfare.

This supposedly practical attitude overlooks another less apparent but equally important problem in New York: a crisis of spirit among its residents. It is not that New Yorkers do not love their city. That has not, after all, been true for over 100 years; money-making and power have been New York's guiding spirit and the city changes too rapidly to be loved. But, unlike the New Yorkers of the past, the people are no longer proud of their city. The reasons for this lack of pride are far simpler than the causes of such overwhelming issues as fiscal crisis or the loss of middle-class citizens to the suburbs. Who can be proud of a city that is too busy or too indifferent to keep its streets clean, maintain properly its once-splendid parks, or keep its landmarks in good repair, much less save them from the wrecker's ball? If our elected officials performed such mundane tasks as street and park maintenance, they might begin to regain the lost confidence of New Yorkers, a confidence that is needed if some of the more complex issues that threaten the city's long-term viability are to be solved.

Some New Yorkers still feel the pride that most once had for their city. Thousands of New Yorkers, both in city government and on their own or in private organizations, have given their time, energy, and money to preserving the city's past and guiding its future development into a more humane and comfortable city. Despite repeated challenges in the courts, New York's Landmarks Preservation Commission is one of the strongest and most farsighted such groups in the nation. Hundreds of designated individual buildings and two dozen historic districts, some of them encompassing a hundred blocks, can no longer be demolished or rudely altered at will. The city has also designated midtown Fifth Avenue, Times Square, and the Lincoln Center neighborhood as special zoning districts, so that any new construction must enhance their visual delights and activities. Before the enactment of these zoning districts, Fifth Avenue was well on its way to losing its nearly round-the-clock mix of open shops, hotels, and restaurants and to becoming another anonymous street of branch banks and airline-ticket offices. Now developers are allowed to erect buildings that are taller and cover more ground than zoning usually permits only on condition that the first floors are devoted to shops and that apartments occupy some of the upper floors.

Since 1960 thousands of New Yorkers have purchased and renovated deteriorating brownstones throughout Manhattan and Brooklyn, thereby not only saving nineteenth-century buildings from eventual demolition, but also reclaiming entire neighborhoods and giving them an affirmative identity. Other New Yorkers have finally stopped deploring the condition of the parks and have started to prod city officials into providing proper maintenance and repairs. When that isn't enough, these concerned New Yorkers have raised money to do the work privately. Walking tours, bus tours, museum exhibits, and books have helped New Yorkers rediscover their city, both its past and its present.

Few things are as exciting for people who are enjoying and improving New York than the view of their city from the top of the Empire State Building. The ascent, by elevator, to the Observation Deck is easier than the climb New Yorkers made a hundred and fifty years ago up the winding stone staircase of Trinity Church's tower, but the delight of those who take the trouble to see the view has remained the same over the years. New York is still a brick and mortar "beehive," though it is now punctuated by the soaring skyscrapers of the 1920s and the boxy glass buildings of the post–World War II building boom, and the view stretches ten and twenty miles in every direction into New Jersey, Long Island, Westchester County, even Connecticut. All the daily nuisances and indignities of life in New York — the dirty streets, run-down buildings, noise, the traffic — vanish here, and, at least for a moment, New Yorkers again ask the rhetorical question posed over a hundred years ago: "Who is so blind as not to see that New York will always be the great city of the western world?"

Index

Abyssinian Baptist Church, 221
Academy of Music, 291
Adams, John, 67
Adelphi Hotel, 80
Aeolian Hotel, 151
Albemarle Hotel, 296
Albion Hotel, 151
Allied Chemical Building, 326
American Hotel, 45, 47, 151
American Institute Fair of 1867, 282
Amsterdam Avenue, 319
Anatomical Museum, 122
Angelis, Dr. de, 95
Apartment building, first, in New York, 294
Appleton's Journal, 320–21
Appleton's Magazine, 254
Apthorpe, Charles Ward, mansion of, 313–14; illus., 314
Argus, 38
Aspinwall, William H., 294
Assaults and burglaries, 114–16
Association for the Improved Condition of Deaf Mutes, 310
Astor, John Jacob, 44, 309; and Astor House, 45–46; and development of Lafayette Place, 57; his system of real estate speculation, 57–58; purchase of Burr's estate in Charlton Street area by, 68
Astor, William B., 58, 172, 177; and Union Club, 212; construction of brownstone row houses by, 250
Astor Hotel, 326
Astor House, 45–46, 58, 92, 149–50, 156; profit for manager of, 159; gas used in kitchens of, 197; survival of, 274
Astor Place Hotel, 151
A. T. Steward & Company, 91, 133, 134, 136, 168, 296; completion of, 85–89; illus., 86–87, 88; Negro burial ground beneath, 184; Chambers Street store of, 274–76

Ball, Black & Company, 136, 284; illus., 139
Ballou's Pictorial Drawing-Room Companion, 212
Bank of Manhattan, 184
Bank of New York, 183, 270
Bank for Savings, 49, 221
Banks: suspension of specie payments by, 234, 256; resumption of specie payments by, 235
Barclay Street, illus., 46
"Barracks," 113
Bathroom (ca. 1860), illus., 190
Battery, 5, 15; residential streets around, 31–33; illus., 32
Bayard, Peter, 34
Bayard family, 120

Beach, Alfred Ely, 282
Beach Pneumatic Transit Company, 282
Beekman, Colonel, 272
Beekman family, 248
Beekman Place, 248
Bell, Alexander Graham, 279
Bell Company, 279
Belmont, August, 175, 177, 317
Benkard residence, 293
Bird, Isabella Lucy, 116, 135–36; on Broadway, 126, 129; on Taylor's restaurant, 141; on St. Nicholas Hotel, 154; on hotel laundry service, 158; on Parish house, 168–70; on Haight mansion, 175
Black and Tan Concert Hall, 290
Blacks, efforts to improve condition of, 93
Bleecker Street, 49; attraction of, 51–52, 54; illus., 53, 291; decline of, 172, 289–90
Blizzard of 1888, 280; illus., 281
Blockfronts, 52–54
Bloomingdale Reformed Dutch Church, 315
Bloomingdale Road, 313, 314–15; illus., 312
Blossom Club, 293
Blunt's Picture of New York, 60–61
Blunt's Stranger's Guide, 1
Boardinghouses, 25; immigrant, 95–96
Boardman, Elijah, 47
Boardman, James, 7
Bode's Restaurant, 269
Bond Street, 49; attraction of, 50–51, 58; illus., 51; spread of row houses to, 73; decline of, 172
Bone-boiling works, 239–40
Boorman, James, 61
Borrett, George T., 89, 126–27
Boston, New York's rivalry with, in trade, 23–24
Boulevard (formerly Bloomingdale Road), 314, 319
Bowery, 52, 57, 246; Dutch spelling of, 58; theaters and amusements in, 120–23
Bowery B'hoys and Girls, 123
Bowling Green, 33–34; illus., 35; secluded mansions of, 36; taken over by trade, 73; destruction of, by fire of 1845, 78–82
Bread and Cheese Club, 211
Bremer, Fredrika, 131
Brevoort, Elias, 167
Brevoort, Henry, residence of, 81, 175; illus., 174
Brevoort family, 120
Brewster's carriage showroom, 293
Brick Presbyterian Church, 51, 222–23, 226, 229, 274; illus., 224
Briggs, Mr., 119
Bristed, Charles Astor, 172, 177, 252; on rise of Fifth Avenue, 174–75; on Third Avenue, 246
British American Guide Book, 156
Broadway, 15, 118, 178; viewed from Trinity Church tower, 5; demolition and building on, 13; desirability of, as address, 34–37; illus., 37, 46, 124, 130, 132, 160–61; popularity of, for shopping and pedestrians and carriages, 37–38; early history of, 38–41; Fourth of July celebrations on, 44–45; lower, taken over by trade, 73; activity and elegance of, 125–27; dandies and ladies of, 127–28; problem of garbage on, 129; traffic on, 129–31, 274; department stores on, 133–35; jewelers on, 136–38; Taylor's restaurant on, 138–41; by night, 143–44; prostitution in area of, 144–48; pornography bookstores on, 148–49; hotels of, 149–59, 286; rebuilding of, 159–63, 270
Broadway Bridge, 274; illus., 275
Brocker & Warren, 78
Brokaw mansions, 326
Bronx Park, 323
Brooklyn Bridge, 117, 322
Brothels, 294–96, 304; of Church Street, 92–93, 102, 144; relocation of, to Greene and Mercer streets, 144–46, 286; on Bleecker Street, 290
Brown, Julia, 294
Brown Brothers & Company, 211
Browne, Henri Junius: on the Bowery, 123; on Broadway, 126; on concert saloons, 146; on men's

clubs, 214; on Nassau Street, 265; on Stock Exchange, 265; on restaurants catering to businessmen, 269–70; on St. Nicholas Hotel, 286; on Bleecker Street, 289–90

Brownstones, 242–43, 250; illus., 251; interior decoration of, 254; rentals of, after Civil War, 257

Brunswick Hotel, 296

Bryant, William Cullen, 211

Bryant Park, 185, 229

Buckingham, James Silk, 127

Builder, 165, 172, 190–91

Bullivant, Benjamin, 33

Burr, Aaron, 67–68, 183

Calvary Episcopal Church, 181

Canal Street, 6; description of area around, 36; laid out by city, 39–40; sewer, 191

Carl Schurz Park, 310

Carleton, Sir Guy, 34

Carlton Hotel, 151

Carroll Hotel, 151

Cary, Josiah, 181

Cathedral of St. John the Divine, 324

Cattle drives, 238–39; illus., 239

Central heating, introduction of, 192–93, 195

Central Park, 184, 229, 236, 260; work on, 250–52, 259, 305; carriage drives in, 257; attraction of, 302; and Metropolitan Museum of Art, 310; West, illus., 316; West, Dakota apartment building on, 317, 319

Century Club, 214

Chambers, John, 34

Chambers, William, 129, 149, 158, 170

Chapel of the Holy Rest, 119

Charlton Street, 67–69

Chase Manhattan Bank, 184

Chatham Street, 6

Cheesman, John C., 159, 163

Cheever, Dr., 216, 292

Chelsea, 203–5, 248–49

Cherry Street: model tenement on, 116–17; mansions on, 117–19; slums on, 120

Christ Episcopal Church, 221

Church of All Souls, 181

Church of the Ascension, 215–16, 225

Church of the Puritans, 216, 292

Church Street, 103; brothels of, 92–93, 102, 144, 286

Churches: real estate trends and, 31–33; on Fifth Avenue, 215–23

City Beautiful, ideals of, 320–21, 323, 324, 326

City Hall, 1, 2; illus., 2; located on Wall Street as temporary U.S. Capitol, 14; Negro burial ground beneath, 184

City Hall Park, 34, 41, 49; view of Broadway from foot of, 37; Fourth of July celebrations in, 44–45; demonstration in, 76

City Hotel, 151

Civil War, impact on New York of, 254–58

Claremont Park, 323

Clarendon Hotel, 290–91

Clark, Edward, 316–17

Clarke, Thomas, 203–4

Clay, Henry, 44

Clubs, men's, 211–15

Coal, price of, 193

Cole, Thomas, 229

Collamore Hotel, 151

Collect Pond, 38, 39–41, 191; illus., 39

College of the City of New York (CCNY), 210–11

College Place, 91; slums of, 93–94

Collyser, Dr., 121

Colonial Park, 323

Colonnade Row, 58, 177; attraction of, 54; illus., 55

Columbia College, 42, 43, 91, 93; moving of, to East Forty-ninth Street, 104

Columbia University campus, 324

Columbus Avenue, 319

Commercial Advertiser, 6; on Dutch city hall, 19; on enlarging mercantile community, 25; ad for Park Place property in, 42–43; on Chelsea, 205

Common Council, 33–34, 38, 59, 229

Comstock & Adams' dry goods warehouse, fire at, 27

Concert saloons, 146–47

Constellation, 150

Construction sites, chaos surrounding, 240–42

"Coontown," 290

Cooper, James Fenimore, 9, 10, 24, 133; his friendship with Philip Hone, 44; on Greenwich Village row houses, 71; Samuel Morse's letter to, 74; on A. T. Stewart & Company, 89; on Fifth Avenue, 173; and Bread and Cheese Club, 211

Cooper, Peter, 181

Cooper Union, 181, 310

Cortlandt Street, influx of dry goods firms into, 98–100

Costar, John G., 45–46, 47

Costar, Mrs. John G., 45–46

Cottage rows, 253–54

Countinghouses, 16–18, 25, 100; illus., 17; in Bowling Green, 73–74; conversion of, into offices, 272

Courier and Enquirer, 111

Cranston, Hiram, 260, 263

Crockett, Davy, 45

Crosby, William, 118, 119

Croton Reservoir, 182, 184–91, 236, 320, 321; illus., 185

Crotona Park, 323

Cruger, Douglas, mansion of, 310–13

Cruger, Mrs. Harriet Douglas, 78

Crystal Palace Exhibition (1853), 151, 154, 229

Curtis, George William, 163, 284

Customs House, 25, 265

Daily Tribune, 95, 118, 221, 252–53, 260; on New York merchants, 18; on Delmonico's, 82; on dry goods trade, 96–97; on Dey and Cortlandt streets, 99, 100; on transformation of Park Place area, 102, 103; on Columbia College, 104; on tearing down of Stevens mansion, 104–5; on poverty and destitution, 107–8; on Five Points, 108; on Old Brewery, 110; on local hoodlums, 119; on the theater, 121; on Broadway, 127, 128–29; on wall advertisements, 135; on Taylor's restaurant, 138–39; on rebuilding of Broadway, 162, 163; on Penniman mansion, 168; on decline of Bond Street area, 172; on New Yorkers' use of water, 187, 189; on sewers, 192; on heating systems, 195; on tenements on East Seventh Street, 202; on Madison Square, 211; on men's clubs, 214; on Brick Presbyterian Church, 223; on Murray Hill mansions, 227; on Panic of 1857, 234; on "Dutch Hill" shantytown, 236–37; on slaughterhouses, 238; on cattle drives, 239; on Civil War's impact, 256; on Trinity Building, 270; on Union Square, 290; on Jerome mansion, 299

"Dakota," 317, 319

Dana, Charles A., 162

D'Arusmont, Frances Wright, 107

Davis, Alexander Jackson, 52, 91

Davis, Richard Harding, 292

Davis, Thomas E., 58

D. Devlin & Company, 136, 282

Delacroix, Mr., 57

DeLancey, Etienne, 38

DeLancey, James, 20

Delancey Street, 203

Delano, Franklin H., 54

Delaplaine, Isaac, 226

Delaware and Hudson Canal, 193

Delmonico's hotel and restaurant, 82–83, 269, 293, 297; illus., 83

Denning family, 13

Department stores, Broadway's, 133–35

DePeyster, Abraham, 34

DeWitt Clinton Park, 323

Dey Street, influx of dry goods firms into, 98–100

Dickens, Charles, 127, 129, 293

Douglass, William, 43

Downing Street (69), illus., 67

Drew, Daniel, 267

Dry goods trade, 304; overwhelming of Park Place area by, 96–100, 107

Dutch city hall, destruction of, 18–19

"Dutch Hill" shantytown, 236–237; illus., 237

Dutch houses, 10; illus., 10
Dyckman family, 120

East River, 5; crowded waterfront of, 14; compared with Hudson River, 15; activity at shipyards on, 20–23; shipyard on, illus., 21; and 1835 fire, 27; shoreline of, illus., 247
East River Park, 323
East Side: decline of, 202–3; growth of, 245–48, 305; loss of landmarks and parks of Upper, 307–10
Edison, Thomas, 279–80
Eighteenth Street apartments, 294; illus., 295
Eighth Street, 59
Elevated railroad, 282–84, 315; illus., 283, 285
Elevators, first buildings with, 265
Eleventh Avenue (renamed West End Avenue), 317–19
Eleventh Street, 59; West, 64; West, illus., 65
Empire State Building, 329
Eolian Hotel, 291
Epidemics: of cholera and yellow fever, 9, 64–66, 113–14; smallpox, 184
Equitable Life Assurance Building, 265
Erie Canal, opening of, 6, 14–15, 193
Evening Post, 66, 95; on condition of streets, 7; on city's growth and change, 9–10; on vessels in New York harbor, 14; on Bond Street, 50; on Mayor Lawrence's treatment by mob, 76; on financial conditions, 77; on fire of 1845, 81–82; on slums of Greenwich Street, 94; on Five Points, 108; on Gotham Court, 116; on Astor House, 150; on St. John's Park, 171; on elegance of Second Avenue, 173; plumber's advertisement in, 186; on heating, 193; on proposal to build college in Madison Square, 210; on growth of New York, 233; on East Side, 245; on Third Avenue, 246; on Harlem, 306–7

Everett House, 291
Exports, 14, 323

F. A. O. Schwarz, 292
Fay's *View in New-York,* 54
Federal architecture, 50; on LeRoy Place, 52; on St. Mark's Place, 58; superseded by Greek Revival, 62
Felton, Mrs., 193
Field, Cyrus W., 273
Fifth Avenue, 304–5, 328; emergence of, as city's most fashionable address, 173–75, 205; mansions of, 175–77, 206, 225–29, 260, 301–2; illus., 179, 241, 258, 300, 303, 311; row houses on, 206, 319; attraction of, 206–10; men's clubs on, 211–15; churches on, 215–23; above Forty-second Street, problem of whether to build on, 235–36, 258–59; construction sites on, 240; fall of, to trade, 293, 299; mansions of, turned into clubhouses, 293–94
Fifth Avenue Hotel, 265, 296
Fifth Avenue Presbyterian Church, 301
Fiftieth Street, 301
Fire(s): to clean out epidemics, 9; of 1835, 26–28; of 1845, 78–82
First Congregational Church, 221
First Presbyterian Church, 31–32, 216, 222
Fish, Nicholas and Elizabeth, 59
Fitch, John, 38
Five Points, 108–10, 120, 147; illus., 109; health of residents of, 113–14
Five Points Mission, 110, 227
Foley Square, 38
Forest, Emily Johnston de, 64
Forty-second Street, problem of whether to build on Fifth Avenue past, 235–36, 258–59
Foster, George, 108, 126, 127, 144
Fourteenth Street: attraction of, 177–78; boardinghouses of, 293
Fourth Avenue, attraction of, 178–81
Francis, John, 211
Franklin, Walter, 117
Franklin Square, 117

Free Academy, 210–11
"Frenchtown," 290
Front Street, 5, 20

Gallatin, Albert, 51
Garbage on East Fifth Street, illus., 115
Gardiner, David, 54
Gardiner, Julia, 54
Gas light: to illuminate homes and streets, introduction of, 196–97; dangers of, 197–99
General Motors Building, 326
General Theological Seminary, 204; illus., 204
Genin (the hatter), 274
Gentleman's Companion, 294–95, 296
George III, King, 34
German Hospital, 310
German Reformed Church, 221
Gilbert, Bradford L., 277
Gilbert Company, 284
Gilman, Caroline, 60, 117
Gilsey Hotel, 296
Gleason's Pictorial Drawing-Room Companion, 154, 158
Godey's Lady's Book, 134
Goelet, Peter, 178, 292
Goodrich's Picture of New York, 36, 196
Gorham & Company, 292
Gosling's Restaurant, 269
Gotham Court (model tenement), 116–17
Gothic Revival architecture, 29, 51; used in new Trinity Church, 83–84; displayed on Fifth Avenue, 175; used for churches, 215, 216, 217
Gough, John B., 146
Grace Church, 96, 217, 219
Graham, Charles, 279
Gramercy Park, 51; George Templeton Strong's move to, 95, 182, 201–2; illus., 180; attraction of, 181–82, 253
Grand Army Plaza, 301, 302, 326
Grand Central Station, 322, 324
Grant's Tomb, 324
Grattan, Thomas Golley, 195
Graveyards, 184, 222
Gray, John A. C., 225

Greek Revival architecture: on Wall Street, 28; on Bond Street, 50; in Washington Square, 62; replaced by Italianate style, 89, 91–92, 270; of Astor House, 150; of Brevoort residence, 175
Greek Slave, 121
Greene Street, prostitution on, 144–46, 286, 296
Greenwich Street, 41–42; illus., 41; and fire of 1845, 80; slums of, 94–95; rebuilding of, 102, 107
Greenwich Village: impact of 1822 yellow fever epidemic on growth of, 64–66; row-house construction in, 66, 69–71; map of (1822), 69
Grinnell, Minturn & Company, 21
Grinnell, Moses, 177; mansion of, 175; mansion of, illus., 176
Griscom, John H., 113
Griswold, N. L. & G., 21–23
Griswold family, 211
Growth and change, 9–11, 165–67

Hahnemann Hospital, 310
Haight, Richard K., homes of, 175–77, 294
Halleck, Fitz-Greene, 211
Hamilton, Alexander, 13, 68, 183
Hamilton Square, 310
Hardenbergh, Henry J., 317
Hardie, James, 1
Harlem, 305; development of, 306–7
Harper's Magazine, 163, 284, 304
Harper's Monthly, 11, 246
Harper's Weekly, 279, 283, 313
Hart, Eli, & Company, 76
Harvey, Charles T., 282–83
Haslem, Henry, 242
Hatfield, R. G., 136
Heating systems, introduction of, 192–96
Herald, 4–5, 151, 171, 201, 205; on Wall Street, 29; on Vauxhall Gardens, 57; on Tompkins Square, 60; on Sixth Avenue, 64; on Bowling Green, 73; on financial conditions, 77; on new Trinity Church, 85; on College Place, 93; on New York's black population, 93; ads by "peculiar physicians" in, 94–95; on dry goods trade, 96;

on transformation of Park Place area, 102; on extravagance, 107; on Gotham Court, 116–17; on Rutgers mansion, 118; on destiny of East Side, 120; on the theater, 121, 122; on American women's love of dress, 133; on Tiffany's 136, 138; on Taylor's restaurant, 141; on brothel raid, 146; on juvenile prostitutes, 147; on *McDowell's Journal,* 148; on *Venus Miscellany,* 149; on opening of new hotels, 150–51; on St. Nicholas Hotel, 152, 156, 157, 158–59; on Union Square, 167, 168, 292; on Parish house, 168; on uptown residential streets, 170; its list of city's 200 wealthiest men, 172; on Grinnell mansion, 175; on Fourteenth Street, 177–78; on sewers, 191, 192; on steam heat, 195; on city slums, 203; on Union Clubhouse, 212, 213–14; on Fifth Avenue churches, 215, 217, 219; on Murray Hill, 226; on Townsend mansion, 227–29; on growth of New York, 233–34; on problem of building on Fifth Avenue past Forty-second Street, 236; on chaos surrounding construction sites, 240, 242; on Beekman Place, 248; on the West Side, 250; on tall houses and handsome streets, 252, 253; on Fifth Avenue's fall to trade, 293
High Bridge, illus., 187
Hoffman, John T., 282
Hoffman House, 296
Holland House, 302
Home Journal, 133; on Pearl Street wholesalers, 18; on new Trinity Church, 84; on rebuilding of Park Place area, 102, 103; on Stevens mansion, 104; on popularity of theaters, 121; department store ads in, 134; on Tiffany's, 136; on Astor House, 150, 197; on St. Nicholas Hotel, 151, 152; on Broadway hotels, 159; on number of buildings in New York, 233
Homosexuality, 148
Hone, John, 77

Hone, Margaret, 43
Hone, Mary, 43
Hone, Philip, 5; on building, 13; on Daniel McCormick, 26; on 1835 fire, 27–28; on Trinity Church, 29, 83, 85; on First Presbyterian Church, 31–33, 216; on the Battery, 33; Broadway mansion of, 34–36, 41; and William Douglass, 43; diary of, 43–44; illus., 44; on Davy Crockett, 45; on Astor House, 45–46; residence of, illus., 46; selling of Broadway mansion of, 46–47, 74–75; temporary residence of, 49–50; on home of William B. Astor, 58; and real estate, 74, 75, 99–100; and Panic of 1837, 76–77; on Ray mansion, 78; on fire of 1845, 79, 81; on Delmonico's, 82; on A. T. Stewart & Company, 89; on Stevens mansion, 91; on Five Points residents, 114; on assaults and burglaries, 114–16; on building sites, 131; on prostitution, 146; on Brevoort residence, 175; on Croton water system, 185; installation of running water and bathrooms in mansion of, 186; investment of, in coal fields, 193; and Hone Club, 211; on Union Club, 212; on Grace Church, 219; on Stock Exchange, 265; and Apthorpe mansion, 313–14
Hopper house, 309
Hotels: of Broadway, 149–59, 286; in Madison Square area, 296
House of Rothschild, 175
Howard Hotel, 151
Howe, Sir William, 34, 225
Howland, Gardiner, 81
Hudson River, 5, 15
Hudson River Railroad, 171–72, 250, 286
Hudson Street, 69–71
Hyde de Neuville, Baroness, 41

I. and L. Joseph bankinghouse, 76
Illustrated London News, 126
International Hotel, 284
Inwood Park, 323
Irving, Washington, 44, 54

Italianate style, 252, 319; replacement of Greek Revival architecture with, 89, 91–92, 270; first New York mansion displaying, 168; mansions on Fifth Avenue, 177; of Union Club, 212

Jauncey, William, 313
Jauncey family, 13, 25
Jay, Peter, 34
Jefferson, Thomas, 51
Jerome, Leonard, 267, 299
Jewelers, Broadway's, 136–38
John Street Methodist Church, 184
Johnson, Bradish, 207–8, 293
Johnson's Gas Fittings advertisement, illus., 198
Johnston, John, 61
Jones, Mrs. Mary Mason, 259–60, 302
Judge, 302–4
Julien, M., 212

Kemble, Fanny, 5, 11
Kennedy, Archibald (Earl of Cassilis), mansion of, 34, 273
Kent, James, 211
King, Charles, 185
King's Handbook of New York, 293, 302
Klinckowstrom, Axel Leonhard, 4, 37
Knickerbocker, 54, 121, 156
Knox (the hatter), 274

Ladies' Baptist Home Society, 310
Ladies' Home Missionary Society, 110
"Ladies mile," 296; illus., 297
Lafarge House, 151
Lafayette Place, 49; illus., 55, 56; attraction of, 54–58; decline of, 172 177, 220
LaGrange Terrace, *see* Colonnade Row
Lamb, John, 13
Landmarks Preservation Commission, 328
La Rochefoucauld-Liancourt, Duke de, 36
Latrobe, Charles, 24
Lawrence, Cornelius, 76

Lawrence, John, 13
Lenox, James, 294
Lenox, William, 175, 177
Lenox Hill, 310
LeRoy, Jacob, 52
LeRoy Place, 52–54, 177
Leslie's Illustrated, 131, 172; on Fifth Avenue, 207, 208–9; on the West Side, 250
Lever House, 327
Liberty Street, rebuilding of, illus., 97
Life Illustrated, 127–28, 163, 181, 217–19
Lincoln Center, 328
Lispenard Meadows, 38, 40, 191; illus., 40
Livingston family, 211
London Terrace, 254
Lord, Samuel, 133
Lord & Taylor, 133–34, 284–86, 292; illus., 134
Lotus Club, 293
Low, A. A., 21
Ludlow family, 13, 25

McCabe, James, 45–46; on Astor's system of real estate speculation, 57–58; on Old Brewery, 109; on the Bowery, 120, 123; on ladies' wardrobe, 133; on Broadway by night, 143; on brothels and bars, 147; on Fifth Avenue churches, 215; on Astor House, 274; on Trinity Church, 276
McCormick, Daniel, 26
McDowell, Reverend, 147–48
McDowell's Journal, 148
McGowan house, 309
Mackay, Alexander, 9, 16, 20–21, 127, 131
Mackay, Charles, 126, 127, 143, 149
McKim, Mead, and White, 324
Madison, James, 51
Madison Avenue: brownstones on, 257; illus., 260
Madison Square, 210–11, 250, 286; opening of hotels in, 296; restaurants and theaters in, 296–98; illus., 298; mansions of, 298–99; as office-building center, 302
Manhattan Club, 293

Manhattan Company, 183
Manhattan Gas Works, 197
Manhattan Gaslight Company, 197
Marryat, Frederick, 74, 150
Marsh drugstore, illus., 307
Martin, William, 314
Maury, Sarah M., 186
Melish, John, 117
Mercer Street, prostitution on, 144–46, 286, 296
Merchants Exchange: located on Wall Street, 14, 265; destroyed by 1835 fire, 27; construction of new, 28, 78
Merchants' Magazine, 24
Methodist Book Concern, 302–4
Methodist Episcopal Wesleyan Chapel, 221
Metropolitan Elevated Railroad Company, 284
Metropolitan Hotel, 151, 159, 286, 296
Metropolitan Life, 302
Metropolitan Museum of Art, 310–13
Metropolitan Opera Association, 327
Middle Dutch Church, 184, 220–21, 222, 273
Miller, E. L., 195
Minetta Brook, 60
Minturn, Jonas, 50
Minturn, Robert B., 93
Mirror, New York, 3, 36–37, 38, 78, 167
Model-artist shows, 121–23
Moffatt, William B., 240–42
Moore, Clement Clarke, 204–5
Morningside Park, 314, 323
Morrison, John, 61
Morse, Samuel F. B., 74
Mount Sinai Hospital, 310
Murray, Robert, 225
Murray Hill, 299; desirability of, 223–31, 253
Mutual Life Insurance Company, 273

Nash and Fuller's Restaurant, 269
Nassau Street, 265; illus., 266
National Advocate, 25
Neilson, Peter, 66, 121

New England Hotel, 270
New Netherland Hotel, 302
New York As It Is, 49
New York Bay, 5; illus., 32
New York Central Railroad, 324
New York Club, 214, 294
New York Elevated Railroad Company, 284
New York Gas Light Company, 196, 197
New York & Harlem Railroad, 229, 244–45, 305
New-York Historical Society, 310
New York Hospital, 272–73
New York Hotel, 159, 260
New York Journal, 140, 141, 279
New York Public Library, 175, 185, 294, 324
New York Stock Exchange, 265–69
New York Yacht Club, 214
Ninth Street, 59
Normal College (later Hunter College), 310
Novelty Hall, 122

Observatory Place, 310
Odeon Theater, 122
Ohio Life and Mutual Trust Company, 234
Old Brewery, 108–10
Olmsted, Frederick Law, 236, 305
Otis, Samuel, 13

Packet, 33
Palmo's Opera House, 121
Panic of 1837, 75–77, 96, 233
Panic of 1857, 231, 233–35, 299
Panic of 1873, 276, 282
Parish, Henry, 168–70
Park Avenue, 248; attraction of, 229, 253; property map of, 230; illus., 230, 308; destruction of midtown, 327
Park Place, 41; upgrading of, 42–43; illus., 46, 99; collapse of, as fashionable residential area, 92–96; overwhelming of, by dry goods trade, 96–100, 107; building of warehouses in, 100–2; rebuilding of area of, 102–4, 107
Parks, 323

339

Pearl Street, 5, 14, 25; disappearance of residential character of, 15; countinghouse on, illus., 17; merchants, 18; widening and straightening of, 18–19; mansions on, 19–20; and dry goods trade, 96, 100
Pearson, Isaac G., 52
Pelham Bay Park, 323
Penniman, James F., 168
Pennsylvania Station, 324–26, 327; illus., 325
Phalon's Hair-Cutting Saloon, 158
Phelps, Isaac Newton, 227
Phelps family, 245
Phillips, Dr., 216–17
"Physicians, peculiar," 94–95
Pintard, John, 1–2
Pintard family, 13
Plaza Hotel, 302
Plumbers' advertisements, 186; illus., 188
Plumbing, introduction of, 186–91
Population, nineteenth century, xvii, 1–2, 201, 322
Pornography, 148–49
Post, Jehiel, 186
Post Office, 220–21, 222, 273
Potts, Dr., 216
Poverty, 107–10; and tenement conditions, 110–13
Powers, Hiram, 121
Prescott House, 151
Prime, Edward, 81
Prime, Nathaniel, 34
Prime, Ward, & King, 34
Prostitutes, 144–48, 149, 294–96, 304; illus., 145
Public transportation: improvements in, 280–84; by-passing of Upper West Side by, 314
Pulitzer Fountain, 324
Putnam's Monthly: on Stevens mansion, 91; on dry goods trade, 96; on Broadway, 125; on Taylor's restaurant, 138; on St. Nicholas Hotel, 151–52, 154; on growth and change in New York, 165, 166–67; on Union Square, 170; on spread of trade, 170–71; on Fifth Avenue, 177; on Fourth Avenue, 181; on houses in upper part of city, 182; on First Presbyterian Church, 217; on New York churches, 219; on Astor House, 274

Ralph, Dr., 95
Randall, John, 41
Randall, Robert Richard, 61–62
Ray, Robert, 78, 81
"Rear buildings," 111–13; illus., 112
Red House Tavern, 309
Restaurant(s): Delmonico's, 82–83; Taylor's, 138–41; catering to businessmen, 269–70
Restell, Madame (Ann Trow Lohman), 94–95, 208–10, 259; residence of, illus., 209
Reynolds, William, 239–40
Rhinelander Gardens, 254
Richmond Hill, 66–67
Riverside Drive, 314, 315, 317; shanty on, illus., 318
Robertson, James, 133
Rodgers, John, 222
Rogers, George P., 61
Roosevelt, Franklin Delano, 54
Ross, J. H., 197
"Row, the," 62–64; illus., 63
Row houses, 66, 68–71, 201; spread of, to Bond Street and Washington Square, 73; illus., 205; on Fifth Avenue, 206
Royal Geographical Society, 116
Royalle, Anne, 20, 37, 196
Rudolph's Restaurant, 269
Ruggles, Samuel B., 51, 181–82
Rutgers, Hendrick, 118
Rutgers, Henry, 118, 119
Rutgers family, 120

Sailors' Snug Harbor, 61–62
St. Bartholomew's Church, 219–20
St. Benedict the Moor, 290
St. Denis Hotel, 151
St. George's Chapel, 272
St. James Hotel, 296
St. John's Chapel, 3, 7, 287; illus., 8; remodeling of, 172; destruction of, 326
St. John's Park, 6–7, 181, 253; illus., 8; decline of, 171–72; purchase of,

by Cornelius Vanderbilt, 286–87, 289

St. Luke's Chapel, 69–71

St. Mark's Church, 59

St. Mark's Place, 49, 60; attraction of, 58–59

St. Mary's Park, 323

St. Nicholas Hotel, 151–54, 163, 286, 296; illus., 153, 155; dining room of, 154–57; conveniences provided by, 157, 158; profit for manager of, 159

St. Nicholas Park, 323

St. Patrick's Cathedral, 208, 259, 301

St. Paul's Chapel, 3, 129, 274

St. Paul's Methodist Church, 181

St. Thomas' Church, 301

Sanford, Porter & Stryker cottages, 249–50; illus., 249

Sanitation and sewage, 7–9, 191–92

Savoy Hotel, 302

Savoy Plaza Hotel, 326

Schaefer brewery, 248

Schermerhorn, Abraham, 74

Schermerhorn, Mrs. Peter A., 294

Schubrick, W. B., 9

Schuyler, Montgomery, 279, 319, 320

"Scotch Ann's," 290

Scott, Winfield, 51

Scribner's, 302–4

Seagram Building, 327

Second Avenue, 49, 58; row houses and mansions on, 59; elegance of, 173; house prices on, 203

Seventh Avenue, 173–74, 250, 326

Seventh Street, East, completion of tenements on, 202

Sewers, 9, 191–92

"Shantyhill," 313

Shantytowns, 236–37, 313

Sidewalks, condition of, 16

Singer, Mr. and Mrs. Isaac Merrit, 208

Singer Building, 326–27

Sisters of Mercy, 310

Sixth Avenue, 52, 64; illus., 70

Skyscrapers: first, 263; illus., 277, 278; "age of," 279

Slaughterhouses, 238, 239

Sloan, Samuel, 189–90

Slum: housing, 111–13, dwellers, illus., 115; district on East Side, 120, 203

Small Parks Act of 1887, 323

Smith, John, 167

Society Library, 294

SoHo district, 286

South Baptist Church, 221

South Street, 5, 20–21; illus., 22

Sperry, Jacob, 54–57

Spingler, Henry, 167

Spirit, New Yorkers' crisis of, 327–28

Spring, Gardiner, 51, 222

Stables, 243–44

Statue of Liberty, 324

Steam heat, introduction of, 195

Steel skeletons, used in buildings, 277–79

Steinway Hall, 293

Stephens, Anne Sophia Winterbotham, 225

Stevens, John Austin, 273

Stevens, John Cox, mansion of, 91–92, 93, 117–18; illus., 92; tearing down of, 104–5

"Stevens' Palace," 91–92, 93, 117–18; illus., 92; tearing down of, 104–5

Stewart, A. T., 85–89, 91, 214, 256, 274–76; Fifth Avenue mansion of, 299–301

"Stewart's Folly," 85, 89

Street plan, grid, 323

"Street railroads," horse-drawn, 244–45; illus., 245

Strong, Ellen (Ruggles), 182

Strong, George Templeton, 79–80, 165, 196; on new Trinity Church, 83; on Greenwich Street, 94; move to Gramercy Park by, 95, 182, 201–2; on the Bowery, 120; on prostitutes, 144, 146; on Parish mansion, 170; on Croton water, 186; fire in home of, 197–99; evening walks of, 201–2, 203; on Fifth Avenue, 207, 235–36; on First Presbyterian Church, 216–17; on Panic of 1857, 234; on Beekman Place, 248; on Western Union Building, 263; and improvements in public transportation, 280; on new Tiffany's, 292

Strong, George Washington, 182, 186

Stuart-Wortley, Lady Emmeline, 156–57

Stuyvesant, Nicholas, William, 59

Stuyvesant, Peter, 58–59

Stuyvesant, Petrus, 59

Stuyvesant, Rutherford, 294

Stuyvesant family, 58–59, 173, 212

Stuyvesant Square, 173

Sub-Treasury building, 25

Subways, first proposed, 282

Sun, New York, 276, 282

Suydam family, 212

Swan, Abraham, 49, 58

Tailer, E. N., 64

Taylor, George W., 133

Taylor's restaurant, 138–41, 284; illus., 140

Temple of the Muses, 122

Templeton, Olivia, 182

Tenement: conditions, 110–13; district, illus., 114; model, 116–17

Tenth Street, 59

Terraces, 52–54

Thackeray, William Makepeace, 133

Theater, popularity of, 121

Thiers Concert Hall, 122

Third Avenue, 59, 246

Thirty-fifth Street, West, 242–43

Thirty-fourth Street, 299, 301; illus., 300

Thomas, Thomas, 102, 212

Thompson, Ida, 295

Thorn, Herman, 273, 313–14

Tiffany & Company, 136–38, 284, 292; illus., 137

Times, 223; on Walton House, 20; on Rutgers mansion, 118, 119; on Lord & Taylor, 133–34; on Manhattan Gaslight Company, 197; on Madame Restell's residence, 208; on New York as place of residence, 244; on Civil War's impact, 257–58; building, replacement of, 274; on Union Square, 290; on Stewart mansion, 301; on West Side, 317; on Penn Station, 324–26

Times Square, 326, 328

Times Tower, 326

Tompkins Market, 50

Tompkins Square, 49, 58, 202, 244; attraction of, 59–60; slum district of, 120

Tower Building, 277

Townsend, Samuel P. "Sarsaparilla," mansion of, 227–29, 243, 299; illus., 228

Trade, 13–14; New York's rise in, 23; rivalry with Boston in, 23–24; loss of Wall Street to, 31; takeover of residential streets by, 73

Travelers Club, 293

Trench and Snook (architects), 102,

Tribune building, 263, 265, 276

Trinity Building, 270–72; illus., 271

Trinity Church, 3, 6–7, 13, 31; view from tower of, 3–6, 7, 329; destruction and rebuilding of, 28–29; shops and hotels once located around, 44; proposal to rebuild, on Tompkins Square, 60; construction of new, 83–85; illus., 84; remodeling of St. John's Chapel by, 172; and Trinity Building, 270, 272; survival of, 276; and purchase of St. John's Park by Cornelius Vanderbilt, 286–87, 289

Trollope, Anthony, 157, 207, 215, 305

Trollope, Mrs. Frances, 5

Tweed, Boss, 282

Twelfth Street, 59; West, 64

Tyler, John, 54

Union Club, 211–15, 223; illus., 213

Union Hotel, 151

Union League Club, 299

Union Place Hotel, 151, 290

Union Square, 51, 159–60; growth of area around, 167–68; mansions of, 168–70; illus., 169; attraction of, 178; influx of shops into, 290–93; brothels in vicinity of, 294

Union Theological Seminary, 294

University Place Presbyterian Church, 216

Unonius, Gustav, 24

Upjohn, Richard, 85, 102, 272

U. S. Steel Building, 327

Van Cortlandt family, 120, 211

Van Cortlandt Park, 323

Van Doren, J. L., 78

Van Rensselaer, Mariana Griswold, 304–5
Van Rensselaer family, 211
Van Schaick, Myndert, 293
Van Wart, Irving, 54
Vanderbilt, Cornelius, 267, 286–87, 301
Vanderbilt, Cornelius, II, 302
Vanderbilt, William Henry, 301–2
Vanderbilt, William Kissam, 301–2
Vanderbilt family, 301–2
Varick, Richard, 13
Varick Street, 326
Vaux, Calvert, 236, 305
Vauxhall Gardens, 57
Venus Miscellany, 149
Verplanck, Gulian, 211
Verplanck family, 13; mansion of, 25
Victoria Hotel, 296
Viele, Egbert L., 299, 315

Waddell, Coventry, 233; mansion of, 51, 225–26; mansion of, illus., 226
Waldorf-Astoria Hotel, 248
Waldorf Hotel, 302
Wall Street, 15; illus., 12, 26, 267, 268; last vestiges of its residential past, 13–14; destiny of, as financial center, 25–26, 265; transformation of, 28–29, 31; Italianate style edifices on, 270
Wallack's Theatre, 292–93
"Wallhigh," 313
Walton, William, mansion of, 19–20, 273; illus., 19
Warehouses, 15–16, 100–2; illus.,

16, 101; in Bowling Green, 73–74
Warner, Samuel, 102
Warren Street, 41–42; illus., 41
Washington, George, 34, 67, 117
Washington, Martha, 118
Washington Arch, 324
Washington Building, 273
Washington Hotel, 273
Washington-Lafayette Park, 323
Washington Square, 184, 252; attraction of, 60–64; illus., 63; spread of rowhouses on, 73; mansions of, 108
Washington Street, 80
Water Street, 5, 20
Water supply, efforts to improve, 182–91
Watson, James F., 171
Waverly House, 79
Wealth, New York's, 322–23
Webster, Daniel, 44
West Side, growth of, 248–50, 313–20
Western Union Building, 263, 265, 276; illus., 264
Wharton, Edith, 259, 319
Whitman, Walt, 129, 244
Willis, Nathaniel Parker, 89; on Trinity Church, 84; on Tiffany's, 136; on Taylor's restaurant, 141; on fashionable addresses, 172; on interior decoration of brownstones, 254
W. & J. Sloane, 292
Wood, Silas, 116
Woods, Kate, 296
Wood's Illustrated Handbook, 178
World, New York, 272, 279
Wren, Sir Christopher, 223